The Origins of War

The Origins of War

Violence in Prehistory

Jean Guilaine and Jean Zammit

Translated by Melanie Hersey

Blackwell
Publishing

French edition © 2001 by Éditions du Seuil

English translation © 2005 by Blackwell Publishing

BLACKWELL PUBLISHING

350 Main Street, Malden, MA 02148-020, USA
108 Cowley Road, Oxford OX4 1JF, UK
550 Swanston Street, Carlton, Victoria 3053, Australia

The right of Jean Guilaine and Jean Zammit to be identified as the Authors of
this Work has been asserted in accordance with the UK Copyright, Designs,
and Patents Act 1988.

Originally published in 2001 by Éditions du Seuil as *le Sentier de la Guerre:
Visages de la violence préhistorique*
English edition published 2005 by Blackwell Publishing
Translated into English by Melanie Hersey

Library of Congress Cataloging-in-Publication Data

Guilaine, Jean.
  [Sentier de la guerre. English]
  The origins of war : violence in prehistory / Jean Guilaine and Jean Zammit;
translated by Melanie Hersey.
      p. cm.
  Originally published in 2001 by Éditions du Seuil as *le Sentier de la Guerre:
Visages de la violence préhistorique* — Verso t.p.
  Includes bibliographical references and index.
  ISBN 1-4051-1259-X (hardcover: alk. paper) — ISBN 1-4051-1260-3 (alk. paper)
  1. Warfare, Prehistoric. I. Zammit, Jean. II. Title.

  GN799.W26G8513 2005
  303.6′6—dc22   2004005856

A catalogue record for this title is available from the British Library.

Set in 10$^{1}/_{2}$/13pt Minion
by Graphicraft Limited, Hong Kong
Printed and bound in the United Kingdom
by TJ International, Padstow, Cornwall

The publisher's policy is to use permanent paper from mills that operate a sustainable
forestry policy, and which has been manufactured from pulp processed using acid-free and
elementary chlorine-free practices. Furthermore, the publisher ensures that the text paper
and cover board used have met acceptable environmental accreditation standards.

For further information on
Blackwell Publishing, visit our website:
www.blackwellpublishing.com

Contents

2 Agriculture: A Calming or Aggravating Influence?

3 Humans as Targets: 4,000 to 8,000 Years Ago

4 The Warrior: An Ideological Construction

5 The Concept of the Hero Emerges

Preface

Is it all just a sign of our times? War is breaking out again in Europe (Serbia, Chechnya, and Kosovo) following a prolonged spell of peace. At the same time violence, the result of economic inequality and social exclusion, is claiming our cities and, at times, our countryside too. Could this explain why prehistorians have recently turned their attention to analyzing and reanalyzing war and conflict? Political and economic factors have always shaped the discipline of archeology, and continue to do so. For some three-quarters of a century (1870–1945), Europe lived either through war or with the threat of war and experienced troop movements, displacements, and deportations. As a result, the focus of history has always been upon events and those involved, upon conflicts, territorial divisions, and dissolutions imposed by foreign intervention. During times of peace, history and archeology as disciplines have both endeavored to adopt a more peace-oriented approach, conducting detailed studies into the daily lives of ordinary people and focusing upon technical developments, changes in the indigenous culture, the progressive taming of nature, and, more recently, human beings as a species.

However, for a number of years, the issue of violence among prehistoric populations has been a popular topic of investigation. The steady increase in archeological evidence has doubtless played a crucial role in bettering our understanding of a field which has long remained inexact and unsubstantiated owing to a lack of documentation. Yet despite all the difficulties associated with this discipline (evidence becoming increasingly scarce the further back in time one goes, difficulty in interpreting certain documents), the view that prehistoric people did not always live in peace and solidarity with one another is still widely held. It is also important to note that prehistory is not a uniform whole but can be divided into periods of time varying in length and characterized by distinct differences in technical, cultural, and economic progress. This diversity is all the more marked at a global level as civilizations flourished and diversified, adapting to the broad range of physical and social environments. In assigning prehistory to the realms of a far-away and long-forgotten era, many a historian has committed the grave methodological error of equating the advent of writing with the onset of an organized world; a mistake not least because all of the oral cultures predating the introduction of writing systems (as well as those oral cultures that continued to exist long afterwards) were highly sophisticated in certain regards, a fact that often fails to be recognized. The archeology of the ancient Near East (where some of the earliest writing systems originated) is particularly revealing. Signs of progress date from well before the advent of writing: the "invention" of agriculture and cattle breeding in the eighth millennium before the common era (BCE), the existence of towns from the fourth millennium BCE onwards, the introduction of relatively stable governing powers maintained by elites or dynasties, social tensions, exchange systems operating over wide areas, and deities that were subsequently developed and elaborated by the rural and later urban populations. In order to arrive at such a high degree of social stratification, it would be difficult to comprehend how prehistoric societies would not have encountered inevitable force, tension, and conflict along the way.

The problem becomes all the more complex when we turn our attention to the earliest prehistoric populations which, over a period of 2.5 million years, never developed agriculture, relying instead upon nature by hunting wild animals, fishing, collecting molluscs, and gathering leaves, roots, and fruit. These societies had very low populations which increased only very slightly over thousands of years. Thus, it is tempting to dismiss them as fraternal, calm, and altruistic societies, feasting on the bountiful fruits of nature: a real Garden of Eden. Conclusive archeological evidence is scarce, making such assumptions impossible to prove or disprove at times. In this work we shall endeavor to present a somewhat less peace-oriented impression of *Homo sapiens*, drawing examples from the most recent hunter-gatherer societies ("Epipaleolithic-Mesolithic"). It is important to bear in mind that, even if the presence of violent behavior in the Upper Paleolithic era can be confirmed, all interpretations of this behavior remain speculative, particularly where the earliest periods of human existence are concerned. For this reason, this work will focus primarily upon the most advanced stages of prehistoric society: the Neolithic and the Bronze Age.

The role of prehistoric warfare has often been underestimated and labeled a minor and very sporadic activity; prehistoric societies are often perceived to have been largely peaceful. Without wishing to relabel prehistoric man as a war-loving monster, we aim rather to challenge this peaceful image somewhat. Ethnography invites us to do just this by highlighting the importance of war in pre-state societies at a social, political, and economic level.

Traditional archeological approaches, which tend to focus upon fortifications, weaponry, and executions, have only been able to identify certain aspects of this social phenomenon which, like violence, is an inherent part of human behavior. Ancient warfare and, in particular, short-lived battles and conflicts rarely left any trace in terms of material evidence. Former battlefields are now anonymous and have often since been transformed into peaceful landscapes. Open spaces, once dotted with shell-craters, have become tranquil golf courses. Graves can only survive under good conditions and thus a great deal of evidence is destroyed over time. Archeologists are well aware that the number of finds relating to a particular period or culture is always very low in relation to the original size of the population. This accounts for the difficulties experts face when piecing together demographic reconstructions and explains why lengthy controversies may follow.

Archeologists rarely have the opportunity to interpret evidence relating to conflict since, for this to happen, delicate conditions need to be maintained over time in order to preserve both human remains and material artifacts. Yet prehistorians cannot fail to acknowledge that violent, if not murderous, encounters must have occurred in prehistory. This is more evident today than ever before, since reconstructing social contexts and mapping their progressive complexity over time has now become more than just an objective of archeology: it is a legitimate exercise in its own right. Essential evidence of violence in oral cultures, hunter-gatherer societies, and tribal populations is also well documented in anthropology, thus adding credibility to the theory that warring factions existed in prehistory. Keeley's excellent work entitled *War Before Civilization* adopts a similar comparative approach, focusing upon prehistoric, ethnographic, and state societies. This is substantiated with statistical evidence which leaves little doubt that violence and warfare featured in pre-state societies.

"Primitive" warfare is not a new topic of investigation, having first been tackled by Hobbes and Rousseau – the bibliography of related works is now endless. This book aims neither to be scholarly nor exhaustive. Aimed at a broad readership and written by a prehistorian and a medical doctor specialized in ancient pathology, the primary aim of this work is to outline certain problems, to discuss particular pieces of archeological evidence, and to raise questions: in short, to present rather than to prove. At no point does this work aim to make generalizations, preferring instead to focus upon a handful of the many issues relating to this complex field – a field made all the more complex by the vast range of cultures that have characterized human society over time and space. The pitfalls of basing this work upon a few select issues are clear; for this reason, it was necessary to delimit the subject matter. Mediterranean and European prehistory and protohistory form the main emphasis of discussion, although examples are occasionally taken from other parts of the world. The main subject for discussion can be summarized in two simple questions: What do we know about the violence and first conflicts of the Mediterranean and Europe? How should we interpret existing evidence? Answering the latter question is far from easy. One view is that confrontations are rooted in a long and distant history. The ideological construction of the warrior thus evolved over time and, once established, led to the emergence and widespread acceptance of an ideal: the hero.

Acknowledgments

The authors are indebted to Maryvonne Naudet and Raymond Videl for their laborious work in documenting all evidence of arrow-inflicted wounds and other injuries dating from the Neolithic in France, a task which took many long months to complete.

They also wish to offer their thanks to Philippe Chambon, Georges Costantini, and Dominique Sacchi for their help in rereading certain passages of the manuscript, making suggestions, and providing information, all of which enriched the text and its content.

Numerous colleagues also offered various invaluable details and suggestions: Angel Armendariz, Joan Bernabeu, Éric Crubézy, Henri Duday, Daniel Fabre, Dominique Gambier, Christian Goudineau, Christian Jeunesse, Olivier Lemercier, Bernardo Marti, Rafael Martinez Valle, Fabio Martini, Oriol Mercadal, Béatrix Midant-Reynes, Marylène Patou-Mathis, Yannick Rialland, Anne-Marie Tillier, and Dr. Joachim Wahl. The authors wish to express their deepest gratitude to all.

Introduction

Bloodshed at the Beginning of History

Before delving into the depths of prehistory, it is useful to gain an initial overview of the beginning of history, a time when the first states and earliest towns, in their thirst for domination, became locked in an endless cycle of conflict. Such instability characterized the cities of Sumer in Mesopotamia from around 3000 to 2500 BCE. At this time, Sumerian city-states were already at war and destroying one another, disputing territories, seizing each others' troops, and employing force to rob neighboring towns of their riches.[1] Treasures from the royal tombs of Ur reveal the full splendor of these riches: gold, silver, and bronze vessels, sophisticated weaponry, and jewelry made from precious metals and exotic stones which include lapis lazuli imported all the way from mines in Afghanistan. One burial ground dating from around 2,500 years ago was found to contain the "Standard of Ur," a double-sided panel decorated with scenes of figures. The panel is made of a mosaic of shells inlaid with carnelian and lapis lazuli and set in bitumen (see plate 1). One side shows battle scenes and prisoners being captured. Chariots, laden with projectiles and pulled by onagers, charge over fallen enemies while prisoners file, stripped of their clothing, before the king and his dignitaries. The central section shows yet more defeated prisoners, again stripped of their clothing, being escorted by a victorious army of infantrymen all wearing helmets and protected by heavy capes. This indicates that there was a real army with infantrymen and chariots of war. Sumerian soldiers actually had a range of weapons at their disposal – pikes, axes, clubs, daggers – and were able to defend themselves with their shields. Their weaponry also included a ceremonial dagger which was a kind of sword with a crescent-shaped blade, resembling a saber. The bow, though less widely used at this time, soon reappeared on the battlefield.

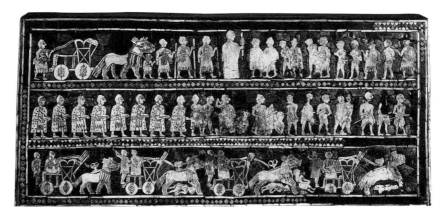

Plate 1 Standard of Ur from one of the "royal" tombs, Mesopotamia,
ca. 2500 BCE. Double-sided panel decorated with a mosaic of shells set in bitumen
and inlaid with lapis lazuli and carnelian, known as the "war" panel. Top row:
prisoners, stripped of their clothing, file before the king and his dignitaries.
Middle row: prisoners followed by an army of infantrymen. Bottom row: chariots
in action, crushing the bodies of fallen enemies. British Museum, London.
© The Bridgeman Art Library.

It is easy to see why, given the uncertain climate at that time, towns
defended themselves by erecting high walls, both as a symbol of their strength
and to provide effective protection for the population and their property.
Urban communities were guarded by high walls. The Uruk wall was the most
spectacular; it surrounded an area of 400 to 500 hectares, was more than
10 km in length, and comprised no fewer than 900 towers.

Art tends to favor the stronger side. The so-called "Stele of the Vultures,"
for example, marks the victory of the sovereign of Lagash over the sovereign
of the neighboring town of Umma in approximately 2450 BCE – it shows the
king and his infantrymen trampling over their fallen enemy.

These internal disputes were brought to an end with the founding of the
first Mesopotamian empire: in 2300 BCE, a Semite by the name of Sargon,
officer to the king of Kish, founded the kingdom of Akkad before embarking
upon a series of military campaigns which took him as far afield as Elam and
the outermost bounds of the Mediterranean.

There is every reason to believe that war dates back even further in
Mesopotamia. Scenes depicted on Uruk "cylinder seals," known to be one
thousand years older than the Akkad empire and several centuries older than
the graves at Ur, confirm the sovereigns' cruelty beyond all doubt; they are

depicted assisting in the cold-blooded execution of defeated prisoners. The execution of prisoners is a commonly recurring theme. Figurines often represent prisoners crouching down with their hands tied behind their backs, awaiting the ultimate punishment.

The Egyptians, generally portrayed as calm and peaceful, occasionally came under the rule of aggressive leaders who had no hesitation in enrolling mercenaries into their armies. Here too, acts of violence are known to have occurred well before the unification of the kingdom. Warfare was a common theme even then, judging by the fresco paintings decorating the plaster walls of tomb 100 at Hierakonpolis, in the region of Edfu; this mudbrick-lined tomb formed a kind of chamber for a notable individual during the second half of the fourth millennium BCE. The paintings decorating the tomb show curved, Gerzian-style boats, perhaps intended to represent a naval battle. There are also scenes of war and hunting: one figure is shown battling with two animals, perhaps lions. Elsewhere two figures confront each other, as if fighting a duel. In another painting, one figure is shown beating three enemies with a club.[2]

Figure 1 Gebel el-Arak dagger (Egypt). Enlarged detail of the ivory handle. Battle scenes are depicted on one side. After Sievertsen, cited in Midant-Reynes, 1999.

Another well-documented piece of evidence dating from this pre-dynastic era is the Gebel el-Arak dagger, which has a sculpted ivory handle (figure 1): on one side, there are scenes of fighting between various individuals and images of sea battles; the reverse side depicts an individual confronting wild animals. Both sides of the dagger show scenes of domination – over man and over wild animals.

These scenes of violence date from a time when Egypt was pursuing a series of conquests and was "manufacturing" power, resulting in the unification of the country under the pharaoh. In each of the various regions, rivalry led representatives from powerful families to assert themselves as leaders – there can be little doubt that such improper seizing of authority did not pass without upset. Tensions must have remained high both between influential towns, still defended by substantial fortifications, and between small kingdoms with their numerous extensions and ever-growing appetites for expansion. Force seems to have played an essential part in aims and interventions, in protecting populations and their possessions, and in subordination. Whether the unification of the country under the pharaoh was triggered by a successful conquest, as is often claimed, or whether, as seems more likely, it occurred in stages alongside the powerful acculturation movements of the day (led by the Nagadian elites and directed at the Delta lands), the image of the sovereign was nevertheless based upon his power and ability to defeat the enemy. War is an element of royal rule and contributes to the institutionalization of the post.[3]

The theme of victory in battle is clearly depicted upon the Narmer palette, which is said to tell the story of the unification of Egypt: the victory of the South over the North (figure 2). The king, wearing the white crown of Upper Egypt, is shown executing one of his subjects who kneels before him, held down by a Horus falcon which is perching upon papyri. At the bottom, two "swimmers" seem to signify naval combat. On the reverse side, the king is shown wearing a red crown to symbolize conquered land; preceded by his standard bearers, he can be seen observing the full extent of the battle – rows of decapitated bodies. This work is far more than just a depiction of tragedy, it is also allegorical: it symbolizes the omnipotent sovereign overpowering all who challenge him. Massacre is shown to be a symbol of authority. Raids were carried out by Egypt upon Nubia, Libya, and the Near East throughout the duration of the empire.

Briefly, the long succession of wars, invasions, and destruction which characterized the Eastern Mediterranean region during the second millennium BCE include: the destruction of the Babylonian empire by the Kassites and Hittites; raids carried out by the Kingdom of Hatti across the whole of the Anatolian periphery; nomad invasions which shook the Assyrian empire; successful invasions by the pharaohs as far afield as Nubia and Syria; and wars directed by the Ramessides against the Hittites and Sea Peoples.

Greek history seems to have been equally violent. In the third millennium BCE, eyries were built in the Cyclades islands and in Kastri (Syros) and concealed behind fortified walls in order to prevent piracy in the surrounding area. In Asia Minor, the second city of Troy erected fortified walls, flanked by towers, on a hilltop; other cities in Anatolia, Syria, and Palestine had similar defenses in place. In the second millennium BCE, the Mycenean cities of

Figure 2 Narmer palette (Egypt), ca. 3000 BCE. On one side (left), the king raises his club to strike his enemy, shown kneeling. The other side (right) shows the king, greatly enlarged in comparison with the other figures, preceded by his standard bearers and observing the battlefield where the bodies of his enemies are laid out. After B. Midant-Reynes.

Mycenae, Tiryns, and Pylos barricaded themselves in behind heavily fortified city walls and set about going to war.

War: An Ongoing Feature of Literature and Religion

Homer, the earliest of the Greek poets, set the tone in praising the virtues of warfare. In the *Iliad*, he describes how the Greeks and Trojans became enraged, thirsting for blood. Even the gods took sides, supporting their heroes. Homer refers repeatedly to the heroes' relentless efforts and describes scenes of horrific fatal injuries and decapitated bodies as the war continued to rage. Such sickeningly morbid details frequently form the focus of his descriptions. The *Odyssey* is just as violent: upon his return to Ithaca, Ulysses massacres Penelope's suitors in cold blood, leading to all-out carnage. So it seems that the Greeks, experts in the writings of Homer, were also schooled in violence and severity.

The works of the three great ancient Greek historians – Herodotus, Thucydides, and Xenophon – are largely devoted to warfare. Herodotus, the "father of history" renowned for having documented many well-known events, describes the battles that took place in the Aegean, Persia, Egypt, and the land of the Scythians. Thucydides devoted himself entirely to his one work, *The History of the Peloponnesian War*, which recounts the bloody confrontations that occurred between Sparta and Athens during the fifth century BCE. Xenophon picks up where this narrative left off in 411 BCE, describing the final stages of this encounter. Later, in *Anabasis*, he describes the fate of those Greek mercenaries who were in the pay of Cyrus, king of Persia, in the battle which brought Cyrus head to head with his brother and tells of their retreat through Anatolia back toward their motherland.

The Tragedians (Aeschylus, Euripides) alternate between accounts of war and family dispute. The works of the Sophists (Protagoras, Hippias, Prodicus) all refer to the advantages and disadvantages of war, some references being more obvious than others. Philosophers often discuss combat in an attempt to assign an ethical and existential value to the individual, enabling him to fight against fate. Even Plato's philosophical writings are scattered with accounts of warfare as, for example, in the *Symposium* in which the trouble-maker, Alcibiades (himself a defeated war leader), describes Socrates's exploits at the battle of Potidaea.

The sacred texts of the great monotheistic religions are no more peace-oriented. The Bible is a collection of military exploits: its exegesis reveals that retaliation, war, revenge, deportations, and the capturing of prisoners were common events. If we recognize that a large proportion of the verses are derived from even older legends, as in the case of the *Epic of Gilgamesh*, then the same glorification of violence can also be identified. Established in the seventh century of the common era (CE), the Qur'an makes no attempts to conceal its tendencies toward holy war or jihad as a way of subjugating or destroying infidels, although the majority of its suras do preach tolerance.

Violent warfare also forms an integral part of India's oldest religions. The most ancient sacred texts, such as the Bhagavad-Gita, declare war to be essential for any would-be hero. The Mahabharata, a Sanskrit epic of more than 200,000 verses, is devoted entirely to the never-ending confrontations between the Kaurava and the Pandava.

But what of ancient China, home of Confucianism and Taoism? Even here, it is said that the king of Qin (from which the European name for China is derived) had 240,000 people decapitated in 293 BCE in an attempt to end the war between Han and Wei. The reign of Huang Di, who brought unity to China in the third century BCE, followed a period of extensive bloodshed.[4] In around 500 BCE, Chinese polemics expert Sun Tzu wrote *The Art of War*, which was apparently considered to be an authoritative work by Japanese military institutions right up to the attack on Pearl Harbor on December 7, 1941.

In Central America, Cortez's conquistadors were appalled by the human sacrifices made during Aztec religious ceremonies, in which thousands of people were put to death in just one day. However, under the protection of the Cross, these very same Catholic conquistadors in turn slaughtered the Mexican populations.

How should we interpret this global barbarity which has infiltrated history from the very beginning? Has violent behavior been glorified and exaggerated over time in the interests of a few omnipotent leaders? Was history written primarily by the victorious and then manipulated for their own gain? Although exaggerations may have been made at times, war is nevertheless present throughout the earliest written works, both literary and religious. However, rather than looking at such written evidence, this study will focus primarily upon prehistoric archeology, exploring civilization before the advent of writing systems. The main objective is to define the behavior of humans before the emergence of the first states – this is essentially an archeological enterprise.

Archeology: Tracking Down History

If this analysis of conflict is to be based upon archeological finds, how can we be sure that this evidence is reliable? Is it really possible to piece together accurate reconstructions of battle scenes and invasions through archeology alone? Where certain styles of ceramics or metal tools have spread over a wide area, this is most likely due to acculturation or even a social exchange system. Yet experts often came to very different conclusions in the past. The wide-ranging distribution of certain objects has often been attributed to conflict and to the movement of people and objects this entails. As a social science, archeology has always been influenced by the prevailing historical and intellectual climate of the time. The popular notion that history revolves around fact and conflict has greatly shaped many of its conclusions over the years. The western world has been defined over time in terms of its invasions: pillaging throughout Europe carried out by bands of Celts, Germanic uprisings against the Roman empire, barbarian invasions, Arab raids, Norman incursions, the Hundred Years' War, and so on. The notion that conflict has regularly ravaged societies, either driving out inhabitants or reducing them to slavery, has long been accepted. The history of France, and similarly that of its neighboring countries, has long centered upon battles; it is often assumed that new geopolitical structures only emerge as a result of conflict. It is this somewhat "military" climate that has prompted archeologists in the past to focus upon the issue of defense mechanisms as symbols of resistance and security, instead of examining the more subtle evidence relating to everyday life.

Furthermore, archeologists have often tended to look to the past when contextualizing the present, even when contextualizing their world view. European archeology, such as it was during the first half of the twentieth century (a half-century ravaged by two world wars with intervals of cautious peace, during which there was little attempt to disarm), attributed changes in civilization to violent splits within a group. Changes in material culture were put down to one culture infiltrating another – it was thought that migration was responsible and that "outsiders" had erased all signs of the previous culture, replacing them with their own knowledge and ways of life. Each phase was thought to last anything from years to centuries, basically until newcomers invaded again, bringing with them a new set of cultural norms. Thus, the emergence of both the first agricultural civilizations and later the first protohistoric civilizations in Western Europe has long been regarded as the end result of a series of migratory movements, originating in the Eastern Mediterranean region and spreading outwards as each population gradually drove out or defeated the local population.

This version of history has since been greatly revised. Theories concerning the significance of invasions, the strength of the troops deployed, the extent of the distances covered, and the resultant upheavals have all since been greatly modified. Archeology began to focus instead upon domestic objects and everyday life. As a result, from the 1950s and 1960s, archeologists began to propose other reasons for changes in material culture, instead of assuming warfare to be the cause. Shifts from one stage in civilization to another were attributed to developments in the local population rather than to nearby or distant groups invading. In short, violent intervention and warfare were no longer considered responsible for such changes; instead indigenous development and progress alone were thought to be the cause.

There can be little doubt that this shift in viewpoint was not entirely "natural." It may well be that the decades of peace that followed World War II in Europe contributed to this more peace-oriented impression of how societies have evolved. Archeologists are also inevitably influenced by their own experiences. Despite their best attempts at remaining objective, their individual insights into the modern world and their own cultures may nevertheless affect their interpretation of the subject matter. The result of this mirroring effect will, of course, vary depending on factors such as the author's experience, age, material and cultural background, and opinions. During periods of migratory movements sparked by warfare, a peaceful vision of the past has tended to prevail, with the widespread assumption that early societies lived side by side in harmony and solidarity. Thus, it seems that present-day circumstances do have some bearing upon the prevailing theories of the time. This notion of prehistoric harmony may well be contested in the near future. Indeed, the wars in Bosnia and Kosovo may well lead some European archeologists to portray the past in less idyllic terms. Without wishing to cast doubt upon the integrity of researchers, it is nevertheless clear that archeological interpretations can never be entirely objective.

War in Prehistory: From the Garrigues of Languedoc to the Temples of Malta

Two examples will serve to back up these assumptions. In the south of France in the third millennium BCE, a Copper Age culture referred to as the Fontbouisse culture (named after a site in the French region of Gard) covered the area from Hérault in the west to the Rhone in the east, and from the Cévennes mountains to the sea. At times groups lived here in open dwellings with no means of defense (no moat, palisade, or walls), and at other times they lived in small communities protected by stone walls, reinforced in places with protruding circular structures. The latter type of site was first discovered during the excavation of the Lébous "castle" in Tréviers (Hérault). The sites were initially thought to have been fortresses, with bastions for further protection. Yet context is just as relevant as architectural evidence. This culture which once flourished upon the garrigues of Languedoc disappeared suddenly in around 2300–2200 BCE, having been replaced by a new population with an entirely different culture: new types of pottery appeared, bronze replaced copper, and material objects began to resemble those found in Northern Italy and the upper basin of the Rhone. Lifestyles also showed marked changes: very little stone was used in construction, unlike the preceding era when stone was the main building material – populations became more mobile again. These transformations were initially thought to be the direct result of a violent challenge from outside the group. It was proposed that the early Bronze Age populations, which inhabited the outer Alps, descended upon Languedoc, burning the fortified settlements to the ground and driving out the inhabitants. As a mark of extreme degradation, some of the dead were buried in the disused turrets.[5]

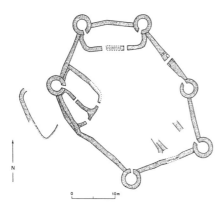

Figure 3 Boussargues (Argelliers, Hérault, France). Layout of the dry stone wall, which surrounded several dwellings, with circular structures built in at intervals, ca. 2500 BCE. After Colomer, Coularou, and Gutherz, 1990.

When a new generation of archeologists in Languedoc excavated the nearby site of Boussargues, another wall-enclosed site, their interpretation of the evidence had little to do with warfare. Despite being surrounded by walls, they thought this small settlement to be a farm rather than a fortress, with the outer buildings opening onto an inner courtyard (figure 3). The small towers in each corner were not thought to be bastions. Instead, it was presumed that they were small drystone, corbelled huts, perhaps for domestic use. Since no loopholes had been built into the wall, there was no clear evidence that the wall was erected for defense purposes.[6] As for the theory that early Bronze Age populations invaded the site, no conclusive evidence was found to this effect. Bronze Age settlers are known to have inhabited a site at Rocher-du-Causse in Claret (Hérault), another walled settlement. However, even here there is no evidence that the site was violently destroyed by these newcomers – in fact, they occupied the settlement themselves. It is even possible that these two groups were not contemporaries and thus never come into contact with each other. In this case, the original inhabitants could not have been forced out of their settlement.

These examples reveal how evidence relating to the history of one type of settlement can produce two entirely different interpretations.

The Maltese archipelago is a similar example in many ways. From 3500 to 2500 BCE, an innovative civilization prospered here, renowned for both its megalithic temples and its hypogea. Over this thousand-year period, Maltese sanctuaries began to exhibit specific, original design features, such as concave facades, trefoil floor plans, small loggias, and altars. Over this same period, rock faces were hollowed out to form artificial caves, each with several chambers. They served the island's farming communities as burial chambers with rooms set aside specifically for burial rituals. This highly distinctive and innovative culture, reflected by their architectural and artistic creations, disappeared suddenly in around 2500 BCE. Many different theories have been proposed as to why this should be, although it was long thought that violent attacks, sparked by jealousy and greed and intended to destroy this resourceful, insular civilization, were to blame. Opinions differed as to where these invaders came from – some thought from Sicily or Italy, whilst others proposed the Aegean or even Anatolia. Whatever the case, it was thought that these outsiders were oblivious to the sacred significance of the Maltese temples and so destroyed them, at times building new settlements in amongst the rubble. They even committed the sacrilegious act of constructing a cemetery for cremating their dead among the ruins of the Tarxien, the largest sanctuary upon the Maltese archipelago.[7]

Unfortunately this theory, which had long convinced experts, began to come apart at the seams when more detailed archeological investigations were carried out. Fresh investigations revealed a significant lapse in time between the temples being abandoned and the arrival of early Bronze Age settlers. In fact, by the time these "outsiders" first set foot upon the island, the Maltese civilization would already have been in significant decline – indeed, it may even have disappeared completely. Thus, it seems that internal ructions rather than violent attacks were to blame for the downfall of the golden age of Maltese temples. What sparked these internal disruptions is not known, though an economic crisis or social unrest are both possibilities. There can be little doubt that more detailed archeological studies have stripped the "military" theory of any credibility.

Corsica: Conquered and Reconquered

When it comes to linking events in protohistory with conflict, Corsica deserves further consideration. Over the years, much debate has centered around evidence of Bronze Age life on the island, raising the question of whether there was an invasion from the Mediterranean. Everything began after World War II when a number of small dwellings, possibly even simple monuments, were identified; these are composed of large blocks generally built up into a point and raised in relation to the surrounding land. The main feature of these small structures is usually a circular tower – a torre – surrounded by walled defenses (figure 4). The torres form the strong point of these structures and, though they are of more modest proportions, they are not unlike some of the nuraghes of Sardinia and the talayots found on the Balearic Islands. This type of architecture, developed during the Bronze Age, was thought to have appeared following the arrival of settlers from outside the area who came equipped with technical know-how previously unknown on the island. Evidence seemed to indicate that Corsican civilizations during the Neolithic and during the initial stages of the "metal" ages showed no marked differences in terms of their structural developments. Indeed, dolmens seem to have

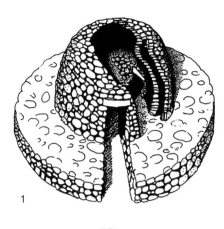

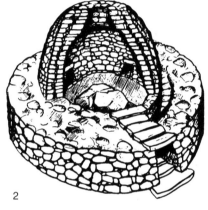

Figure 4 Examples of torres, vaulted structures that were a prominent feature of many Bronze Age sites in Corsica, 2nd millennium BCE: (1) Balestra; (2) Tappa. After Grosjean, 1966.

been their most significant architectural achievement. For this reason, these indigenous populations of the island are termed "Megalithic," whilst the new settlers, having brought new methods of construction to the island, are referred to as "Torreans" (from "torre"). The differences between these two populations were so vast that one can only assume that they must have been involved in disputes with each other. But in attempting to substantiate this theory, the situation becomes all the more complex.

Ever since Prosper Mérimée, Inspector-General of Historic Monuments under the July Monarchy, identified the first Corsican menhir-statues, a number of these unusual stone-sculpted monuments have been discovered. These upright stone statues were clearly a long-standing tradition on the island. Examples range from simple menhirs with vaguely human features to magnificent statues bearing elaborate anatomical detail. The "Megalithic" civilizations on the island became expert stonecutters, constructing dolmens and sculpting menhirs. However, during the second millennium BCE, this indigenous and peaceful population was suddenly attacked by invaders who seized the south of the island where they landed. It seems that even when confronted by violent hordes of invaders armed with swords and bronze daggers, the islanders still relied primarily upon their bows and stone-headed arrows. With no choice left but to hand over their land, the "Megalithic" population withdrew to the north of the island and waited for more stable times to arrive. The Torreans, by contrast, settled in the south and set about erecting their trademark citadels complete with torres throughout the area, demonstrating their superior strength, architecturally speaking.

Warfare and ambush between the two groups were common occurrences. Whenever the indigenous islanders killed one of the Torrean leaders in battle, they sculpted a stone statue bearing his features (figure 5). It is thanks to these humble sculptors that we have an idea of how these brutal Torreans would have dressed, looking fearsome in their horned helmets and breastplates or leather vests and carrying long swords. The Torreans themselves showed few artistic tendencies. They seem to have shown no interest at all in these statues, either smashing them or using them as crude stone tools to construct their fortresses. It seems that this is what occurred at Filitosa, a Torrean site in Southern Corsica where many of these statues, crushed into pieces, were re-used as building materials in the walls of some of the dwellings. So the Torreans, unlike the indigenous islanders, seem to have had no aesthetic appreciation.

These formidable newcomers were undoubtedly pirates. Disruption and destruction were not uncommon in the Eastern Mediterranean at this time owing to the displacement of populations over land and sea. Some of these communities have been christened the "Sea Peoples" and spread such great disruption and confusion as to trouble even some of the most powerful pharaohs of the time. In around 1179 BCE, Ramses III put a stop to the situation by inflicting a crushing defeat upon the Sea Peoples. The walls of

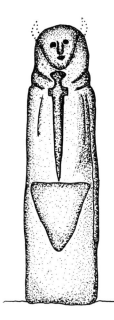

Figure 5 Cauria 2. Sculpted monolith (figure armed with a sword, a helmet with horns, and a loincloth (?)), intended to represent a Torrean "invader." After Grosjean, 1966.

Ramses's temple in Medinet-Habu, close to Thebes, were adorned with images of this victory, upon his command. The pharaoh's enemies, as they appear in these scenes of naval combat, have some features in common with the Torrean figures depicted upon the menhir-statues – both are shown wearing protective vests and, in particular, two-horned helmets (figure 6 and plate 2). The reasons for these similarities are clear: the "Sea Peoples" who fought against the pharaoh were the exact same "Sea Peoples" who invaded Corsica just a few centuries earlier; they were undoubtedly the Shardana referred to in many texts. It seems likely that they settled initially in Sardinia (the name of the island is thought to be derived from these settlers – the similarities between the words "Shardana" and "Sardinia" are evident); from here, they were naturally tempted to try their luck at conquering neighboring Corsica.

Figure 6 Detail of a fresco from the Medinet-Habu temple (Egypt), showing a scene from the battle between Ramses III and the Sea Peoples (ca. 1179 BCE). The image shows a warrior, one of the "Shardana." After Arnal, 1976.

Following several hundred years of prosperity, the Torrean civilization finally collapsed. The indigenous descendants of the "Megalithic" civilization, occupying the north of the island, had little sympathy for these "intruders" and eventually reconquered the island, bringing to an end this lengthy period of foreign occupation.[8]

This is a fascinating history, even if warfare does have a frequent part to play. Unfortunately, it is entirely speculative. The lack of written accounts means that experts must rely upon inadequate material evidence to reconstruct this sequence of events. In attempting to fill the gaps in history with speculation, in this case concerning migratory movements, archeological theories often come unstuck. Indeed, archeology as a discipline will begin to lose credibility if it is forced to rely entirely upon such unsubstantiated theories.

Plate 2 Filitosa (Corsica), armed Bronze Age statue, second millennium BCE.
The figure is equipped with a sword complete with cruciform hilt and a bronze
dagger. © AKE-Images/Eric Lessing.

The theory proposed above covers many of the features that frequently play a part in history: invasion and warfare, victorious new settlers armed with superior technological knowledge (in this case architectural skills and bronze weaponry) yet incapable of adapting to local tradition (such as the menhir-statues), eventually resulting in the courageous indigenous population resisting the invaders and regaining control of their "freedom."

The flaws in this theory soon become clear. Firstly, there are "Torrean" sites in both the north and south of Corsica – thus, there was no cultural segregation upon the island. Furthermore, research indicates that stone structures did not just make a sudden appearance at some point during the second millennium BCE; instead it seems that they were the result of a long process of development which began at least 1,000 years earlier, if not before.[9] The "Torreans" merely represent one stage in Corsican prehistory, a stage characterized by external influences at a time when the Mediterranean region was beginning to open up. As for the broken statues, it is likely that they were sculpted and then destroyed by the "Torreans" themselves whenever they wished to challenge their ancestral heroes. This provides a much simpler explanation than the alternative, which sought to describe the scarce archeological evidence in terms of fact and warfare and looked to the east (always the east!) for answers when all else failed.

Violence and Aggression Before Humans

With these warnings on interpreting evidence out of the way, it is time to investigate the origins of human aggressiveness. Firstly, it is useful to analyze aggressiveness in primates and more generally in higher-order mammals in order to substantiate our theories with biological evidence. From a Darwinian perspective, the main evolutionary mechanisms in operation actually indicate that there is a strong link between aggressiveness in our closest animal ancestors and aggressiveness in hominids. However, humans are unique in targeting this aggressiveness for maximum impact. This line of research has been followed up by zoologists and more specifically by experts in animal behavior. Their work has resulted in a new perception of primatology – the discipline devoted to the study of those primates most closely related to humans. This discipline, originally restricted to laboratories and animal houses, has now become one of the standard behavioral sciences, renowned in particular for having developed a new understanding of animal aggressiveness.[10]

The results obtained during research are directly relevant to determining the biological components that underlie violent behavior in humans. These results can be divided into three categories depending on the situation in which the individual is placed: (1) the individual against members of the same social group, (2) the individual and the rest of the group against other groups of the same species, and (3) the individual and/or the rest of the group against other individuals and/or groups of another species.

The first instance concerns the level of aggressiveness exhibited by individuals in a social group of animals, be it a pack or herd, toward other individuals within the same group. Evidence indicates that aggressive behavior materializes during crisis situations sparked off by the drive to survive and reproduce. Fighting between male members of the group determines which individual is most dominant and thus most capable of securing the fertile females. Paleolithic paintings often depict such seasonal clashes between male ibices, stags, and other mammals. Such behavior is also common among the big cats (lions), prairie dogs, and chimpanzees. It is important to note that these struggles tend to result only in minor injuries (bites, scratches, or blows); there are no brutal killings.

Among predatory animals (carnivores such as felines and canines), confrontations between individuals within the same social group frequently erupt when prey is being shared out, particularly when such food is scarce. Squabbles and fights break out as individuals chase each other around the prey, awaiting their share. Intimidation tactics often result in biting and serious injuries.

It has been known for aggressiveness to be taken one step further among the big cats, most notably lions; females, sometimes accompanied by a dominant male, have been observed killing and devouring the cubs of another female. This behavior is far from common and seems to occur most notably during severe food shortages. Chimpanzees have also been observed exhibiting this extreme behavior, though again very rarely. In this case, however, there is no evidence of omophagy, i.e., animal cannibalism, occurring.

Another level of violence (if one can apply the term to animal behavior) can arise as a result of confrontation between two social groups, usually carnivores such as felines, lycaons, and hyenas. Such confrontations are almost always prompted by attempts to seize or defend territories valued for hunting or predation. Anthropoid apes (chimpanzees and gorillas) also carry out such attacks. Identifying the reasons for such behavior in predatory carnivores and apes is far from easy. Whilst the instinctive urge to gain control over territories rich in prey may well lead to fighting, other less specific reasons have also been suggested by ethologists following research carried out by Morris. It is claimed, for example, that modifications of an ecological niche and specific pathological traits can trigger abnormal behavior.

The problem becomes all the more complex in the case of apes, which are known to throw projectiles and even use branches as clubs when carrying out assaults on other groups. Could this be how the use of weapons in pre-human species first came about?

New research has also revealed a tendency to expel certain members of a social group among certain species of ape. Whilst this generally prevents a female from mating with her offspring, it also leads to aggressive behavior within the group. This "biological" attempt to prevent incest (which the authors in question claim to be Darwinian behavior) is highly significant: it indicates that more complex social relations may have evolved in pre-human primates, a complexity which is not exhibited by the other species of carnivorous mammal discussed here. This behavior is accompanied by changes in the cerebral capabilities of these apes which may have been responsible for the emergence of new behavioral patterns in early humans and their descendants with violence becoming a kind of "cerebral" behavior, at the center of new urges and desires.[11]

Aggressiveness between different species, on the other hand, is related primarily to predation. Whereas felines and canines hunt for prey, pre-hominid apes were omnivorous. The Australopithecines, by contrast, are often compared to vultures since they frequently devoured the remains of herbivorous mammals left behind by predators. It is even possible that Australopithecines may have exhibited a kind of "proto-fighting" behavior prior to actual hunting, a behavior that would have continued to evolve throughout the Paleolithic.

It is likely that predatory strategies and techniques became more complex and "human-like" as cerebral capabilities evolved, as outlined above. As well as leading to the development of hunting, this evolutionary process may also have triggered more violent behavior with the same weapons being used both in hunting and in fighting.

Thus it seems that a certain amount of biologically driven aggressive behavior is directed at animals of the same species and becomes particularly fierce when motivated by competition for sexual partners or food, though it is very rare for any individual to be killed during such conflicts. By contrast, playful interaction, rest, and "civility" all play an important part in feline behavior.

When confrontation between different social groups within the same species does occur, intimidation seems to be preferable to inflicting injury; violent behavior is reserved for crisis situations when competition for hunting territories is rife. Deaths often occur when individuals become isolated from the group (due to immaturity, old age, or illness), thus losing the protection offered by the group setting.

Murder is particularly rare among the apes and most notably among our closest relatives, the anthropoid apes. Confrontations tend to involve the use of projectiles. Incest is also prevented by aggressive, though not fatal, moves to exclude certain individuals from the group.

If carrying out such research into our closest ancestors does indeed play an essential part in identifying the beginnings of human violence, both on an individual and a group level, then it seems that, as human beings, we cannot resort to the excuse that our violence is a product of our pre-hominid evolution; it is the human brain alone which has made us the most dangerous of all animals.

Warfare: Nature or Culture?

Violence and conflict are frequently discussed as though they are specific to the period from the Neolithic onwards. This perspective is based upon a more "materialistic" view of human behavior – it is only since the emergence of the first agricultural civilizations that humans have accumulated wealth and surpluses which have, in turn, led to greed and competition. Capitalization and signs of prosperity are certain to trigger feelings of greed in the less well off.

It is, however, of greater interest to turn our attention to hunter-gatherer populations which tend not to amass supplies long term (except perhaps for the more civilized hunter-gatherer societies) and thus envy is less common. In view of this, it is useful to investigate whether or not they, too, are faced with conflict in times of crisis and suffer from this apparent necessity to initiate confrontation at regular intervals. Two different perspectives may be adopted here, one based upon archeological evidence and the other upon anthropological fact. Although material evidence relating to battle is often lacking, many prehistorians consider it likely that violent clashes have taken place between different groups since the Paleolithic. Leroi-Gourhan believes this to be the case. He claims that hunting and warfare form part of an aggressive behavior which is inherent in human beings and has been since "Australanthrope" times and possibly even earlier. In his view aggression, i.e., the use of violence, is essential in so far as it is a technique for acquiring food. Hunting is essential for survival and thus aggression is an essential means of subsistence. Seen from this perspective, warfare is merely an extension of hunting – an "equivalent"of hunting. War, like hunting, is "natural"; essentially it is "man hunting."[12]

This view has sparked many responses. Clastres, in particular, challenges this interpretation, claiming that biological and "natural" factors cannot explain social behavior; instead sociological factors are relevant here. Warfare, he maintains, is a human and cultural phenomenon – the result of acquired, not innate, behavior. Clastres's theory draws an important distinction between aggression as an action, used to obtain food (i.e., hunting), and aggressiveness, a human behavior relating to warfare. Furthermore, he points out that, whilst hunting is a means of providing nourishment in the form of animal flesh, warfare rarely results in cannibalism. Thus, the role of sociological factors should not be underestimated by focusing too heavily upon biology. "Primitive warfare is not linked in any way to hunting; it is not deeply rooted in the reality of man as a species, but rather in the social being of primitive society. The universality of primitive warfare indicates that it is cultural, not natural."[13]

Others consider that primitive warfare is the result of poverty and is triggered by economic factors similar to those which brought about agricultural production and capitalization in the Neolithic. In the case of hunter-gatherer societies, however, resources tend to be scarce. It is thought that this may lead to goods and territory being seized from neighboring groups. This theory is based upon a somewhat impoverished view of prehistoric society, yet research has indicated with near certainty that early societies were perfectly capable of meeting their nutritional requirements, albeit at a cost to their limited time and energy. In view of this, it seems that the reasons for warfare must lie elsewhere.

According to Clastres, primitive societies (hunter-gatherers and "primitive" farmers) actually enjoy war. The vast quantity of ethnological literature written between the sixteenth century, when America and its so-called "savages" were first discovered, and the nineteenth and twentieth centuries, when westerners ventured into the remaining unexplored areas of the world, reveals that the indigenous populations of America, Africa, and Melanesia as well as nomads in Australia and farmers in New Guinea all took to battle with enthusiasm (plate 3). Chronicles, travel reports, and accounts written by religious, military, and administrative figures regularly describe war-like situations and warrior-like behavior. "Primitive societies are violent societies; war forms the very fabric of their social existence."[14] This may well be equally true of western prehistoric civilizations.

On a more general note, Keeley's work attempts to compare prehistoric populations (tribes existing before the formation of "primitive" states) and civilized populations (familiar with written script and with a certain degree of centralization in place). Keeley endeavors to prove that warfare between pre-state populations has resulted in greater bloodshed than modern-day or contemporary warfare. Studies of ethnographic populations

Plate 3 Battle scene among the Dani of Papua New Guinea, early 1960s. © Film Study Center, Harvard University.

have revealed significant death rates during periods of conflict (figure 7): 32.7 percent (of the total population) among the Jivaro (59 percent of males), 20.9 percent among the Venezuelan Yanomami-Shamatari (37.4 percent of males), and between 15.5 percent and 18.6 percent among certain groups in Papua New Guinea (Dugum Dani and Mae Enga). Only 2 percent of the population was killed in warfare during the Western European wars of the seventeenth century, while the French military encounters of the nineteenth century resulted in 3 percent of the population being killed.[15] Warfare seems to be more frequent in pre-state populations than in modern-day societies. Furthermore, murder and pillaging still occur in societies traditionally considered to be peaceful. It is, however, worth noting that violence is absent from some societies, for example, the Mbuti Pygmy population of Central Africa and the Shoshone and Paiute populations of the Great Basin.[16]

The theory that warfare occurred in the Upper Paleolithic societies of the West seems entirely plausible, in view of the constant levels of aggression displayed by present-day hunting populations such as the American Indians.

Many have sought to contrast primitive warfare with modern-day warfare. Primitive warfare operates on lower numbers, often involving individual

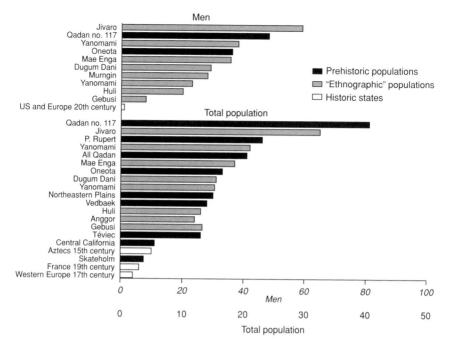

Figure 7 Percentage of men killed (above) and percentage of total population killed (below) in warfare across a range of societies. After Keeley, 1996.

volunteers who are not "specialists" and have no elaborate strategic plan. It tends to take the form of confrontation, with no authority figure on either side, and participants are undisciplined and unorganized. By contrast, "modern" warfare brings together professional armies prepared for combat, organized into distinct and rigid hierarchies and issued with highly effective weaponry. There are, however, certain similarities between the two. In most societies, for example, it is the adult males who engage in combat. The techniques adopted also reveal a certain continuity in the aims of warfare, particularly when viewed from a broad chronological perspective. Humans have always had deadly weapons and the most advanced technological developments of the day at their disposal such as the bow, invented toward the end of the Pleistocene era, and early metallurgy, applied in the production of weapons (daggers, swords, and spears) several thousand years later. These weapons were used over thousands of years, right up until guns and crossbows made their first appearance. This will be discussed in greater detail later in the book.

Exchange or Battle?

Is humanity's natural state to be at war or at peace? Do archeology and anthropology offer any answers to this question? Prehistorians and ethnologists alike have been criticized for frequently failing to address the issue of warfare in their work.[17] Both actual and potential conflicts have passed unnoted and, as a result, primitive societies have often been portrayed as peaceful. This omission could partly be explained as follows: the "savages" first discovered in America in the sixteenth century lived in stateless societies, i.e., with no one individual or individuals dominating or being dominated, and thus these societies can essentially be described as "incomplete" or in their infancy; war and violence tended not to occur, since they result from conflict and dispute between states and are thus products of a more recent stage in human evolution. However, although violence is reportedly unknown in some societies, the vast majority of ethnographic studies are full of references to warriors and ongoing conflicts in "primitive" societies. Even as early as the seventeenth century, Hobbes notes that these "savages" seemed to have a thirst for war. He claimed that the constant disruptions stemmed from the lack of any state or government in these societies – there was no authority figure to establish and oversee social organization. According to this philosophy, humans cannot fully develop their capabilities in the absence of discipline; without laws and regulations, humans are destined to endure solitude, acrimony, rebellion, and dispute. This state of continually mistrusting others creates constant conflict: *"bellum omnium contra omnes* (war of all against all)."[18]

Clastres describes this frequent need for war as a means of resisting the state, perceived to be a body which integrates and restrains the individual, almost like shackles. He claims that "primitive" societies fight in order to retain their individualism and liberty – they refuse to be dragged into a system in which the powerful dominate. After all, these "primitive" populations tend to divide, not unify, and strive for independence, not centralization. Through warfare, this resistance is periodically expressed. Its main aim is to maintain a regular dispersal of the population. In this sense at least, "primitive warfare is the means to a political end," a logic of difference, in order that inequality, division, and exploitation by a superior body (the state) are systematically avoided.

This autarkic ideal does not by any means prevent exchange from taking place between societies, although this does tend to be a last resort. Exchanges are kept to a minimum and societies strive to be self-sufficient, in so far as this is possible. Alliances between groups, facilitating the circulation of goods, are established with great mistrust and tactics may be used to buy time. Exchange agreements are only ever entered into grudgingly, with resignation. Furthermore, alliances are never permanent and are often broken – inconsistency and betrayal are primary reasons for breaking agreements, often sparking conflict. It seems that war takes place most frequently between neighboring populations which, due to their close proximity, are commonly tied by alliances and exchange systems. Thus, exchange is nothing more than a tactic, whilst war is an actual institution. Violence is neither anecdotal nor transient, rather it is of central importance. "Primitive societies are violent societies; they are essentially warlike." Their thirst for political independence and rejection of submission leads them to form as few alliances as possible, thus reducing the risk of integration – after all, even the slightest deviation from this could lead, sooner or later, to the formation of a state.

This view stands in direct contrast with the theory proposed by Lévi-Strauss who claims that alliances and exchange were at the very heart of human interaction in early societies. He believes that war is merely a brief downside to union and communication, a temporary deviation which, despite its often deadly consequences, quickly highlights the need for alliances. What better way for two conflicting groups to make their peace than through marriage and forming new acquaintances, thus reducing the risk of further conflict and strengthening cooperation.[19] Humanity tends toward union and regrouping. As Lévi-Strauss famously put it: "War is an exchange gone wrong; exchange (of people or goods) prevents war."

Although these two theories clearly contradict one another, they do highlight two consistencies in human behavior: the need for peace and contact and the desire to strive for freedom and reject constraint.

Was there a Paleolithic "War"?

The word "war" should be understood in its most general sense here – the sense is not one of armed conflict but rather of bloody clashes between small groups, raids carried out on neighboring parties, ambush attacks, and even individual murders. If this definition of war is deemed to be valid, hunter-gatherer societies must be viewed in an entirely different light. It would no longer be possible to perceive these "abundantly stocked societies," amply provided for by nature, as peaceful, incapable of harming others, and guided by an immeasurable generosity. Indeed, this definition of war dismisses the image of the Paleolithic as being a Garden of Eden, instead presenting it as a lengthy era during which, at times, man had no hesitation in slaying his fellow man.

The very suggestion of this is always greeted with a certain degree of reluctance since humans have always tended to portray their origins in a more favorable light. Even for some researchers, the idea of a mythical Golden Age, a paradise on earth in which humans lived alongside their gods (or God) as their equal, was more than merely a utopia. Several well-respected prehistorians had no hesitation in likening this blissful image to the Paleolithic, perceived to have been "a kind of Eden where Stone Age man lived in symbiosis with nature."[20] According to this line of reasoning, prehistory can be divided into two phases of varying length, each exhibiting marked differences in human behavior. Throughout the majority of the Paleolithic, humans would have lived a wild and natural existence (natural in the sense of being close to nature), thriving upon the fruits of their natural environment. From the Neolithic onwards, humans would have begun to "distance" themselves from nature, rejecting nature and becoming unruly, "unnatured," and violent, forced from then onwards to work hard to ensure a basic subsistence and secure a future.

New skills acquired during the Neolithic, the new Stone Age, may well have led to the cultivation of plants and the domestication of certain species of animal. However, these beneficial changes were accompanied by highly detrimental developments such as warfare. In the words of Chavaillon:

Successful first attempts at agriculture, cattle breeding and constructing dwellings (whether individual or non-individual dwellings), farms and villages would have led any unscrupulous or ravenous neighboring groups to desire similar luxuries. And so security for one group became temptation for another. During the Paleolithic, man sought food on a daily basis; he had only his prey to defend. Neolithic man, by contrast, stored and amassed food supplies – cereals were stored in silos and herds put out to graze in paddocks. The sturdy dwellings and defended villages also ensured a relatively secure lifestyle. However, man soon became prey himself, his material wealth motivating the deprived and dishonest to seize these possessions.

The Neolithic brought about more than just new techniques and ways of living; war too emerged as a way of acquiring land, livestock, and material goods. Defeating an enemy also results in the destruction of the enemy's shelter and community. Whilst Paleolithic man lived off game, wild plants, and vegetation, villagers driven from homes demolished or burnt down found themselves destitute, often having lost their essential hunter-gatherer instincts. War gradually became part of everyday life and made its mark upon the landscape. The numerous village fires led to the regular construction of new buildings, thus widening and raising the base of the original site. This eventually formed a layered mound, each layer representing one stage of habitation. And so war, too, can provide a means of archeological reconstruction.[21]

Some of these claims could be discussed in greater detail in strictly archeological terms, such as tells and tepes, the name given to artificial mounds formed by the continual accumulation of debris upon a site, each layer forming upon the debris of the previous settlement. Many of these stratified sites are the result of constant rebuilding, replanning, and remodeling of villages as layouts were constantly reassessed. This often required the existing dwelling or area to be flattened first, usually through setting fire to the buildings, as was the case at certain sites associated with the Vinca culture in the Balkans.[22] Fire also served as an effective means of eradicating insects and disease. It is, however, possible that some of these settlements were destroyed in fires linked to warfare, although distinguishing between deliberately started yet "peaceful" fires and fires linked to pillaging is no easy task, indeed it is often impossible. And, of course, there are always accidental fires!

What is more interesting and lies at the very heart of this debate is the potential dichotomy between "natural" and peaceful Paleolithic man and Neolithic man, assumed to be more civilized, "cultured," distanced from nature, and violent.

It is important to note that the human species – *Homo sapiens* – has remained the same for some 200,000 years, whether we are referring to the Paleolithic, Neolithic, or the present day. There has been little variation in human intellectual capabilities over this period, despite humans becoming increasingly distanced from nature over time; this can be attributed, most notably, to the growing number of technical advances made by humankind. There is no denying that today, as a species, we inhabit a highly artificial environment; despite this, our biological makeup and mental capacity are the same as those of our Cro-Magnon ancestors.

For this reason, any theory seeking to contrast the Paleolithic as a peaceful period and the Neolithic as an era characterized by warfare must be based purely on cultural factors; although humans undoubtedly derived great benefits from the introduction of culture, such as the cultivation of cereals and domestication of animals – essentially artificial food sources – these developments also brought tension.

Although there is no doubt that conflict frequently revolves around ownership of material goods, this does not explain all inter-community clashes. The breakdown of alliances, causing or taking offense, ongoing animosities, and the notion of "inherited enemies" are all equally valid reasons as to why simple quarrels may turn violent, yet none of these reasons is linked to agricultural production. Thus, it may well be that these causes of conflict date back to beyond the Neolithic.

It is also worth noting a particular shortcoming of science, which has had a tendency to accept certain popular conceptions held by our own culture, using "objective" evidence as proof. By drawing contrasts between hunter-gatherers, thriving on the riches of nature, and farmers, forced to work "by the sweat of their brows" in order to keep up with their agriculture and livestock, the antagonism between the original earthly paradise and the time of the Fall from Grace (when humankind is said to have fallen from God's favor, having been forced to work ever since) is recreated, albeit at a more scholarly level. Confirmation of this is supposedly provided by the scientific and cultural communities, which have combined "hard" proof with popular, naive, and mythical views – the result is pure fiction. In fact, science has merely drawn upon the banal notions and unfounded assumptions that lie deeply rooted in the human mentality and culture.[23] The result is an accepted viewpoint presented as a complex idea, a pitfall which prehistorians researching the origins of our species must avoid. It is important to question any commonly held conceptions and obvious explanations, for these tend to be based upon cultural responses and present a biased view of primitive civilization.

Ritual Warfare and War between "Great Men"

The conventional view of bloody conflict should not neglect to take account of ethnology, which documents many conflict situations that often have little to do with widespread war and violence. In addition to the violent encounters that spring to mind whenever there is mention of hostilities and groups attacking one another in the name of revenge, invasion, or pillaging, there are also ritual wars, the aim of which is to identify the most courageous individuals from two given groups. These conflicts can be compared to a kind of game or sport in which it is necessary to adhere to very specific conventions.

Laburthe-Tolra divides warfare among the Beti of the Cameroon into three categories; he identifies two types of bloody warfare – brutal violence, for which there are no rules, and widespread plundering. These formidable confrontations are also accompanied by a third type of encounter – ritualized, organized warfare, which is treated like a game.[24] The author draws an interesting parallel between ritual warfare and *abia*, a game of chance in which a die is used: players may end up destitute, reduced to slave status. Ritual warfare may also be a violent kind of a game in certain situations; participants can try their luck either peacefully by playing or physically by fighting.

This analogy is reflected in the vocabulary of the Beti: they talk of "dying" or "being killed" instead of losing a game. In the same vein, war is like a gamble, "risking everything, physical and material." This game-like side to war can be explained by the theory that there is always an element of chance in the outcome of any battle, although those who deserve to win always have courage, dexterity, and strength on their side. "Going to war is like throwing a die; the individual's powers of survival are determined solely by unseen forces; it is merely a matter of revelation, of the individual deciphering his fate under the mysterious eye of chance; he does this with some haste – going to war is the making of a man."[25] According to this theory, in pursuing such bloodthirsty games the individual aims to make clear his intentions, to risk and eliminate chance as a factor, whilst at the same time attracting the attention of others, increasing his standing, ensuring he is held in the highest esteem and gaining in wealth. Ritual warfare is a risk which, if taken, may allow an individual to prove his worth, gaining him notoriety and affluence. Clearly, ritual warfare has great social and economic benefits. The successful individual attains his new status following union as well as violence; among the Beti, the successful individual "offers his sister's hand in marriage to the brother of the deceased as a gesture of peace. The result is the formation of a new alliance, assuming the large-scale game which constitutes this small-scale war adheres to the necessary rules."

Among certain populations, ritual warfare is accompanied by bloody duels, designed to bring exceptionally courageous individuals face to face in battle. Godelier examines such behavior among the Baruya of Papua New Guinea, a population characterized by its constant inter-tribal conflicts, ended by the redistribution of agricultural land and hunting ground. Although skillful archers came head to head in battle, they still maintained a certain distance from their enemy; similarly, ambush attacks were not uncommon, though never serious. However, it was not unknown during confrontation for the bravest warriors to break away from the two warring sides to engage in direct, violent conflict; their aim was to smash their opponents' skulls using stone cudgels. These fierce warriors were known as *aoulattas*. Their prestige was attributable to their bravery and dexterity as well as to magical talents, thought to explain their speed, precision, and deadly (and somewhat supernatural) powers.[26] Having killed his enemy and recovered the body, an *aoulatta* was entitled to eat his victim's arms and legs in order to obtain power, whilst the other warriors smeared themselves with the victim's blood. Despite this, the warriors gained very little in terms of material wealth – protecting the village against pillagers and intruders was considered to be their role and fate. Their prestige meant that they were respected as a source of authority, even during times of peace, and were active in resolving disputes within the community. However, if ever they took advantage of the situation to profit from their status, they were condemned and punished. They were also forbidden from killing an enemy during times of peace since only the tribal assembly was accorded the power to declare war.

In primitive society, ritual warfare, battles between warriors, and duels can also serve as a means of limiting confrontation and losses. In this sense these limited confrontations (limited both in terms of the number of participants and level of danger involved) provide a means of settling a disagreement with a minimum of risk. These forms of consensus between populations offer a way of reducing and minimizing the extent of violence – they attempt to establish a peaceful existence. Any necessary clashes still occur periodically, yet are controlled as best they can be by minimizing their extent. Even if ritual warfare does result in some fatalities or casualties, this is strictly limited. Traditional warfare, by contrast, places no restrictions on violence, and thus there are greater numbers of participants and victims involved.

Prehistoric Man: Neither Brutish Nor Docile

Popular depictions of prehistoric humans tend to be comical; they generally portray a very different picture to the one presented in this work. Many comic strips depict prehistoric man as a rather brutish figure: his head sunk into his shoulders, surly and distinctly unintelligent, he leaves his damp cave in search of food, club in hand. His spouse is not much better off: her hair is pinned up using two bones and hygiene is not her strong point as she wanders around among scraps of discarded food. This laughable creature is the popular artistic portrayal of prehistoric man, and yet prehistoric humans were actually responsible for painting some of the great artistic works in Lascaux, Altamira, and Chauvet.

However, some attempts at presenting the opposite view have also been made. Over the last couple of centuries, certain artists have focused more upon everyday life in primitive society, often portraying prehistoric man as calm and serene. One scene, for example, shows an elderly man with a beard, the grandfather of the group, passing on his advice to the intrepid, muscular hunters. Large-breasted women, often topless (regardless of the climate!), watch over their playful children. All around, there are lush and wholesome scenes of nature; life is calm and tranquil.

These two conflicting impressions are, of course, just caricatures. However, they are not as harmless as they may appear. They convey two very different views of prehistoric humans in their simple and mundane fashion. The second stereotype portrays these first humans as Olympian creatures, as lambs basking in original innocence in their lavish surroundings. The first, by contrast, evokes the impression of an almost animal-like existence: the human species would have had a long way to go to rid itself of such a barbaric lifestyle and become gradually "civilized." These simplistic impressions can be transposed, exaggerations aside, onto a more ideological plane.

The theory of the noble savage revolves around the idea that primitive life was free of any aggression and cruelty, thus there was no reason for conflict. The supposedly non-violent nature of human beings and the peaceful natural world were said to complement each other "ecologically." As we have already seen, two similar theories favor the notion that the first humans were peaceful. The religious viewpoint sees human destiny as a gradual deterioration: at the outset, humans inhabited a bucolic setting beside God, yet made the mistake of attempting to defy their Creator. Humans were thus expelled from Paradise and condemned to a life of toil and strife. Thus, humans are never satisfied, their destiny amounting to an endless search for this paradise lost. The scientific view is that Paleolithic life was relatively easy since nature presented so many possibilities and, at this time, there were fewer populations to share them. Humans were, therefore, able to profit from the situation by balancing the many resources at their disposal. Many anthropologists have also expressed this view – some even conclude that Paleolithic man had a great deal of free time at his disposal since obtaining food would have taken very little time at all. The arrival of the Neolithic tolled the knell of this golden age as humans became slaves to work: there was a regression of sorts as servitude began in earnest – a gradual descent into Hell.

The other view of the history of humankind is linked to the notion of progress. This viewpoint claims that savage man in his wild and shabby state, barely able to survive, gradually began to leave behind his inferior status through sheer persistence; by working hard and applying himself, man finally took control of nature. Thus, his destiny is one of continual improvement. Man is seen to be in control of his own plight and depends upon himself alone. Even works written much earlier on the subject, which based their arguments upon economic factors (Varro) or technological developments (Lucretius), have tended to focus upon the various stages in human evolution (from an initial state of ignorance through to developing agriculture and metallurgy) before humanity attained its superior status. Written during the nineteenth century, Morgan's evolutionary classification describes early humans as "savage" (and cannibalistic!). It is claimed that humans passed through a series of successive stages, making economic and social progress along the way, to become "barbaric" (but creative) and finally "civilized" with the advent of writing.[27] This same theory was adopted by Marxist philosophers and skilled prehistorians alike.

Our preconceptions about prehistoric humans are usually linked to specific philosophical theories. It is essential that these apriorisms are eliminated from the debate, which should be based solely upon objective evidence. Brief analysis of the two theories discussed above reveals that both adopt an evolutionary stance: the first revolves around the idea of moral decay and a nostalgia for the distant past, whilst the second praises progress, improved living conditions, and the broadening of knowledge. Whilst one theory sees humans as moving continually away from nature to detrimental effect, the other claims that work and culture carve a path toward a positive future.

But what if fundamental human behavior and reactions have not changed? What if humans never were the innocent lambs nor the violent brutes that certain caricatures have made them out to be? What if humans always were the same complex and emotional beings they are today, with a tendency at times to react harshly or violently? And what if the notion of the noble savage, good-natured and innocent, is nothing more than a myth? What if humans always have had a certain liking for confrontation and a need for domination which have been regularly expressed over time? With the aid of historical and ethnographic examples, it is possible to prove that conflict has always taken place.[28] Thus, why should we assume that prehistory was a peaceful period? It seems highly unlikely that there would have been a peaceful interlude spanning several thousand years in the midst of conflict.

This is the line of argument that will be adopted here. There is no denying that anthropological evidence relating to the Paleolithic is scarce, thus any conclusions drawn may well be debatable; this applies in particular to the many thousands of years spanning the Lower and Middle Paleolithic. For this reason, it is much easier to start with the appearance of our own species – Homo sapiens sapiens or modern humans.

Another apriorism which requires further discussion is the role of demographic variation in triggering conflict. One of the main arguments supporting the notion of a peaceful Paleolithic focuses upon the limited population at that time. Although attempts to reconstruct the demographic structure of prehistoric populations have always sparked fierce debate among experts, many estimates have nevertheless been made, taking into account the number of sites, the synchronic and diachronic nature of these sites, comparable anthropological models, levels of technology identified, and so on. These estimates always propose very low population densities. Population densities were also undoubtedly very uneven, given that certain "tribes" were prone to regrouping in more "profitable" areas with more prey and milder climates, compared to other areas where conditions were much more difficult. It is estimated that, at the very end of the Paleolithic, the world population totaled only 2–3 million.

Thus, the question arises of whether or not there is any correlation between the number of individuals inhabiting an area and the reasons for conflict. War is often held to be a means of regulating demographic pressure. However, there is no close correlation between the frequency of warfare and population density, even though there are clearly fewer grounds for war where population densities are lower. This is because the significance of population density as a factor varies according to the area's economic potential (dependent upon environment and natural or artificial fertility of the land). It is also important to take levels of technological development into account, since this may have some bearing upon the relevance of local data.

The jungles of Malaysia and Central Africa as well as the Great Basin in North America are all areas with low population densities where conflict is rare.[29] But do these examples reveal a more general trend?

In fact, it all comes down to a community's ability to resolve social problems by implementing rules, ethical codes, or even more drastic measures in order to maintain peace. Keeley contrasts the Natufian culture of the Levant from around the eighth to the sixth millennia BCE, a period characterized by a notable rise in population, increased social complexity, and a gradual settling of populations, with the Mesolithic period in Central Europe in the sixth millennium BCE, where population density was likely to have been much lower. In fact, there are very few indications of any tensions having been present in the first case, yet there is evidence of non-accidental death having occurred during the latter Mesolithic period.

One of the central arguments in this debate is that Paleolithic society must have been peaceful owing to its small population. It is widely held that mutual help, cooperation, and a pooling of efforts are essential for survival in a small population. The fluidity of small groups, their wide-ranging territories, and their tendency to regroup at times for hunting purposes all indicate that cooperative relationships are beneficial, thus tensions are unlikely to arise. This viewpoint is strengthened by the theory that humans are at a great disadvantage if they only have limited control over nature. Cooperation would have been essential in order to subsist and survive where productive forces were not sufficiently effective; by forming unions, insufficient levels of manpower on the part of the individual could be overcome.

Testart refers to such solidarity in what he terms the "rule of sharing," which he claims comes into play where hunting is concerned. The idea is that a huntsman who has made a kill shares his prey with his fellow hunters. "Sharing functions as a means of 'social insurance' in that the successful hunter knows that, should he return empty-handed in future, he will be fed in turn by one of his more fortunate fellow huntsmen."[30] Hunting heroes come and go – they are celebrated immediately after their success, but soon slip back into anonymity. This system certainly requires a degree of selflessness, but is hunter-gatherer solidarity entirely flawless? After all, the solidarity of these societies has been regularly called into question. Rather than claiming that hunter-gatherer societies (and especially the "more advanced" societies of the Upper Paleolithic and Epipaleolithic) were largely based on solidarity, we propose to look at this from a different angle: if it was indeed logical for these societies to maintain peaceful relations, how then could groups and individuals have succumbed to violent conflict? Can archeology shed any light on this matter?

The Issue of Sacrifice

In 1958, one of the authors of this work came across two bodies, one lying on top of the other, in a Neolithic tomb dating from 4000 BCE in Cournanel (Aude, France) and concluded, perhaps a little too hastily, that one of the two individuals had been sacrificed; ritual sacrifice was, after all, not unheard of in antiquity.[31] The issue arose again some years later when the remains of a young woman holding a very young child were found buried in the Gazel cave in Cabardès, France, thought to date from a late stage in the Early Neolithic (the beginning of the fifth millennium BCE). Whilst it is conceivable that both died from the same illness, it is nevertheless possible that one of the two died a premature death with the other being forced to follow into the afterlife.

In fact, there are numerous examples dating from prehistory whereby several individuals were buried simultaneously in sealed tombs. Sealed tombs are entirely different from collective tombs, like the majority of the megalithic tombs and hypogea. Collective tombs are reopened each time an individual dies, rather like modern-day tombs. By contrast, sealed tombs also contain many bodies but are only opened for the funeral ceremony, after which they are sealed for good. Multiple burials seem to date back a long way; tombs containing several corpses have been discovered in Qafzeh (Israel), the earliest dating from the Middle Paleolithic (one child and one adult, possibly female). Similar tombs also date from the Upper Paleolithic: at the Barma Grande site (Grimaldi, Italy), a triple burial (one adult male, one adult female, and an adolescent) was discovered. In the "Grotte des Enfants" cave, also in Grimaldi, the body of an elderly female was found lying in a flexed position on top of the corpse of a young male, whilst in Dolni Vestonice (Moravia, Czech Republic), a young female was found lying between two males. Two adolescents were placed together in tomb 3 in Sungir (Vladimir, Russia), and at the Riparo del Romito site (Cosenza, Italy) one female was buried next to a dwarfed male.

There is always the possibility that such individuals were buried together because they died at the same time, following an epidemic, famine, or conflict, for example. However, the alternative also warrants consideration – that certain individuals were sacrificed to mark the death of one or several members of the group. Theories fluctuate between these two ideas – either that several individuals died at the same time and were thus buried together, or that certain individuals were selected to be buried with the deceased individual(s) in order to accompany him/her/them in death. The notion of sacrifice underlies the latter theory, with other human "lives" being offered to the deceased.

This theory does not apply solely to those tombs which contain multiple corpses; it is also possible that some of those buried in individual tombs may have been deliberately killed.

Sacrifice is the ritual execution of a living being – often a human, although animals may be used as substitutes on occasion. Sacrifice involves much more than making an offering to the gods or spirits – it is a bloody and sacred ritual. Sacrificial victims may include anyone from captured enemies, convicts, and outcasts to members of the community – children, adolescents, and adults alike. If sacrifice is purely a matter of violence that results in the death of an individual, then can it not be likened to murder? This question forms the basis of a long-standing anthropological debate. Two introductory points should be made here: menstrual blood and sacrificial blood are mutually exclusive, meaning that women may not carry out a sacrifice. Similarly, blood shed in murder should be distinguished from sacrificial blood, since a murderer may not perform a sacrifice.[32] A definite symbolic distinction is therefore made between murder, perceived to be a negative act, and sacrifice, which is supposedly positive. In any case, from an objective viewpoint, violence clearly plays a part in both murder and sacrifice, even though the latter is ritualized and supposedly beneficial. Sacrifice has been subject to many differing interpretations over time – it is widely held to be a religious gesture, a duty, and a means of purification. By sacrificing an individual (or an animal substituted for an individual), the wider group is guaranteed redemption of a kind. Girard claims that the violence displayed during sacrifice is a solution, a means of controlling the violence of individuals within the community.[33] It is a social mechanism for maintaining peace within the group, rather like the incest taboo which prohibits sexual relations occurring within the family group, thus avoiding any related violence. Sacrificial rituals, however violent they may be, actually protect society. "The vicious circle of reciprocal violence is replaced by the vicious circle of ritual violence which is both creative and protective."[34] The victim takes the blame and receives the punishment, taking the place of all potential victims. The victim is responsible for preserving the world, becoming the focus of any problems and enabling society to be saved through his or her purifying death. This is a reenactment of the original murder, required for social equilibrium to be maintained.

However, this theory cannot completely overlook the severity of the act in question – an act which many have condemned, from antiquity right through to the present day, highlighting the similarities between sacrifice, murder, and war. Others have claimed that sacrifice, like war and crime, reflects an instinctive need for death – an act which, once committed, appeases a situation.[35] Sacrifice can also be seen as a means of controlling violence, essentially providing an outlet or cure – an act which aims to make a situation more "civilized." Finally, it should be noted that those who practice or encourage sacrifice do not perceive it as an act against nature. On the contrary, sacrifice gains the approval of the whole community.

Archeological evidence relating to oral cultures certainly struggles to differentiate between sacrifice and murder, particularly since many ethnographic studies have revealed that murder – on demand – often forms part of an exchange system. This is the case in Oceania where, following a quarrel, a life is taken in revenge; the murderer is considered to be an avenger, not an executioner. Those who were close to the victim show their thanks by giving gifts, thus adding to the "murderer's" prestige. Here, a complex system of social relations is in place in which men and women, living and deceased, are exchanged. These dramas are essential to maintaining the social equilibrium, which is highly dependent upon the ever-changing network of alliances. Thus, murder is one way of regulating society and is expressed through these social relations: it becomes an intrinsic part of local custom.

Testart notes that sacrifice generally takes place in societies with rigid hierarchies, i.e., where religious or social systems form a pyramidal structure: there is one (or many) highly esteemed and revered divinity (or divinities) to whom the sacrifices are dedicated, an executioner who performs the sacrifice, and a victim.[36] The act of choosing a victim alone demonstrates the vast divide which separates those in charge and those who must obey. Sacrifices are often arranged by kings, princes, or potentates, for example. The killing of several individuals "one after the other" is typical both of nascent states (Egypt, Mesopotamia) and rigidly structured chiefdoms (European protohistory, Oceania). If this is the case, how then can similar killings in more ancient times be explained? According to the theory proposed, they could have been part of a bloody ritual and custom – this violence may not necessarily have been an attempt to please a deity.

Is Prehistoric Violence "Readable"?

Is there any archeological evidence to demonstrate the many facets of pre-historic violence? It is possible to draw up a list of the violent behavior most likely to have been practiced by Stone Age humans, but finding archeological evidence will often prove difficult. Firstly, it is necessary to structure the theoretical propositions in a way which enables them to be proved or disproved.

There are many different motives for and means of committing homicide, be it deliberate or accidental; homicide may be premeditated or may be the result of a brawl or more brutal and spontaneous violence. It may take the form of murder, execution, slow death following torture, death following a period in captivity, poisoning, and so on. There are many ways of dealing with the victim's body. It may simply be disposed of, for example, thrown into the sea or into a river. This seems to have been the case in Northern Europe; here, several bodies discovered in peat bogs and dating to prehistoric times were found to show definite signs of violent death – slit throats, strangulation, and hanging. Alternatively, the body may be burnt, buried, or concealed in a well-hidden or far-removed hiding place such as a swallow hole, cave, or fissure in a rock face. Given this tendency to discard or conceal all human remains, the difficulties of investigating such behavior immediately become clear.

Another possibility is that the body may be abandoned on the spot where the individual died, in which case it would soon be eaten away by vultures, carnivores, and birds of prey. It may also disappear completely as a result of ruthless taphonomic processes, i.e., natural biological processes and physicochemical conditions which affect the decomposition of living organisms after death. However, in some cases, it seems that bodies were consumed. There is evidence of cannibalism having been practiced throughout prehistoric times; it has been the subject of many heated debates which will be discussed at greater length at several points subsequently in this text. The entrails – the brain, liver, and heart – are certainly eaten, while muscular tissue and bone marrow (extracted by crushing the long bones) may also be consumed. However, only the bones remain to aid archeologists in their research.

It should be noted that the remains of these victims were sometimes buried "as normal" in a cemetery. Most evidence from the Neolithic, in the broadest sense of the term, is derived from such burials.

But aside from individual killings, it is collective aggression, bringing one group of humans face to face with another, which comes closest to revealing the origins of warfare. Finding proof is no easy task. Archeologists must rely upon remains in communal graves, bodies bearing various injuries and amassed in family graves, cemeteries in which relatives placed their dead alongside the bodies of their enemies, and corpses abandoned where they fell and which have gradually fossilized over time through sedimentation.

Human sacrifice is a rather exceptional case. It deserves a mention as it is still an example of homicide and exceptionally violent behavior, even though it is often disguised as a religious ceremony – the victim is prepared psychologically or medically beforehand (through taking euphoric or analgesic substances) and the aim is "salvation." This practice also forms part of myth and historical fact: the Bible, for example, describes the (averted) sacrifice of the son of Abraham, the *Iliad* tells of the death of Iphigenia and, on a more historical note, the sacrifice of Carthaginian children to the god Moloch, Caesar talks of sacrifice in his *Gallic Wars*, and the Aztec holocausts witnessed by Cortez's conquistadors were only halted through even harsher barbarities.

Some of these collective sacrifices dating from the very beginnings of history were fueled by a ruler's craving for power, as the archeological evidence demonstrates: individuals were killed in order to follow their "master" or sovereign into the other world. Rulers during the first Egyptian dynasty, the "kings" of Ur, the "sovereigns" of Kerma, Scythian princes, and Chinese emperors all took many of their dependants with them in death.

Chastisement and punishment also deserve a mention. These acts include beating, whipping, mutilating, amputating, branding, and any other means of harming humans or animals as a means of suppression. During prehistoric times, captives, prisoners, and defeated enemies may have been punished collectively, in addition to the corporal punishments inflicted upon individuals. Violence was, therefore, used as a means of imposing a sentence. The victim was singled out as a social outcast and even marked as the property of the ruler or group as a whole. It goes without saying that only detailed anthropological studies will be able to determine the level of suffering endured by these victims, and only then providing that the injuries inflicted left some mark upon the bones, since the flesh is rarely preserved. Rape too has probably long been a frequent occurrence, although this is impossible to prove; rape may have taken place at the same time as the injuries were inflicted upon the victims' bodies.

The question of whether or not slavery played a part in prehistory is difficult to answer. Very little is known about slavery in hunter-gatherer societies in particular, although it seems likely that abductions and prisoner taking have always featured in society. However, in the absence of any evidence to this effect, prehistorians have tended to avoid the issue. Slavery is often the result of conflict between communities. In the western world, for example, slavery gradually began to emerge as soon as conflict became a more regular feature – around the second or third millennium BCE. It is important to exercise a degree of caution because most western settlements at this time (during the Copper and Bronze Ages) were only small-scale, although some are known to have spanned several hectares (Los Millares in the southeast of Spain). However, even where settlements were small, there is no reason why confrontations on a smaller scale couldn't have taken place, resulting in populations being displaced or driven out of certain areas, with the most skilled craftsman or craftsmen, etc. being captured. As will become increasingly clear, scenes of execution depicted in the art of the Spanish Levant from the Neolithic onwards make such hypotheses distinctly plausible. In the East, such scenarios are known to have occurred thanks to texts from Mesopotamia dating from the third millennium BCE; all indications are that the construction of towns from the end of the fourth millennium BCE (Habuba Kabira, an Uruk settlement) created social settings in which frictions were a frequent feature, often resulting in prisoners being captured and perhaps even slavery.

One further aspect of violence is ritual mutilation. As we have already seen, physical aggression can be masked as religious or social, even festive or playful behavior. Markings such as slashes and tattoos were found upon Similaun man, Scythian remains, and mummies from Northern Europe, and could be the result of violent behavior. The "Capsian" populations of North Africa (dating from the eighth to the fifth millennia BCE) are known to have inflicted osteological lesions upon themselves by voluntarily extracting their incisors, canines, and even premolars. This often led to more serious complications such as hemorrhaging, secondary infections, and chronic handicap and can thus be classified as acts of second-degree violence or aggressiveness.

Finally and purely hypothetically, it is worth mentioning the possibility that all or part of the human body may have been put to material use following homicide or fatal injury. The entrails and fat, for example, may have been used in medication, trophies, and tools. Human bones may have served to produce other instruments. In the Bédeilhac cave (Ariège, France) a sharpened fibula dating from the beginning of the Bronze Age was discovered, and similarly in the Tuteil cave in Montségur (Ariège) an ulna was found which had been carved to form an awl. A fibula from the Ganties-les-Bains cave (Haute-Garonne, France) is thought to be Neolithic in origin. There is a hole in one end, whilst the other has been fashioned into a point. Whoever used this tool undoubtedly had very agile fingers; it also showed signs of undergoing rotational movements. It is thus possible that this tool was used as a spindle for making textiles. Although these bones may have been removed following natural or non-violent death, it is nevertheless worth emphasizing that parts of the body may be put to a wide range of uses following death.

This introductory chapter has sought to demonstrate the wide range of issues that arise when investigating the topics of violence and war in prehistoric times as well as highlighting some of the epistemological approaches applied to interpreting such behavior. We shall turn now to tracing the archeological evidence relating to this study, inevitably incomplete as it is, through time.

Chapter 1

Violence in Hunter-Gatherer Society

What can we conclude about our earliest ancestors? Are there any indications of violence having occurred among early humans? Murder, infanticide, and cannibalism are rare among chimpanzees, but cases have been documented. However, drawing conclusions about our own species is much more difficult. There is, for example, no definite evidence of organized burial having occurred at any point throughout the entire Lower Paleolithic period (spanning several hundred thousand years), thus it is impossible to make any interpretation. Human remains discovered in layers of deposits are often incomplete, dismembered, and mixed up with animal remains and domestic waste. What can be deduced from these rare and disordered bones? Not a great deal. As for the fractures and breaks found upon some hominid bones, these deformities may simply be the result of post mortem processes such as fossilization, physical impact, or the subsidence of brecciated sediments.[1] The discovery of human bones amongst food waste again raises the much-disputed question of whether cannibalism was ever practiced. It seems all the more likely that cannibalism did indeed occur when taking into account the behavior of our closest primate relative, the chimpanzee, known to consume the flesh of its own species on occasion. Yet there may also be many other explanations – tombs may subsequently have been dismantled, bodies may have been abandoned where they fell with these remains subsequently breaking up, the bones may have been attacked by vultures, or there could have been a lapse in time between the human remains and the surrounding food waste being discarded in the same place. The positioning of these remains may even be an indication that human bodies were dealt with in a particular way following death. This seems to have been the case at the Tautavel cave site in the Corbières region of Southern France where human remains were found scattered among stone artifacts and partially consumed animal remains, all dating from the local population some 450,000 years ago.

In fact, there is no evidence of any deliberate attempts to bury the dead before the Middle Paleolithic (approximately 200,000–35,000 years ago). Fossilized human remains found prior to this period show no sign that populations had any awareness or understanding of death at this time, for this would be reflected in some attempt at protecting the body of the deceased and shielding it from any potential damage, perhaps by placing it in an enclosed location to ensure its preservation. Deliberate burials at Qafzeh (Israel), La Ferrassie (Dordogne, France), and La Chapelle-aux-Saints (Corrèze, France) indicate that this stage in the evolution of culture was reached around 100,000 years ago and lasted until the disappearance of the Neanderthals.

It should, however, be noted that deliberate burial, both in the Middle Paleolithic and even earlier, only represents one practice – there were a great many other funerary rituals that would undoubtedly have been considered equally respectable. Examples include simply abandoning the corpse, allowing the flesh to decay either through natural processes or "aided" by wildlife, for which the body could either be confined or exposed to the open air, dismembering the skeleton, breaking and sometimes cutting open some of the bones and consuming the flesh, and, in particular, breaking the long bones in order to eat the marrow and fat, etc. they contain. Some of these practices are certainly shocking to the modern world, in which we are conditioned to view burial or cremation as standard practices. The very idea of cannibalism can, therefore, be sickening. Yet it is important to realize that none of these rituals should be considered barbaric or repellent. To those who practiced them, these rituals were normal and accepted ways of dealing with the bodies of the deceased, whether the aim was to preserve all or part of the body or to dispose of it entirely.

Besides burying or abandoning the corpse, the body was often "manipulated" during prehistoric times – certain bones were selected, others were rearranged, and specific bones were removed as part of rituals or beliefs, the significance of which is no longer known. Humans have adopted many and varied practices for dealing with the dead. This work will focus upon those that relate to violence.

Neanderthal Man and Cannibalism

It is with some difficulty that anthropologists and prehistorians have attempted to pinpoint the reasons behind Neanderthal attitudes toward the dead. Yet with many of the original observations now being rather dated, some of the evidence being in doubt, and certain theories being revised after having been based upon incorrect interpretations, many of these early hypotheses are little more than misleading for researchers. Many theories, for example, have focused upon the extraction of organs from the skeleton and in particular from the skull. The Mount Circée skull (discovered near Rome) is a well-known example frequently referred to by experts. The skull was found resting, upside down, in a small gap surrounded by large stones. The right temple was smashed and the foramen magnum widened, which many concluded to be the result of a ritual involving the skull being "emptied" of some of its contents (possibly for consumption?). This theory has, however, recently been disproved: the damage was caused, quite simply, by hyenas! Similar conclusions have been drawn regarding the skull discovered in Steinheim (Germany), thought to be much older – approximately 200,000 years old. Again the foramen magnum has been widened – could this have been for the purpose of extracting the brain?

Was Neanderthal man prone to violence? Vallois implies he was, after studying the skull of Fontechevade man (Charente, France). He claims there are signs of the skull having received a fatal blow to the top of the upper left part of the head. According to the author, this injury may have been inflicted with a sharp object while the individual was still alive.[2] But is this merely an isolated incident with no statistical significance? The Mousterian human remains discovered in the Skhul cave at Mount Carmel (Israel) are also frequently referred to in such debates. The head of the femur and the coxal bone have both been pierced, probably with a hard-wood spear (figure 8).[3] It has often been claimed that these are the earliest known cases of injury. However, anthropologists today do not consider this evidence to be particularly significant.

The Neanderthal skeleton discovered in the Saint-Cézaire cave (Charente-Maritime, France) in 1979 is an interesting case. In fact, this specimen is one of the later Neanderthals because it is associated with an advanced industry of the Upper Paleolithic: the Chatelperronian culture. It can be dated to around 36,000 years ago. Recent reanalysis of these fossilized remains identified a fracture, 36 mm long, upon the dome of the skull; the injury was inflicted by a sharp object. This is, therefore, undoubtedly a case of violence. However, the injury was not fatal – scarring of the bone reveals that the individual survived this blow.[4]

Claims that such evidence is indicative of Neanderthal cannibalistic behavior have always raised many questions and sparked great debate among prehistorians. Before debating this issue, it is useful to summarize the facts. The Krapina cave (Croatia), a Mousterian site thought to be approximately 100,000 years old, has probably aroused most interest and is often said to have contained evidence of the earliest cases of cannibalism. Among the Neanderthal remains (of at least 14 individuals), there are also many fractured human bones. The grooves upon these bones indicate that they were dislocated and

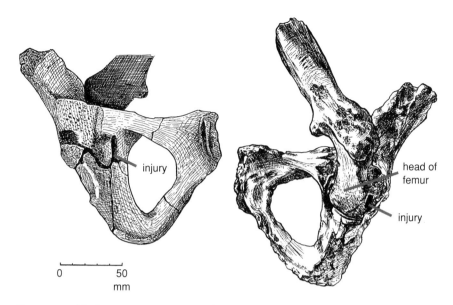

Figure 8 Shkul cave at Mount Carmel (Israel). Mousterian human remains reveal that the head of the femur and coxal bone have been pierced, probably with a sharp instrument according to McCowan and Keith, 1939.

then stripped of their flesh, possibly to make use of the meat. The breakages, which run parallel along the long bones, indicate that they were intentionally broken, perhaps in order to extract the marrow. Some of the bones have also been burnt. All of this seems to suggest that humans made use of the body following death. Some experts dispute this theory, claiming that there may have been natural causes for the various changes in the state of these bones, post mortem, or even that the bones may have been damaged during excavation. Recent reexamination of the evidence, however, seems to confirm the first theory.[5] Further research has also revealed that these remains were not, as has often been assumed, buried in an early grave which was later disturbed, so unearthing the remains. In fact, these remains were never buried in the first place. They were discovered in amongst the remains of animals killed for food; these bones too had been stripped of their flesh in the same way. There is no doubt that the human bones show signs of fracturing, though opinions as to why this should be are many and varied. Some experts see this as little more than a funerary ritual in which the body would have been cut up and the bones broken. This practice has been observed among certain groups of aborigines in Australia and offers an alternative to the cannibalism theory. The practice of breaking the long bones, however, is often interpreted as an attempt to extract and consume the marrow. Indeed, hunter-gatherer populations frequently used this technique to extract animal bone marrow, at least until the early Neolithic.[6] Seen from this perspective, it is possible that cannibalism was practiced at Krapina and if this is the case, cannibalism can be said to date back much further, to some 100,000 years ago. The subsequent transition to the Neolithic and even later periods would not necessarily have caused such behavior to die out. Thus, cannibalism may have been practiced throughout the duration of prehistory.

Krapina is not an isolated example. The issue of Neanderthal "cannibalism" has regularly resurfaced in response to more recent discoveries. In the Hortus cave (Hérault, France), for example, fragments of long bones were discovered which had been cracked lengthways, perhaps a deliberate attempt at extracting the marrow. These long bones were found in amongst the remains of animals which had been hunted, killed, and consumed.[7] It is thus tempting to see humans as prey. This matter became the subject of debate again recently, following research carried out at the Moula-Guercy cave in Ardèche (France). At this Mousterian site, it would seem that stags and ibices were consumed along with the bodies of two adolescents and two adult males.[8] The techniques used to break open these animal bones were also applied to the human bones; in particular, the same practice of breaking the long bones to extract the marrow was used. The bones even show similar signs of damage caused by the flesh being cut away from the bone. Indeed, 50 percent of the human remains show such traces of damage, a very high percentage in view of the fact that only 14 percent of the remains of animal prey bear such markings.

Cannibalism may, in fact, be an even older practice dating right back to the Lower Paleolithic. The Trinchera Dolina site in the Sierra de Atapuerca (Ibeas de Juarros, Burgos, Spain) is an interesting case. In layer 6 of these deposits, which paleomagnetic dating has placed as at least 780,000 years old, the highly fragmented remains of six bodies were found. Certain paleontologists classified these remains as a new species: *Homo antecesor*. These human bones were discovered in amongst faunal remains and lithic artifacts. Cut marks upon the bones, at points where the muscle is attached, reveal that the bones were stripped of their flesh using sharp stone tools. Thus, it seems that some humans dismembered and probably then consumed other humans in the same way as they consumed herbivores, the remains of which were scattered around the area.[9]

Despite this, experts are still not in agreement as to the possibility of Neanderthal cannibalism. Many argue that the signs of damage found upon human bones are the result of funerary rituals and do not represent an attempt to consume human flesh – the bones would firstly be dislocated, stripped of their meat, and then broken. There are indeed many different ways of treating the dead body and certainly some cultures do go so far as to break and crush the bones; however, such practices alone do not confirm the theory that the human flesh and bone marrow were consumed. Sharp tools would have been required in order to carry out these rituals effectively. The posterior part of a skull found in Marillac (Charente, France) provides evidence of such tool use, as the skull bears markings which suggest that the individual may have been scalped. The Engis 2 skull (Belgium) indicates that this individual suffered a similar fate.

The difficulties of interpreting such evidence are due in part to the nature of the action involved. In terms of the flesh and the marrow (whether they are consumed or merely disposed of), or indeed the bones (whether they are removed, cleaned, or even ritually broken), the techniques for removing the flesh and dismembering the body tend to be the same in all cases, thus similar marks are left upon the bones. These markings merely reveal the nature of the human intervention involved – no great deductions about the motives behind this behavior can be made based upon the markings alone. The contrast between the view that the human flesh was consumed and the theory that funerary rituals involved treating the body in some way is not as stark as it may seem: the two rituals are not necessarily mutually exclusive – there may have been instances of both being practiced.

Even if the theory that Mousterian groups practiced cannibalism is held to be correct, the reasons for the consumption of the human flesh still need to be addressed. If this cannibalism was purely a means of nourishment, then humans in this case were mere prey. If, however, this was ritual cannibalism, then the aim may have been to incorporate the dead into the bodies of the living. This dilemma frequently arises in discussions on prehistoric cannibalism and still divides paleontologists today since both theories could be deemed valid, depending on the scenario in question. Ritual cannibalism should be seen as a kind of "privileged relationship" between the living and the dead; it is in no way a barbaric act. In this sense at least, it would be wrong to label it a "primitive" act. However, philosophical judgments are bound to resurface in response to such theories. This is clearly an issue that requires further investigation.

Prehistoric Cannibalism

There are still a great many implications underlying the controversy over the significance of prehistoric cannibalism (even once we have come to realize that this is not the barbaric act that our cultural conditioning would have us believe). Two theories will serve as a backdrop to this debate. Those who hold with the theory of cannibalism as a means of obtaining food and maintain that prehistoric humans would not have hesitated in killing one of their fellow humans and eating the flesh, just as if it were a crude aurochs steak or a haunch of reindeer, consider prehistoric humans to have exhibited rather animal-like behavior, even up until more recent times. Such sporadic and unscrupulous aggressiveness on the part of prehistoric man, directed against his own species for the sole purpose of obtaining food, has led modern-day moralists to conclude that prehistoric humans were a rather curious and not very commendable species, lacking any respect toward others and thus not worthy of further consideration.

How is it possible to revere a species which has no hesitation in killing and even eating members of its own kind? Yet even seen from this perspective, surely it is possible to try to determine the influence of the psychological stimuli underlying this behavior. If we stick with the theory of cannibalism as a means of nourishment, then eating human flesh and drinking human blood seem to be a means of obtaining strength, through the ingestion of the blood. Human flesh and the flesh of animal prey are, in this case, the same – both are linked to the same impetuous desires. This rather tarnished view of humankind would certainly be contested by those who regard humans as superior, perfect beings, as a species which has consistently bettered itself and come to dominate nature over time through its intelligence and cultural developments. Seen from this perspective, humans are essentially unique in having transformed their natural environment through the cultural innovation they have perfected over the generations. Prehistorians studying early humans have persistently portrayed the species in a positive light, as more and more fossilized human remains have been discovered and the details of human technical knowledge and social relations gradually emerged. Neanderthal man, for example, has been progressively "reassessed," having long been portrayed as rather brutish and narrow-minded in many earlier reconstructions of the era (though admittedly these tended only to present a very superficial overview). Neanderthals are now considered to have been more "presentable" than was first thought and are classified as belonging to the species *Homo sapiens*. As a result, fewer and fewer "primitive" characteristics are now associated with Neanderthals, whereas previously they were defined by such traits. It is now claimed that Neanderthals abandoned scavenging in favor of sophisticated hunting techniques, that they were responsible for the first organized burials (and were therefore capable of metaphysical thought), and that they were experts at managing their need for raw materials in order to manufacture tools. The very suggestion of this *Homo sapiens* having consumed human flesh has always taken the edge off this more positive image. There have even been attempts to minimize or exclude examples such as Krapina from the debate – it has been argued that these few examples represent localized events. Others have claimed that cannibalism is a feature of certain unusual rituals which, far from being barbaric, denote a special relationship between the "consumer" and the "victim." This relationship may be characterized by kinship or friendship ties or may be purely an attempt to acquire another individual's energy and vigor (in the case of an enemy or even a close relation). Whatever the reason, it is claimed that the "victim" is never just "meat," but is instead the main focus in a process that concerns the relationship between the two parties involved. This process expresses a ritual bond and is steeped in its own specific ideology. Seen from this perspective, cannibalism is far from being an animal-like activity. Indeed, it could even be claimed that there is something grand, even sublime, about a ritual like this, which lacks any tendency toward violence.

These different perspectives reveal that archeological finds can often give rise to many varying interpretations. This is nothing new. Just as there are many different interpretations of historical periods, the same is true of prehistory. Any event or find can trigger any number of different explanations. Studying prehistory involves more than just analyzing our scientific knowledge of humankind's earliest past – debating the origins of various customs and practices is just as much a part of the exercise. In this case, even interpretations proposed by the most thorough experts in the field are inevitably colored by an element of subjectivity determined, subconsciously, by personal judgments which are themselves influenced by culture-specific factors. It may be that this "cannibalism" was little more than the logical conclusion of a symbolic system that involved murder and bloody rituals.

After all, isn't culture responsible for making such "dramas" essential to the functioning of society?

Suspicious Disappearances in Charente (France)

It is necessary to jump forward in time to investigate whether or not further, more detailed research has led to the confirmation of any of the proposed explanations for the condition of these human bones (either cannibalism or funerary rituals involving the flesh being removed and bones broken).

European hunter-gatherer societies will remain at the focus of this discussion for the moment, though the final stages of their existence are of greater interest here, i.e., the Mesolithic from the ninth to seventh millennia BCE. It immediately becomes clear that the controversy over whether or not cannibalism was practiced is just as marked for this era. Indeed, there is even more evidence in support of the cannibalism theory from this period.

Some 20 km to the north of Angoulême in the village of Agris (Charente, France), excavations at the "Grotte des Perrats" cave have revealed the remains of at least eight individuals – five adults and three children – which may be relevant to this discussion. There are indications that these bodies were treated in various different ways: bones appear to have been deliberately broken and the flesh removed, leaving many markings upon the bones. These remains were then discarded in amongst the remains of other animals (large ruminants, suidae, carnivores, and birds) killed for food or other purposes by the local population. All of these remains were found lying in amongst a mass of scattered rocks, showing no signs of pattern or organization. A highly detailed study recently concluded that all of the damage to these human remains was inflicted by Mesolithic humans and that secondary factors hardly had any effect at all (carnivores, compacting of sediments, the weight of stone blocks, pressure from surrounding walls, preferential destruction, bone fractures due to the mechanical properties of the bones, etc.). Thus, humans alone were responsible for this damage.[10] But why was this damage inflicted? For Boulestin, there can only be one explanation: to remove and eat the bone marrow. This would explain why those bones which only contain spongy tissue (the sternum and patella) were systematically destroyed, being of little value. The long bones, by contrast, and in particular the humerus, femur, and tibia, were fractured at several points, as if to prevent any of their contents being wasted. Although fewer breakages were found upon the smaller bones, also exploited for their marrow, they were still used to their full potential. Skulls were also broken open in order to extract the brain. It is thought that this sequence of events went as follows: head severed from the rest of the body, ears cut off, eyes removed, lips and nose possibly removed, tongue taken out, and mandible separated from the skull. Following this, the scalp may well have been cut away from the skull with a large median incision, enabling the flesh to be stripped away. The flesh seems to have been removed much more extensively from the only child's skull found here – the frontal bone, for example, shows many signs of incision. The brain could be retrieved by breaking the skull across the frontal bone, along the sides (parietal and/or temporal bones) or underneath by enlarging the foramen magnum. At the "Grotte des Perrats" cave site, damage to various parts of the skulls seems to indicate that the main aim was to remove the bone at the top of the skull in order to extract the brain. Such damage to the skull may not have been inflicted solely upon those recently deceased – some victims may have been alive when struck; indeed, this may have been the cause of their death. In particular, this may have occurred in cases where there are signs of damage to the front of the skull, although this hypothesis would be extremely difficult to prove. However, it is clear that the multiple injuries upon the human skulls and other bones in Agris are unlikely to have resulted from the bones being separated from the muscle and then broken as part of a strict ritual. Boulestin sees this practice as a butchering process in which the extraction of the marrow and brain represent the ultimate acts. One of the most convincing pieces of evidence in favor of this theory is provided by marks indicating that these bones were "chewed" upon. These marks are not the same as those caused by dogs or other carnivores gnawing upon the bones, rather they resemble marks left behind by humans consuming the flesh, as has been documented in numerous ethnographic studies. There are thus a number of factors which, though they are not always found elsewhere, support the theory that cannibalism was practiced in Agris toward the end of this exclusively hunter-gatherer era.[11] The issue of cannibalism arises again in conjunction with the peasants of the Neolithic, which will be discussed later in the text.

Cain's Predecessors

Should archeologists limit their theories to the evidence available or assume that such evidence will always fall well short of the reality of the situation, a reality which is very difficult to piece together? Studying anthropological relics from the Middle and Upper Paleolithic in accordance with the first of these two alternatives would lead one to conclude that aggressiveness was uncommon during this period. Rare cases of injury could be put down to "insignificant happenings" between individuals or to isolated events. A study of the fossilized human remains dating from this period (taken from a test region – Southwest France) in order to research the health and paleopathology of the population seems to confirm this. Of the remains of 209 individuals studied (many of which were only partially complete), American anthropologist Brennan identified only five bone fractures (of which two dated from the Upper Paleolithic), the causes of which are not known. Brennan also includes several controversial examples on her list: the Cro-Magnon II remains with an injury to the left frontal bone, the Magdalenian skeleton from Laugerie-Basse with a fracture to the temporal fossa, the remains of a Magdalenian female found in Sorde with an injury to the right parietal bone, and the La Quina 5 specimen, the remains of a young female with damage to the right humerus. If the discussion is limited to the 165 Upper Paleolithic fossils studied by the author, only ten or so recognized cases emerge. These account for just 6 percent of the total.[12] This percentage should be spread out across this lengthy period of time spanning more than 20,000 years. However, the low population should also be taken into account – at this time the population across the whole of the European continent totaled only several

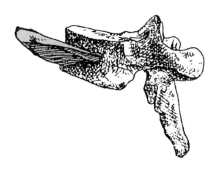

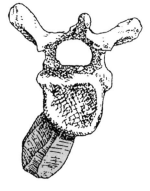

Figure 9 Montfort-sur-Lizier (Ariège, France). Quartzite blade lodged in a human vertebra. After Begouen, Cugulières, and Miquel, 1922.

tens of thousands. Can a systematic relationship between low population and good social relations be established in view of this?

Were the Cro-Magnons peaceful? It is unlikely. The scarcity of evidence means it is impossible to make generalizations, yet it is clear from some of the examples that violence was used and with the aim to kill. A child's remains found in Grimaldi (Italy), thought to date from Gravettian times in approximately 25,000/22,000 BCE, were found to contain the point from a projectile lodged in the vertebral column. In the San Teodoro cave (Sicily) the remains of a young woman, dating from 12,000 BCE, were found with a flint point lodged in the right of the pelvis.

The Montfort site in Saint-Lizier (Ariège, France) is an interesting case. Among a cluster of Azilian remains found in a cavity here, a cervidae vertebra was discovered which had been cut through completely using a flint blade, presumably severing the spinal cord. In 1894, at the surface of this very same site, among deposits thought to be either Magdalenian or Azilian, i.e., dating from between 13,000 and 8000 BCE, Miquel unearthed a quartzite blade lodged in a human vertebra (figure 9).[13] This demonstrates that violence was not inflicted upon animals alone.

The many human bones discovered in the Maszycka cave in Polish Silesia are much more difficult to interpret. These finds comprise the remains of 16 Magdalenian individuals, all grouped together and all largely incomplete – there are approximately 50 bones in total. The remains have clearly been singled out and comprise mostly fragments of skulls, jaws, and collarbones. These are the remains of three males, of which one was an adolescent, and five females, two of whom were only young. The remains of the other eight individuals cannot be clearly identified due to their immaturity and a lack of evidence. The bones show signs of damage, the result of chipping, incisions, and chewing which seem to date from the time when the site was occupied. This has led to talk of cannibalism, with victims supposedly being decapitated and dismembered outside the cave. Only a selection of the bones were then taken into the cave and sorted for ritual burial. The sorting and selection of bones in this way could not have been carried out by carnivores (hyenas); this is definitely the result of human activity. Thus, it has been proposed that a massacre would have taken place, followed by the consumption of the human flesh and the ritual and symbolic burial of some of the remains. It is possible that these killings were carried out by an enemy group, possibly "Eastern Gravettians," who disliked the idea of Magdalenian settlements spreading eastwards.[14]

Let us leave prehistory for a moment and turn our attentions to myth. The "first murder in history," recounted in Genesis 4, seems strangely anachronistic. It concerns the two sons of Adam and Eve, two "Neolithics," Abel being a shepherd and Cain a farmer. Cain offers God the fruits of his labor, only to find his offerings met with indifference. Abel, who sacrifices his animals, i.e., sheds blood, has his efforts accepted. Cain becomes jealous and angered that his own efforts were not accepted and kills the innocent Abel. As a result, Cain is condemned to roam as a nomadic shepherd in order to redeem himself of the murder he has committed. However, he is not forced to disappear altogether. In fact, he benefits from a certain degree of protection, establishes the very first town, and has a long line of descendants, one of whom is Tubal-Cain who invented metallurgy. Thus it seems that sacrifice and violent murder do feature in Genesis and are even, to a certain extent, justified. The bloody sacrifices made by Abel earn him divine recognition. In fact, these acts are considered to be a source of life, a means to regeneration. Cain, who had up until this point never committed bloodshed of any kind, received a punishment relative to his crime. The death of Abel is considered to be a sacrifice in itself – Cain had no choice and was incapable of resisting the violent act that led him to make this sacrifice.[15] Thus, execution takes on the role of a sacred and founding act, a ritual required in order for social structures to be established. For this reason, societies have always resorted to execution as an irreversible and legitimate act.

There is no doubt that the text of Genesis demonstrates the existence of a degree of social functioning within this agricultural and pastoral context. As has been seen already, the act of murder did not make its first appearance with the onset of agriculture and animal breeding; it was already present in Paleolithic society. Incorporating the mythology of the Bible, the first cases of murder should not be assigned to the Neolithic but rather to Eden itself and the paradise inhabited by its population, living off the fruits of nature. Logically speaking, the first murderer should have been Adam himself!

The Paleolithic art of Western Europe, dating from various points over the last 20,000 years, is of primary importance and provides valuable insight into the issue of violence during the Paleolithic. Despite this, humans rarely feature in the paintings and carvings of the last Ice Age. In particular, there are no paintings like those of the Spanish Levant art which show groups of men fighting. One of the most well-known portrayals of violence is undoubtedly the "well scene" in the caves at Lascaux (dating from ca. 15,000 BCE) (plate 4). This painting shows a man, outstretched and probably dead, falling down before a bison. Despite having inflicted this fatal injury, the bison too is seriously injured. Its entrails are trailing and it is probably close to death. On one of the sculpted limestone blocks at the Roc de Sers site in Sers (Charente, France), another scene is depicted. This is thought to be a Soultrean site, dating from approximately 18,000 BCE. One section seems to show a stocky bull charging at a human figure. But can this "man hunting" by a dangerous animal actually be interpreted as violence? The problems of interpreting the image arise from the fact that the exact relationship between the animal and the

Plate 4 "Well scene," Lascaux (Dordogne, France). Tragic confrontation between a man shown collapsing and an injured bison, ca. 15,000 BCE.
© N. Aujoulat, CNP – Ministère de la Culture.

individual in question are not known, thus there remains an element of doubt. Similarly, the Villars cave (Dordogne, France) contains a painting of a bison heading directly toward a man. The man seems to have injured the animal with a spear. His pose would indicate that he is about to dodge the animal.[16]

Even though human conflict barely features in this artwork, violence toward animals is evident – there are many images of animals that have been struck by spears or projectiles. This theme is present in artwork spanning a period of at least 15,000 years, the time span thought to separate the artwork in the caves at Cosquer and Niaux (France). However, caution should be exercised when interpreting these images, since the "hunter" or person responsible for causing the injury to the animal is never featured. Furthermore, whilst some of the animals certainly seem to be seriously injured, others look as if they can barely feel their injuries. In the latter case, these may not have been hunting scenes – there may be undertones of violence. Leroi-Gourhan suggests that some of the animals may have been painted earlier with certain features being added later. The projectiles, for example, may have been painted in during specific ceremonies. The animal would have been symbolic – it would be selected and then sacrificed as part of a ritual, its flesh being pierced with arrows. Essentially, it is claimed that the images portray a ritualizing of violence.

The theme of murder also seems to feature in Paleolithic art, if one of the scenes in the Cosquer cave in Provence (France) (plate 5) is anything to go by. The artwork shows a human-like figure falling onto his back, diagonally,

Plate 5   Cosquer cave (Bouches-du-Rhône, France). Anthropomorphic figure, falling backwards after being struck by arrows, ca. 20,000 BCE.
© N. Aujoulat, CNP – Ministère de la Culture.

Violence in Hunter-Gatherer Society   53

arms and legs raised. The head is small and rounded and the shape of a nose can be made out. The leg is made up of two convergent lines. The raised, disproportionate arm has been heavily scratched into the rock. The individual, seen falling backwards, has been struck by many projectiles: a spear pierces his chest and a javelin, complete with two barbs, enters his back, going right through his body and head and out the other side. The scene is thought to date from the second phase of the Cosquer cave, in around 20,000 BCE. It seems, therefore, that murder and capital execution played a part in both the thoughts and customs of the day.[17]

Scenes of humans being struck by projectiles and either injured or killed do feature in Upper Paleolithic art, though again examples are far from common. A loose pebble from the Paglicci cave in the southeast of Italy was found to have been engraved with such an image in around 21,000 BCE. The pebble shows a human-like figure which has been struck by several spears from the head down to the pelvis. Rupestrian art also includes several diagrammatic figures which seem to have been injured by various projectiles (figure 10). In

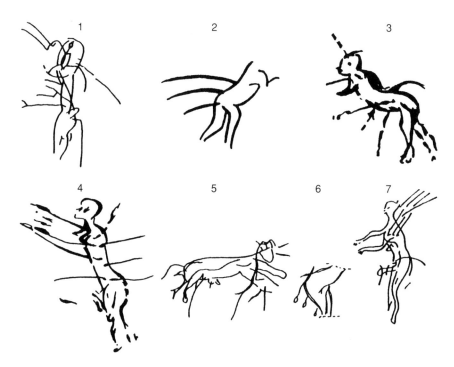

Figure 10 Paleolithic art depicting human or anthropomorphic figures injured by arrows: (1) Paglicci cave (Italy); (2) Cougnac (France); (3) Cougnac (France); (4) Pech-Merle (France); (5) Combel (France); (6) Gourdan (France); (7) Sous-Grand-Lac (France). After Dams, 1984.

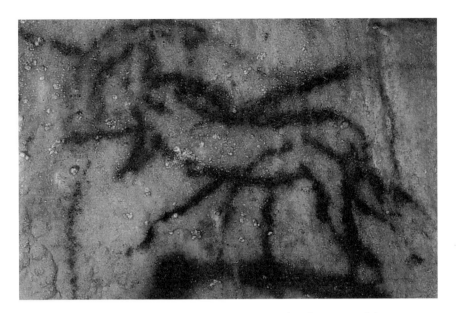

Plate 6   Cougnac cave (Lot, France). Anthropomorphic figure, struck by arrows, ca. 20,000 BCE. Photo M. Lorblanchet.

Cougnac (Lot, France), a decapitated body is shown, struck in the back by three projectiles, whilst another individual has been struck by seven spears all over his body (plate 6). In the Pech-Merle cave in Cabrerets (Lot, France), one individual is shown to have been hit by arrows all over his body, both from the front and from behind (plate 7). In Combel, part of the same network of caves, a human-like figure with an animal-shaped posterior (like the example

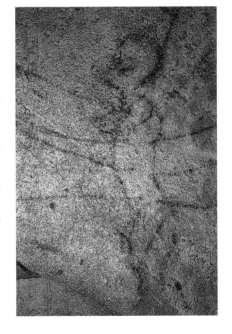

Plate 7   (*right*) Pech-Merle cave (Lot, France). Anthropomorphic figure, struck by projectiles, ca. 20,000 BCE. Photo M. Lorblanchet.

from Cosquer) can be seen collapsing, after having sustained several injuries. A carving upon a bone from Gourdan (France), showing only the pelvis and legs of a human figure (similar to the example from Cougnac), shows several arrows penetrating the victim's legs and rear. Also of interest is a rock engraving discovered in the cave at Sous-Grand-Lac (France). Like the bone carving from Gourdon, this engraving too is thought to belong to the late Magdalenian era. The engraving shows a figure injured in both the neck and back by a number of projectiles. Arrows also appear to have struck this individual's posterior and penis. These various examples are all the more significant in light of the fact that human figures are rarely featured in the parietal art of the Quaternary. The examples demonstrate that Cro-Magnons were indeed violent and that this violence often proved fatal.

Sicily: Torture in 10,000 BCE?

In 1952, another treasure was added to the examples of Rupestrian art from the Mediterranean region with the discovery of rock engravings upon the walls of the Addaura cave on the slopes of Monte Pellegrini, near Palermo (Italy). This artwork was completed at various points in time. It features animals (equidae, bovidae, and cervidae) and humans. It is the human figures that are of particular interest here, the majority of which all feature in the same well-known prehistoric art scene (figure 11). The engraving is generally thought to date from the "Late Epigravettian." This culture is thought to have existed during the transition period between the Paleolithic and the post-glacial era, in around 10,000 BCE. Nine figures are shown standing upright, in various positions, surrounding two horizontal figures. All of these human figures appear rather curious: several have a beak and a prominent mass of hair (or even a headdress or bonnet), which is raised in the rock. Three of the figures are lacking this unusual headwear. The figures on the periphery seem to be moving in a specific way – they are standing with their legs apart, either bent or moving. It appears that they are either dancing or moving rhythmically. They also seem to be moving their arms in an equally lively manner: two individuals are holding their arms in an "orant" pose, while others seem to be moving them in turn (one arm raised, the other bent). One figure is holding his arms forward, with three other figures making more reserved gestures. But the most striking positions of all are adopted by the two figures in the center. Lying with their stomachs to the ground, their legs are completely bent back to the extent that their feet are level with their rears and heels almost touching their buttocks. One of the two figures has his arms hanging free, whilst the other seems to have them folded tightly

Figure 11 Addaura cave (Sicily). Complex rock engraving showing human figures with beaks, along with a cervid. Epigravettian, ca. 10,000 BCE. After Mezzena, 1976.

behind his shoulders and neck. In addition to having their limbs bent back, each figure also has a rigid penis, perhaps an erection.

This curious scene, in which each individual seems to play a very specific role, has naturally sparked many different interpretations.[18] Starting with the unusual nature of this "ceremony," each of the individuals present "plays" a specific part, as is reflected by the curious headwear, dynamic movements, lively actions, and often unusual positions adopted. This picture seems to show a kind of ritual dance taking place around the bodies of two adolescents, forced to adopt a rather acrobatic pose, which is designed to restrict their movement. It has even been suggested that these young men were thrown from one person to another around the circle, with those doing the throwing having their arms raised and those catching holding out their hands. As for the penis being clearly depicted, it is possible that the adolescents were wearing protective penis gourds. Others have suggested that the scene represents homosexual activity, though as the two bodies are facing away from each other, this seems highly unlikely.

A more widely held view is that these two individuals were not gymnasts of any kind but "victims" selected to take part in a magical, propitiatory ceremony (figure 12 and plate 8).[19] The nature of the pose which they have been obliged to adopt suggests that they were "victims" of an appalling and painful sacrifice. Forced into a very uncomfortable position with their legs bent right back to their rears, these victims would have had to endure a terrible death – an organized strangulation. A cord was tied around the neck and ankles of each victim. The tensed position each individual was forced to adopt and the effort of keeping his legs bent in this way would cause him to tire and gradually relax his muscles, so unbending his legs. In doing so, the cord would tighten around the neck, leading to strangulation. In Sicily, *incaprettamento* is the name given to death by asphyxiation as a punishment; it was the method once used to punish anyone who had broken the rules of the Mafia. More detailed examinations of the figures from Addaura have revealed the presence of a taut cord linking the neck and feet. The different poses adopted by each individual could represent two different stages in the suffering of these "victims of torture." The figure shown with his arms hanging down may have already abandoned all resistance and may be dead. The other, with his hands around his neck, could be attempting to undo the knot before it strangles him. Could this be an initiation ritual? Such rituals are often characterized by cruelty and pain, with the aim of making the initiate stoical and able to resist suffering. It is equally possible that this scene represents a sacrifice. It is not, physiologically speaking, impossible that these victims would have had an erection in this situation. Strangulation may be accompanied or followed by several reactions: a discharge of feces, protrusion

Figure 12 Addaura cave (Sicily). "Initiates" or "torture victims": the two figures are shown to have their legs bent back and feet tied by a cord, which forms a slipknot around their necks. After Blanc.

of the tongue (which seems to be the case here), and a partial or full erection, with or without the emission of sperm – all due to a relaxation of the sphincter muscles. However, the theory that this was a cruel initiation ritual designed to test the mental and physical capacities of these two adolescents should not be dismissed.

Baron Blanc, an eminent paleontologist, compares this custom with initiation rituals carried out by various other societies and examines the cruelty they involve. During initiation rituals, initiates may be required to kill an

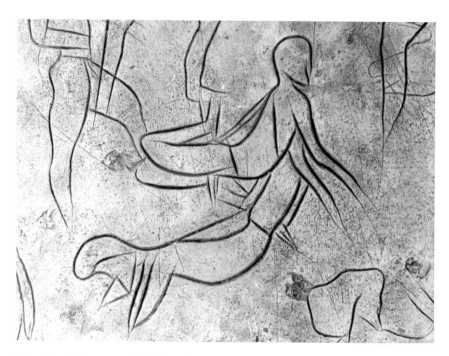

Plate 8 Addaura cave (Sicily). Paleolithic rock engraving, ca. 10,000 BCE. Detail of the two "initiates" or "victims of torture." Their legs and feet are tied together and a taut rope links their feet to their necks in a slipknot. © Ikona, Rome.

enemy and bring back his head, eat human flesh, undergo anal penetration, have their bodies tattooed, or be circumcised. All are tests which aim to shape the personality and prepare initiates for adversity – both are essential in securing status as a man and a warrior. Coming close to death (through semi-asphyxiation in the case at Addaura) could be one of the conditions that must be met in order that the initiate may reproduce one day. Whether the Addaura scene depicts a sacrifice or simply torture, the ceremony probably involved magic and regeneration: the death or strangulation of the "victims," their apparent erections, and the dancing or invocations on the part of the spectators are all indicative of this. It is also important to emphasize the dramatization of events which characterizes this rather supernatural atmosphere, reflected in the use of masks or unusual headdresses and the presence of officiants wearing beaks. The "victims" endure this suffering in order to be stronger in life or to commit themselves to sacrifice. They may be participating in a "mystery" intended to bring about regeneration.

From the Throwing-Stick to the Bow and Arrow

Humans have regularly strived to make new weapons that are more effective than those already in use. This is because one of their main aims has always been to contain, subjugate, and even eliminate any potential enemies. Can this behavior be traced back through time? Some certainly think so. In one of the opening scenes of Stanley Kubrick's *2001: A Space Odyssey*, two groups of Australopithecines go all out to attack each other, throwing stones, fighting with their bare hands, and even using a large mammal's bone as a weapon. Is this portrayal true or false? The fact that it refers to an era so far back in time, along with the lack of evidence, leaves the subject open to interpretation.

With a better understanding of the technical innovations which have enabled violence to inflict greater damage over time in the form of mechanical weaponry, this theory seems all the more plausible. Some would argue that these weapons were designed to improve humans' ability to hunt and were intended, first and foremost, for use in acquiring essential food. And this is certainly true. However, it was not long before such weapons were turned against fellow humans. This behavior seems to have increased greatly during the Upper Paleolithic, when humans invented the first reasonably powerful devices for propelling projectiles beyond the range that could be reached if thrown by hand. Upon striking their intended target these projectiles, which generally had very sharp tips, were even more likely to cause injury or death and could be thrown from a much greater distance. Before these inventions were made, striking a particular target would undoubtedly have involved simply throwing a stone, a sharpened section of wood, or a primitive spear. During the intermediate stage, piercing implements would have been attached to reasonably long handles to form weapons. Blunt projectiles were also used over a long period of time. These included throwing-poles, boomerangs, and so on – essentially, weapons that cause death or injury by inflicting a frontal or lateral blow, by crushing the flesh and bones. The popularity of such missiles is reflected in Rupestrian rock engravings and paintings from various eras, many being more "recent." Hand-held weapons were also used, such as rocks, sticks, cudgels, and, of course, the "club" dating from more recent times (clubs from the Neolithic era onwards – often symbols of prestige – and maces used in more recent historic times). Bolas form another group of weapons used in hunting (or warfare). These missiles consist of round stones strung together on cord. The stones are swung round and then hurled at the animal prey, like the weapons used by the ancient Gauchos of the Pampa region. This weapon serves to break and bind the animal's limbs simultaneously.

The introduction of mechanical weaponry was characterized by the application of technological developments to predation and violence. Hand-made instruments, such as the bow, sling, and throwing-stick, were used to propel weapons. The greater distances and precision that could be attained enabled more damage to be inflicted. At the same time, such weapons would have led to the emergence of new tactics and strategies. New organizational strategies would have developed in confrontation situations; engagements with the enemy and "command functions" would have become more "collective," and "proto-mechanized" combat would have developed, allowing for all kinds of long-distance attack.

The throwing-stick was used effectively in hunting during the Upper Paleolithic. This instrument is placed between the hunter's arm and the projectile and enables spears and arrows to be launched with greater force. The decoration often found upon the stick (handle) or the end piece, which is often carved, indicates that this weapon may also have been an ancient work of art. Only by holding this light weapon and using it to fire a spear at a fixed or moving target can this deadly combination of weapons be fully appreciated.

The bow was even more effective. It is likely to have been invented toward the end of the Upper Paleolithic (in around 12,000/10,000? BCE), although some claim this weapon was first developed in Solutrean times (ca. 20,000 BCE) because stemmed arrowheads and flint barbs, which could be attached to wooden arrow shafts, were developed at this time.[20] It has even been suggested that the small points found in La Gravette, dating from 25,000 BCE, could be arrowheads. The invention of the bow led to a mechanization of human aggressiveness, enabling humans to make rapid developments and fire weapons over greater distances at levels unrivaled until the invention of firearms. In fact, the bow became the subject of a myth which still exists today. The bow and its partner, the arrow, are used in advertising campaigns and as logos for numerous products. Even in this context, they are used as a kind of metaphor for war, representing a mercenary battle. In architecture, the strength of the bow-shaped structure is put to use in supporting various monuments: indeed, Roman arches probably constitute the most important feature of our earliest cathedrals after, of course, the manpower of the Romans themselves. On a more trivial level, it is worth noting that images of virility tend to involve a flexing of the muscles and erection of the penis, like the tightening of the bow. The rainbow, the electric arc, Cupid's bow, the bow of Diana the Huntress and of Joan of Arc are all words and expressions which relate to bows or bow-shaped objects and portray the bow – which made its first appearance with the last of the great hunters – as a quasi-magical object.

The First Bows

Despite debate as to when the bow was first invented, it is generally thought to date roughly from the very end of the Paleolithic. This theory is based on flint points, thought to date from this time, which were probably attached to arrow shafts as arrowheads. It is thought that the fragmented specimens discovered in Stellmor, near Hamburg, could date from the Ahrensburgian period, around the ninth millennium BCE. They were found along with a hundred or so pine-wood arrows which varied in length between 85 and 100 cm. The arrows were feathered and the ends had been split to allow the flint arrowhead to be attached. However, it is not until much later, during the Mesolithic, that there is definite evidence of bows being used. Bows dating from this period have been found, both complete and broken, along with an increased number of arrowheads. Examples of bows are rare, but some have been found in the peat bogs of Northwestern Europe and Northern Russia, where the wood was preserved by the silt-rich sediments. Similarities in their morphology are immediately evident.[21] Two elm-wood bows were discovered in Holmegaard (Denmark) and would originally have been 1.5–1.6 m long. The most complete of the two reveals a slight narrowing at the center, presumably to provide a handgrip for the archer. The handle also gradually becomes thinner toward each of the two pointed extremities. The second bow is broken and of a similar type. These weapons have been dated to the eighth to seventh millennia BCE ("Maglemosian").

Other examples are thought to be more recent and date from the time when Nordic cultures began to develop ceramics (Ertebölle culture). One such example is the Muldjerg bow, which is 1.7 m long and carved from elm-wood. The Braband bow is another example. It was found incomplete, was fashioned from ash-wood, and had a wide central section and narrower, though still thick, extremities.

Among the "Mesolithic" discoveries, conifer-wood bows found at the Vis-Moor I site in the region of Lake Sindar were convex and asymmetrical with different-shaped extremities (figure 13): at one end, they have a small appendage which often, though not always, contains a hole for attaching the string; the other end simply narrows at the base. These bows are generally 1.4–1.5 m long and form the most common type. At this same site, a fragment

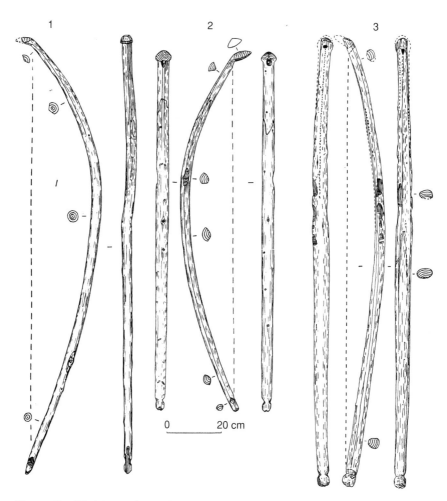

Figure 13 Vis-Moor I (Russia). Mesolithic bows, seventh to sixth millennium BCE. After Bourov.

of a bow with a double curvature was discovered. This model undoubtedly dates from very early times, though some have claimed that this model is more sophisticated and relates to protohistoric times. The third type of bow is of exceptional proportions – 3.5 m in length! The Vis-Moor I site, dating from the seventh to sixth millennia BCE, was also found to contain numerous other wooden objects, including several arrows.[22]

The bows depicted in the battle scenes of the Spanish Levant have long been thought to date from Mesolithic times. These bows appear to be relatively

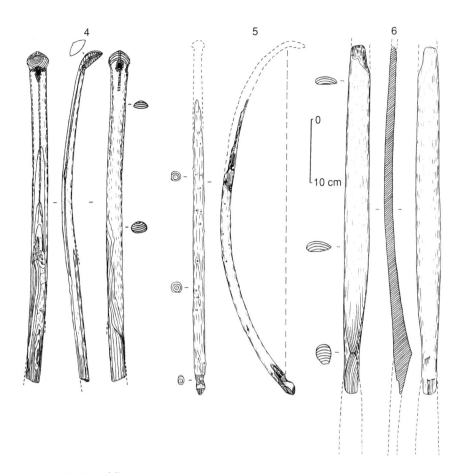

Figure 13   (*cont'd*)

unsophisticated – they are convex and seem to be of small proportions, judging by their size in relation to the height of the archers (figure 14).

Bigger bows are also depicted, shown to be even larger than the archers themselves. Among these imposing weapons, some models have a double curvature, as portrayed in one battle scene upon the walls of the Minateda rock shelter (Albacete, Spain). Some have argued that the morphology of these bows dates the paintings of the Levant to a much more recent point in time. However, this type of bow is known to have been used in the sixth millennium BCE or even earlier by hunter-gatherers in Russia. Claims that the art of the Spanish Levant dates from the later Neolithic should focus upon the types of arrowhead in use. Where the shape of arrowheads can be

Figure 14   Art of the Spanish Levant showing various types of bow: small and convex bows and even large bows, often with a double curvature. After Dams, 1984.

clearly determined, they are leaf or triangular shaped with "ailerons." These designs were very rare in the earlier phases of the Neolithic and only became more common during the course of the fifth millennium and, of course, throughout the fourth and third millennia BCE.

It is also useful at this point to mention the bow found with the body of Similaun man in the Austro-Italian Alps dating from ca. 3200 BCE, although this does require some deviation from the topic of hunter-gatherers under investigation here. This Copper Age individual was found with a large bow (182.5 cm long) made of yew, though it is thought that the bow may have been unfinished due to the thickness of the mid-section (greater than 3 cm) – this section is usually narrowed to create a handgrip. This hypothesis seems to be confirmed by the fact that the surfaces of the bow are not finished off and there are no holes or nocks at either extremity where the string would be attached. Thus, the weapon was not ready for use.[23] The quiver, by contrast, consists of a bag made of chamois leather and attached lengthways to a hazel-wood stick with leather straps. Of the 14 arrows it contained, two are complete, although broken. The feathering upon the arrows is sophisticated and is held together by a vegetation-based tar, strengthened by thread tied around the shaft and tipped with feathers. The flint arrowheads were then slotted into a notch on the arrow shaft and held in place with thread and a birch-wood-based tar. The remaining 12 arrows are composed of slender viburnum sticks, 80 cm in length and with a notch at one end where the flint arrowheads would be attached. Thus, it seems that Similaun man was very poorly equipped to face attack, with an unfinished bow, unfinished arrows, and two damaged arrows.

Conflict in Sudan

A site in Sudan – a slight distance away from the north bank of the Nile, halfway between Wadi Halfa to the south and Djebel Sahaba, an eminence to the north – was the setting for one of the first conflicts documented in archeology and anthropology. "Site 117," as it was named by the American and Finnish teams that began excavations here in 1965 and 1966, is a cemetery where the remains of at least 59 individuals (male and female adults as well as children) were discovered. This site is of interest firstly in terms of its age. Features of the stone industry discovered here indicate that the site is related to the Qadan culture, dating from 12,000 to 10,000 BCE, i.e., the Upper Paleolithic, or even the "Epipaleolithic." The dead were placed in oval graves with flattened bases, covered with thin stone slabs. Individual tombs as well as tombs containing two to five individuals were identified. The most

common scenario was for the body to be placed in the grave with the legs bent, resting on its left side with the head tilted to the east and facing south. The arms were also often bent and the hands placed level with the skull (plate 9).

These individuals were not buried with any funerary treasures or possessions. Quite the opposite in fact – the lithic remains found in the tombs were clearly parts of the weapons and projectiles used to destroy this population. Such artifacts were often found to be lodged deep within certain skeletons at various points on the body – inside the ribcage, at points along the vertebral column, in the palate, and in various other bones. Fragments found next to the human remains probably struck the flesh rather than the bone itself.

Plate 9   Double burial in Djebel Sahaba (Sudan). The sticks show the angle at which projectiles struck these victims during the massacre, ca. 12,000–10,000 BCE. Photo F. Wendorf.

From a technical point of view, some of the projectiles were stone fragments with a thick, blunt edge, fashioned into a point (figure 15). However, among the artifacts are more primitive stone fragments, which have been only slightly shaped, and even some scrapers. The morphology of these stone instruments seems to suggest that they were not used as projectile points yet, despite their unlikely use in warfare, they were nevertheless discovered among the weapons.

It would appear that a large proportion of those buried at "site 117" were massacred, since their bones bear the signs of various blows and injuries.[24] Yet these unfortunate victims were still entitled to a proper burial. Their remains were presumably recovered by the survivors who were anxious not to abandon their dead without burying them in some kind of tomb, however basic. However, the violence that occurred here is reflected in the funerary rituals: some graves contain several bodies. One such tomb was found to contain an elderly male (individual 25) and three adult females (individuals 28, 34, and 37). Two of these females died from projectile wounds to their bones. The third female and the male were both found alongside arrowheads, which presumably inflicted fatal wounds to their flesh.

Another grave contained the remains of two females killed by spears and two children, whose remains revealed no signs of damage (individuals 100, 101, 102, and 103). The very fact that the bodies were buried in groups suggests that even these immature individuals are likely to have died as a result of aggressive behavior, though possibly of a different kind. Two other graves, situated fairly close together, were found to contain five and three bodies respectively and were perhaps originally both part of the same much larger grave. These multiple burials suggest that the individuals contained in each grave were probably buried and killed at the same time. The group of five individuals (individuals 26, 27, 29, 31, and also probably 36) includes one child, two males, and two females (figure 16). Three of these adults had been struck by projectiles, though some also showed signs of various other injuries. Close by, the incomplete remains of three other adults were discovered, the sex of which could not be determined. They may well all have been buried in the same grave originally.

Another grave was found to contain the remains of two children (individuals 13 and 14), struck by projectiles at the point where the skull meets the cervical vertebrae. They had also received several violent blows. Excavation of a grave containing two males (individuals 20 and 21) revealed both to have died of multiple injuries, whilst a female

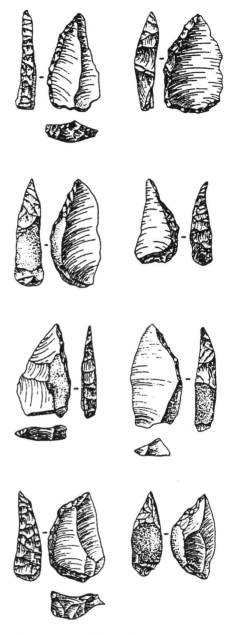

Figure 15 Djebel Sahaba. Site 117. Types of projectile point that would have been attached to arrows or spears, used in the massacre of individuals at site 117. After Wendorf, 1968.

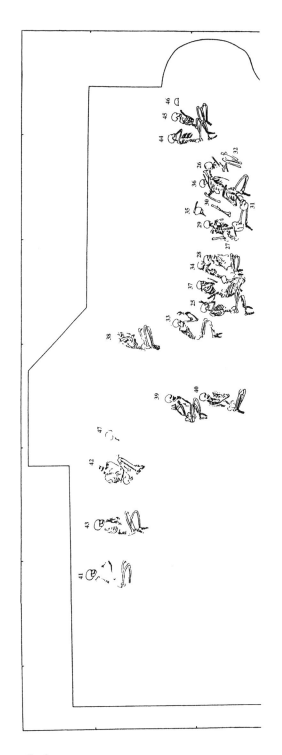

Figure 16 Djebel Sahaba. Site 117. Partial plan of the burial ground, 12,000–10,000 BCE, showing the location of the various graves containing the dead. After Wendorf, 1968.

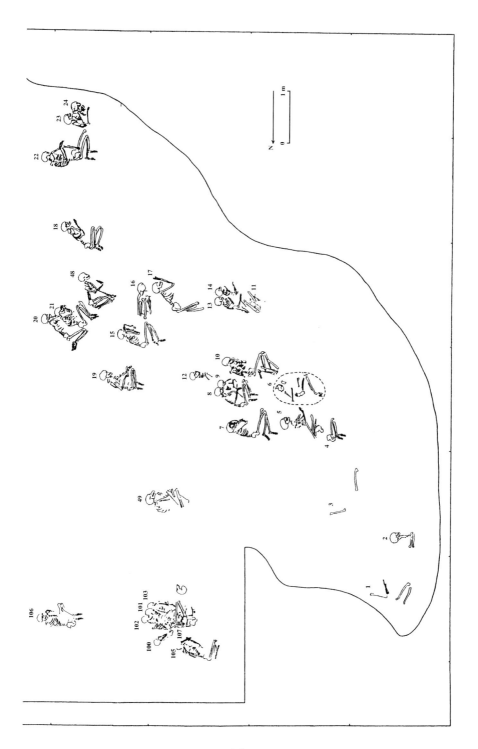

and a child (individuals 23 and 24) discovered in another "double" grave were found to have been struck by projectiles. Several other individuals suffered the same fate, though it is not known whether or not they once laid in one of the larger graves or in separate, adjacent graves. These individuals include a child (individual 47) and several males (individuals 17, 33, 38, 42, and 106), all found alongside various weapons that may well have been the cause of death.

Of these 59 individuals, at least 24 were killed by arrows or violent blows – indeed, the actual figure is probably much higher. It is likely that many of the other bodies found in these same graves died in equally tragic circumstances. Partial remains are all that is left of many bodies, though these individuals too probably died in violent circumstances. Thus, without speculating too much, the number of individuals killed can be placed at approximately 30, half of all those buried here.

It would seem that this population suffered "mass" violence affecting all age groups – young and elderly males, adult females, and children.[25] This was clearly more than just a confrontation between the adult males of two different communities; the population was suddenly confronted by an enemy wishing to destroy it partially or entirely. The massacre of the children in particular, and perhaps also the women, may have been an attempt to systematically rid this area of its population. Indeed, these attackers would not have wanted the women to survive and give birth, thus counterbalancing any losses suffered by the population. The fact that some of the graves contain only parts of the body (most notably the long bones) raises the question of whether the skulls may have been removed by the enemy as trophies. Certainly, this would have been a bloody attack and not just a case of simple tensions between groups occasionally resulting in a few men being killed. If these graves do not date from roughly the same time, as has often been assumed, then it would seem that this population was periodically attacked, with sections of the group being massacred regardless of their age and sex. The ferocity of these attacks, and the violence they involved, places a large question mark over the argument that tensions were less common during this period, the Final Paleolithic, when lower population densities are often thought to have made such barbaric acts untenable. This theory should undoubtedly be revised – the notion that "fraternal" attitudes were prevalent in the Paleolithic certainly shows its limits here.

Coveted Land

The clashes that occurred in Djebel Sahaba are thought to have been triggered by the appropriation of territory bordering the Nile, this land being potentially rich in resources (fish, waterfowl, and mammals inhabiting this riverside ecosystem). Furthermore, the close proximity of the Second Cataract of the Nile made the area even richer in terms of yielding food. On a more general note, as soon as hunter-gatherer communities began to turn to a more sedentary lifestyle – swapping a nomadic existence for a more settled lifestyle – the question of which land to occupy and cultivate became an important issue. Clearly, areas that could meet the nutritional needs of the population through being rich in animal life and vegetation were highly sought after. Logically, it follows that territorialization and the division of land would have begun as communities became more settled, possibly triggering conflict and disagreement. Territories most likely existed right through prehistoric times, varying in size depending upon the nutritional demands of the group, their needs, manpower, ability to obtain food, and difficulties in meeting these requirements. However, population densities remained low since it was necessary for groups to remain fluid and exogamous and to show solidarity in certain cynegetic activities. There would, therefore, have been few grounds for dispute; indeed, disputes may have been limited to disagreements between individuals. These territories would also have been vast and only very loosely defined, enabling bands to lead a nomadic existence over large areas of land without greatly prejudicing their other interests.

The problem probably emerged as soon as hunter-gatherer groups became larger and more advanced and began to lay claim to certain areas of land, particularly those rich in resources. Prehistorians claim that the first sedentary lifestyles (or tendencies toward a more sedentary lifestyle) have tended to develop in a range of areas, all rich in food supplies: river estuaries, coastal regions which offer several ecological niches (the edge of the sea and nearby pools, forests, and inland areas), and valleys alongside mountainous regions which present a wide range of ecosystems over a limited area due to changes in altitude. Such topological and ecological diversity creates small pockets of land which support a wide range of animal and plant species; these species are specific to particular biotopes and geographically limited. The choice of a location in which to settle is thus strongly influenced by the resources available and whether or not these resources will meet the nutritional needs of the group all year round. It is for this reason that the Natufian populations of the Near East settled early on in Galilee at locations where they could easily collect grasses, hunt gazelle, and fish all year round over a small area. Similarly, fishing "villages" on the Pacific coast of South America came to depend upon the resources offered by the sea. Mesolithic communities in Portugal and Northern Europe settled at points where they could benefit both from a sea or lake as well as nearby forests or grasslands. In Africa, oases and certain riverside locations would have prompted the same regrouping and gathering of populations. The switch to a more sedentary lifestyle on this small scale would have led to boundaries being defined and territories marked. At the same time, this tendency to settle would have brought about greater unity within groups, with attempts to strengthen group identity and create cultural tags to mark out a group's "own" space and distinguish it from that of its neighbor. Natural boundaries began to play a specific and vital part at this time, continuing up to the Epipaleolithic and possibly beyond.

Coming back to the case of Djebel Sahaba, the specific socioeconomic context behind this massacre (or massacres) on the banks of the Nile needs to be determined. Soon after this time, the region began to make new technical breakthroughs and even developed more complex lifestyles. Just one to two thousand years later, some of the oldest ceramics to be found on the African continent were made here, and similarly in Sarurab and Saggai, far in advance of the Near East. Around the same time, the domestication of cattle may have made its first appearance at a self-sufficient dwelling in the lower Nile region. In around 7000 BCE, some 100 km west of Abu-Simbel, small communities began to settle close to temporary lakes; hut-like dwellings were constructed from lightweight materials, accompanied by storage pits. This site is not considered to have been a fixed cultural province throughout the Epipaleolithic; instead it appears that these were "progressive" communities which hunted gazelle and lived on sorghum, wild millet, and local grasses. Can we assume from this that the changes that occurred a long way upstream from here were the result of the local community being unable to manage their environment and cohabit with their neighbors? The number of deaths in Djebel Sahaba – approximately 30 – indicates that the population here was much larger than that of small hunting groups. Some members of the group must also have run away or left temporarily and later returned to bury their dead. Furthermore, burial grounds of this type are virtually unknown in the Upper Paleolithic – at this time, individual tombs were by far the most common. Generally speaking, burial sites were not organized into larger burial grounds until the final stage of this era or until Mesolithic times. "Site 117" may, therefore, have contained an unusually large population for that time which would have led to differences in social organization and interaction between groups.

Some problems still remain unresolved, such as the actual size of the group. It has been suggested that this burial ground was not just used occasionally but may well have "functioned" over two generations. Burying the dead together at a fixed location in this way indicates a degree of attachment to the area of land; territories were perhaps already defined.

Incidentally, ethnology provides other examples of hunter-gatherer communities which are both stable and vindictive. In central California, for example, such communities live in fixed villages with facilities for storing acorns. They have a marked social hierarchy, yet conflicts nevertheless break out between villages over the ownership of territories and over harvesting and fishing produce. This undoubtedly represents a more advanced "stage" than that of "site 117." But when exactly did the situation change, causing the hunter-gatherers of the late Paleolithic to experience such tensions?

Conflict during the Mesolithic

Djebel Sahaba is by no means the only illustrative, frequently cited example. Archeologists have been able to identify some of the tensions that characterized highly coveted areas during the Mesolithic and led to killings. These deaths occurred in particular at natural boundaries such as rapids, mountain passes, and other breaks in the landscape, locations where food supplies are in rich abundance within a relatively small area. Balakin and Nuzhnyi, in particular, stress the importance of rivers as natural boundaries and a source of food. They also emphasize the role of rapids, which break the natural flow of the water. Such steep slopes create a range of ecological niches across a small area. Perhaps, like these authors, we should draw a parallel between those killed by projectiles and buried close to such coveted environments and the competitive behavior such environments trigger.[26]

At the Sarai Nahar Rai cemetery (India), situated close to the Ganges rapids and thought to date from the tenth millennium BCE, the remains of three individuals were discovered (one male and two females), all killed by microlithic arrowheads.

In Southeastern Europe, many rapids interrupt the flow of the Dnepr River. A series of burial grounds dating from the Epipaleolithic-Mesolithic era follows the path of the river, tending to be located alongside these natural features and the biotopes, flourishing with fauna and flora, that surround them. Alongside the third set of rapids, at Voloshkii, is a burial ground dating from the early Mesolithic. Of the 19 bodies discovered here, all buried with their legs bent, three had been struck by narrow flint points with a sharp barb and reinforced edge. This may have been one of the earliest known uses of the bow, used to propel light and sharply pointed arrows.[27] Previously, murder weapons took the form of javelins or other projectiles (often launched with a throwing-stick or similar device) or blunt, heavy, or sharp instruments, used to strike the enemy directly.

The Mesolithic Age cemeteries I and III in Vasilevka alongside the Dnepr, dating from around 9000 BCE, were found to contain the remains of individuals injured by projectiles: two of the 25 bodies at the first site and seven of the 45 bodies at the second. At the Vasilevka III site, two females are also thought to have died from violent blows to the body.

Alongside the Danube, at the Schela Cladovei burial ground (Romania), close to the Iron Gates, two individuals were found to have died after being struck by arrows.

Violence resulting in death was clearly a feature of those hunter-gatherer societies in Europe and Asia which settled alongside rivers. However, seaside and lake regions were just as highly coveted (figure 17).[28]

This was the case in Popovo, to the east of Lake Onega (Russia), where a burial site was found to contain the body of a female who had been struck in the right shoulder by a bone point. In tomb K of the Mesolithic burial ground in Téviec (Morbihan, France), a young male was buried, having been struck by two arrowheads in his sixth and eleventh thoracic vertebrae.

Figure 17   Map of the ancient world showing Mesolithic sites where deaths have been attributed to projectile injuries: (1) Djebel Sahaba; (2) Sarai Nahar Rai; (3) Voloshkii; (4) Vasilevka 1; (5) Vasilevka 3; (6) Schela Cladovei; (7) Popovo; (8) Téviec; (9) Skateholm; (10) Bogebakken; (11) Columnata; (12) El Bachir.

Remains of individuals thought to have been injured or killed were also discovered at burial grounds in Scandinavia, dating from the more advanced stages of the Mesolithic or from the period when Neolithic technologies were first beginning to emerge. At burial site I in Skateholm in Skåne (Sweden), which contained the remains of 64 individuals, several of the bodies showed signs of having suffered violent injuries (one male had a sharp arrow lodged in the pelvis). In Bogebakken, close to Vedbaek (Denmark), a trapezoidal point was discovered, lodged in the long bone of a young male (tomb A). Excavations at this same site yielded a grave containing three bodies one of which, a male, had been struck by an arrowhead between the second and third cervical vertebrae. At other sites (Korsor Nor and Tyhrind Vig in Denmark), individuals were found to have received several blows to the head.[29]

A Capsian burial ground in Columnata (dating from the seventh or sixth millennium BCE) contained more than 100 graves. One female was found to have been struck by a slender projectile in her first lumbar vertebra. The skull of another female showed signs of scarring, probably the result of an inflicted injury. Similarly, a male was found to have two thin stone slivers lodged in his thorax.[30] In the El-Bachir cave in Bousfer, south of Oran (Algeria), a flint arrowhead was discovered, lodged in the skull of a child, dating from Epipaleolithic or Neolithic times.

These are, however, only isolated examples; unlike the burial ground in Djebel Sahaba, Sudan, there is no sign of "collective" violence having occurred.

As mentioned above, economic factors, such as the desire to seize land rich in resources, have often been blamed for these violent attacks. Social factors may also have played a part: competition may have arisen between individuals within a group in response to demographic expansion or attempts to acquire more land. In either case, the emergence of leaders could not have passed without some degree of tension. This air of competition among hunter-gatherers may well explain the situations described above: "a settling of scores" as part of an internal struggle for power, perhaps? As has already been suggested, the transition to the Neolithic may have heightened any emerging social inequalities: the need to manage the food supplies obtained during gathering and fishing expeditions would have led to a degree of competition among hunter-gatherers. It seems likely that certain individuals would have acquired even greater responsibilities with the emergence of agricultural production. Those in charge of these early agricultural communities would have required the authority to control economic production and regulate tensions between family units and intolerant individuals.

The Enemy: Mutilated and Tortured

When one of the authors examined a body discovered in a swallow hole in Gigounet (Tarn, France), thought to have died during the late Neolithic, ballistic analysis of the impact revealed the individual to have been stretched out on the ground and possibly already dead when struck by bow and arrow.[31] The body seems to have been dealt a *coup de grâce* as it lay on the ground.

This tendency to "kill" an individual several times, even though he may already be dead, has also been noted at burial grounds in the Ukraine (Voloshkii, Vasilevka I and III), where many skeletons were found to have been struck by several spears. Detailed studies into the trajectories of these projectiles, which struck their target at various angles, seem to confirm the theory that these individuals were already lying on the ground when struck, perhaps dead, yet the attack continued relentlessly.

The case of Djebel Sahaba is perhaps even more enlightening. Individuals 20, 21, and 44 from this burial ground in Sudan were all struck by several arrows, ranging from six to in excess of 20. Ballistic analysis has again revealed that these bodies were massacred several times over. The aim was presumably to destroy these individuals forever, to ensure that they could never live again. Through such extreme violence, their bodies were deliberately damaged in an attempt to reduce them to nothing, permanently.

Balakin and Nuzhnyi point out that the ferocity of these attacks makes it unlikely that this was ritual warfare, i.e., war as a game or spectacle.[32] This behavior is documented in ethnographic literature – the aim is to rule out any chance of the enemy being reborn and any possibility of seeing the enemy live again. This has often been compared to the atrocities committed by the American Indians during guerrilla warfare against Caucasian soldiers attempting to conquer the Great Plains. The bodies of these soldiers, killed by the Sioux or the Cheyenne, were often found to have been struck several times over. Some had been hit by roughly 20 arrows, with one soldier being reportedly struck 105 times. Secondary injuries were also common – blows to the body, scalping, evisceration, removal of the organs, emasculation, and so on.

One nineteenth-century ideological picture seeks to contrast American "order" with "barbarity" on the part of the savage American Indians (figure 18). Soldiers from the federal army, impeccably dressed in their uniforms, are shown observing a battlefield and the ruthless damage inflicted by the "savages" and seem to be filled with great sorrow. The bodies of the American soldiers are shown to be rather gruesome; they have been reduced to skeletons and struck all over by arrows. The scene emphasizes the differences between

Figure 18 Nineteenth-century artwork showing American cavalrymen visiting a battlefield where white soldiers and Indian tribes have fought one another. The soldiers' remains are shown to have been pelted with arrows following their death. After Bergman, 1987.

the supposedly civilized whites and the barbaric Indians; the implication is that the latter disrespected their enemies even after they had been killed.

In addition to their determination to destroy the bodies of any slain enemies, there is also a state of mind which leads the warriors to see war as a status-enhancing activity. It is not enough just to kill the enemy; the body must also be injured and mutilated. No effort is spared in destroying the body and belittling the enemy's spirit and aura (especially in cases where the deceased was a particularly courageous combatant). The victors scorn their defeated enemies and aim to destroy them, physically and spiritually. As a result, they gain prestige and admiration themselves.

This would explain why parts of the body were often taken as trophies, such as the scalp. Similar behavior was exhibited by the Celts, who often removed the heads from the bodies of their enemies, though admittedly this occurred much later in time.[33] Such customs also seem to have been practiced at one time in the south of the Gaul region where skulls were fastened to or embedded in niches in lintels or steles. These were undoubtedly the skulls of defeated enemies and served as trophies, perhaps even as talismans.

The fact that the skull was so highly valued may indicate that this was a custom of a different kind, perhaps a funerary ritual, which sought to give prominence to this part of the body.

The discovery of skulls and other human remains in ditches at certain Neolithic sites could indicate that the head or limbs were initially displayed

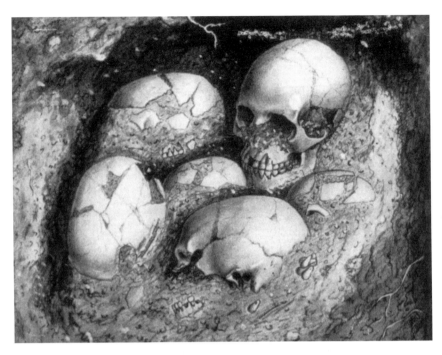

Figure 19 Ofnet (Bavaria, Germany). One of the burial pits, primarily containing the skulls of adult females and children. Some of the remains from Ofnet show signs of violent blows to the back of the head. After Boule and Vallois, 1946.

and then subsequently abandoned as crude and anonymous remains. Or perhaps these were the remains of ancestors and thus fulfilled a magical role. Going back even further in time, there is also the case of the "burial" pits discovered in Ofnet in Bavaria (Germany), generally thought to date from the Mesolithic, though this is often disputed (figure 19). At this site, two pits were found to contain 27 and six skulls, respectively. Of the 33 individuals discovered here, with the exception of four adult males, all were females (nine) and children (20). The skulls were mixed up with ocher and ashes. There could be any number of explanations as to why these skulls were grouped together in this way – perhaps these individuals were voluntarily decapitated (after being selected?) and their skulls then placed together in these specially prepared pits. Perhaps the skulls were trophies, taken from defeated enemies. Or there may, of course, be other explanations. Recent studies have revealed that six of these individuals (four male adults and two children) were struck across the back of the head with an axe. Thus, the skulls may have been grouped together following an act of violence. A similar case is Hohlenstein Stadel (Germany) where three skulls were discovered, two of which showed signs of injury, the result of blows to the head with an axe. Could it be that the tragic incidents that occurred at these two sites saw some of the last groups of hunter-gatherers attacked by "outsiders" (Neolithic populations?), armed with axes? In this case, these piles of skulls could be buried trophies.

It should also be noted that the Natufians of Palestine are known to have removed the skulls from certain bodies long before this and that this custom continued throughout the Near East for two to three thousand years. The severed and plastered skulls from the Southern Levant and skull niches in Cayönü in Southeastern Anatolia bear witness to the importance attached to these practices throughout the Pre-Pottery Neolithic B period in the eighth millennium BCE. In this case, these skulls were not trophies taken from defeated enemies, rather they belonged to members of the community. The aim was to either "restore" these individuals to life, probably because they possessed certain desirable qualities or had a beneficial input, or to store the skulls of ancestors in order to preserve their accounts and memories. Even though the motives behind the Ofnet customs may well have been very different, the treatment and gathering of skulls in this way in post-glacial Europe nevertheless indicates that the skull had a very specific role to play in the myths and rituals of this era.

Chapter 2

Agriculture: A Calming or Aggravating Influence?

In 10,000 BCE, the relationship between humans and nature underwent great changes. For more than 2 million years, humans were completely dependent upon their environment, obtaining food from their lavishly stocked surroundings through hunting, fishing, and gathering wild plants, berries, and fruits. Humans lived according to the natural resources at their disposal and were unable to progress beyond this state, such was their dependence upon their surrounding environment.

In around 10,000 BCE, this situation changed. Humans began, slowly at first and then more rapidly, to free themselves of this dependence, at first controlling and later dominating nature. By domesticating plants and animals, humans began to produce their own food, both vegetation and meat. This allowed humans to increase food production, as required, to feed more people and to make their surroundings more artificial and better suited to this new human existence. However, it would be wrong to assume that these progressive developments, which play a crucial part in the history of humankind, merely improved food production and other economic factors. The Neolithic was also accompanied by changes in humans themselves – they began to perceive their relationship with their environment differently, to fill their surroundings with symbolic significance, to change their behavior toward others and to see their own role differently, having gained control over the environment upon which they had previously been dependent. Thus, humans too underwent great changes on a cultural, ideological, and psychological level. Yet when humans are already in control of the animal, plant, and mineral worlds, what kind of relationship can they have with others of the same species? Did this progressive domestication lead certain individuals to go one step further on the road to hegemony? History has, unfortunately, revealed such fears to be well founded and violence began to take on various different forms from the advent of farming onwards.

The Neolithic in Europe: A Peaceful or Dangerous Conquest?

Agriculture had many birthplaces the world over, one of which was the Near East where wheat, barley, and legumes were first cultivated. However, there were many other epicenters for these changes in food production – Northern China, China's Yangtze region, Southeast Asia, Oceania, Central America, the Andes and their outer margins, and Saharan-Sahelian Africa. The Near East is of particular interest here, since this region was responsible for Europe (as well as parts of Asia and Africa) shifting toward an agricultural economy. Small groups of farmers and stockbreeders from the North Levantine and Anatolian regions set out to "conquer the West," in search of new land from around 8500/8000 BCE. They gradually introduced completely new ways of living to populations that had previously been dependent upon hunting and gathering. This would have been a very slow process, taking more than 2,000 years to reach the western shores of the Mediterranean and even longer to reach the mouth of the Rhine. The spread of agriculture affected two main areas initially: the Mediterranean region and the Danube and its tributaries in Europe's more temperate areas. This led to a frequent restructuring and to variations in economic decisions (choice of which plants to cultivate and which animal species to breed) and cultural features (morphology of houses, stone implements, ceramics, walls, symbolic objects, funerary rituals, etc.). In short, there was no standard model corresponding to the monolithic culture – part of the Near East – and reproduced accurately right through to Western Europe. Instead, there were different cultural models, these differences being all the more marked the greater the distance from the epicenter.

But there is one important question underlying this trend, which saw the first agricultural communities gradually introduced to the European continent spreading out from the Euphrates to the Atlantic – what was the atmosphere at the time of this diaspora? Was this a slow and peaceful process, a colonization with no real story behind it? Or did these developments occur under more difficult circumstances, in a hostile environment? Europe was certainly not unpopulated when these first agricultural communities appeared on the scene: indigenous communities, descended from the great Paleolithic civilizations, populated the continent. The real difficulty lies in gauging the actual population density at the time. Apart from a few specific regions (Northern Europe, Portugal) with a somewhat higher population, overall pre-Neolithic civilizations seem to have had rather small populations. A reasonable estimate would put the population at the time of an area like France in the

25,000–50,000 bracket. Sites dating from the "Late Mesolithic," i.e., the period immediately preceding the arrival of these farming communities, perhaps even overlapping with them, are rather rare. In certain regions, some of these sites are known to have existed simultaneously with the first agricultural settlements, almost as if, in certain areas, the hunter-gatherer lifestyle resisted the supposed advantages of agriculture for a time. This was the case particularly in Northern Europe, where the cultivation of crops began later than across the rest of the continent.

But how were these new arrivals greeted by the "indigenous" population? Some researchers play down this initial contact, claiming that the new techniques (cultivating cereals, stockbreeding, and ceramics) were simply adopted by the local population. According to this theory, Europe's last hunters would have simply borrowed or acquired this knowledge, gradually learning to copy this behavior. Essentially, they would have transformed themselves by adopting these new procedures. Even if this hypothesis does hold true for certain areas, a large part of the Neolithic lifestyle was nevertheless introduced by groups of intruders (even though this spread resulted in only limited displacements at each stage), which explains why this was a relatively slow process. The Neolithic "system" in fact involved an entirely different way of life from the hunter-gatherer lifestyle in terms of technical knowledge, day-to-day routine, the agricultural calendar, relationship with and control of the environment, and systems of symbolic values. The tale ends with the indigenous population disappearing – either they were killed or became integrated into the Neolithic culture through acculturation.

It is not yet known whether the first encounters between hunters and farmers were peaceful or whether local populations in fact courageously sought to defend their amply stocked hunter-gatherer territories against the intruders. It has often been claimed that indigenous populations were so taken with this new way of life and the psychological impact of seeing flocks of sheep and fields of wheat that they would have failed to put up any resistance, handing over their arms and knowledge freely to side with these "outsiders." It has also been suggested that, in the temperate regions of Europe where more forested areas were springing up due to a gradual warming of the climate in this post-glacial era, hunting groups were so few and far between that farmers arriving in and around the Danube region would have faced virtually no opposition. It seems logical to assume that the reaction to each encounter was different, ranging from hospitality to defiance and even, at times, confrontation. Yet regardless of whether the new methods of production were eventually adopted and local populations and migrants ended up interbreeding, questions still remain: Were there feelings of insecurity? Hostile relations? Did the newcomers experience any initial difficulties in claiming areas of highly coveted land, especially along riverbanks, since these areas were frequently sought out for hunting and fishing purposes due to their rich abundance of fish and waterfowl? In Europe's more temperate regions, any particularly fertile areas such as valleys, fluvial basins, and loessial terraces would have attracted these farmers, characterized by their Linear Pottery culture. Thus, it seems likely that there would have been a certain degree of competition between these newcomers and the indigenous population. This is all the more likely in view of the limitations of nature which these first farmers had to overcome (such as the need to deforest certain regions). These pioneers also demonstrated their mobility through their continual spread westwards, which brought about constant modifications and replications of this colonizing front.

New research has revealed that some indigenous areas, although not densely populated, nevertheless had a greater population than was previously thought. As a result, the advance of these first farming communities would have involved the despoliation of certain territories. This is likely to have triggered feelings of animosity among certain groups, determined to defend their hunter-gathering and fishing territories. It has often been remarked that tensions are likely to have been at their most acute in the zones where farming and hunting grounds met. This may explain the existence of fortified Neolithic sites, which were typically defended by a system of trenches, usually combined with a palisade; these areas were perhaps once situated at borders between hunting and farming grounds. There is nothing new in the construction of such fortified sites at border locations; invading groups have always tended to defend their territory in this way along the borders. Keeley even proposes that economic factors were responsible for the division of territories in Northwestern Europe – on the one side were those living upon the land conquered by the farming communities, whereas the other side was still occupied by hunting communities. Often, there was a kind of no man's land in between, spanning some 20 to 30 km.[1] However, this climate of uncertainty would not have been permanent and peaceful relations would also have existed at times between these two groups with their different ways of life. It is known, for example, that the farmers were often provided with the high-quality flint they required for their tool-making by the indigenous population. The role of interbreeding and cultural exchange among these neighboring populations should not be underestimated.

These theories, which aim to describe the conquering of Europe by agricultural communities and the nature of the resultant relationship between locals and newcomers, are largely speculative and are based upon different interpretations of the archeological evidence. However, they are certainly worth postulating. Many models throughout history have attempted an ideological ranking of the two groups concerned: the intruders are generally considered to be economically, technically, and therefore also culturally superior; the indigenous population are seen to be backward and behind the times. Furthermore, it should be noted that confrontations always seem to turn to the advantage of the intruders, as in the case of the Romans and the Gauls, the whites and the American Indians, and so on. These are factors which should be taken into account when debating the spread of these agricultural communities across Europe and other areas of the world which became home to Neolithic communities. It is not unusual for the victorious to class their defeated enemy as barbaric, although they are often far more barbaric themselves. Certain Neolithic communities from the Danube region certainly seem to prove this – Talheim is one such example.

The Talheim Massacre

Some of the conclusions drawn by archeologists from their research have been based upon notions that are difficult to accept. The theory discussed above, detailing how Linear Pottery cultures came to spread a new lifestyle based upon agriculture and animal husbandry throughout temperate Europe, has also sparked other ideas. These farming communities were once thought to have shown solidarity (in overcoming the difficulties posed by the forested areas) and to have been closely bound by kinship ties, enabling friendly relations to be maintained with neighboring groups. As a result, and due also to their low populations, it seemed likely that there were no wars or tensions. It was also proposed that women, thought to be behind the new agricultural techniques, may have dominated the social group as a result of their economic role. Thus, an air of serenity and tenderness was thought by some to have prevailed within these groups. Of course, these were just possible interpretations, yet they conjured up very calm images. For this reason, when evidence of carnage was found in Talheim close to Heilbronn in Baden-Württemberg (Germany) dating from 5000 BCE, i.e., from the time of Europe's earliest farming communities, these images were called into question and archeologists were forced to minimize their idealization of these "farmers of the Danube," whom they had previously considered to be so inoffensive.

The site was excavated in 1983 and 1984, following the discovery of some rather mysterious-looking bones during gardening work (plate 10). It emerged that these bones came from a communal grave containing the remains of 34 individuals (18 adults and 16 children) all piled on top of one another and all having suffered a violent death.[2] Various fragments of pottery enabled the

Plate 10   Talheim (Baden-Württemberg, Germany). Communal grave dating from the Neolithic, ca. 5000 BCE, during excavation. Photo Dr. J. Wahl/Dr. H. G. König. Landesdenkmalamt Baden-Württemberg, Archäologische Denkmalpflege, Osteologie.

site to be dated: the event took place during an advanced stage of the Linear Pottery period. Meticulous research enabled the original position of each of the bodies in the grave to be established, in spite of the difficulties in identifying the remains of each individual (figure 20). The skeletons were, in fact, completely jumbled up and the limbs entangled with one another. These bodies were evidently thrown quickly and carelessly into a pit for disposal. The weight of the earth would then have compressed these remains.

At some point, this population evidently faced a violent attack. Numerous blows and signs of injury to various parts of the skeletons reveal that the "assailants" were determined to finish off their victims. Anthropological studies

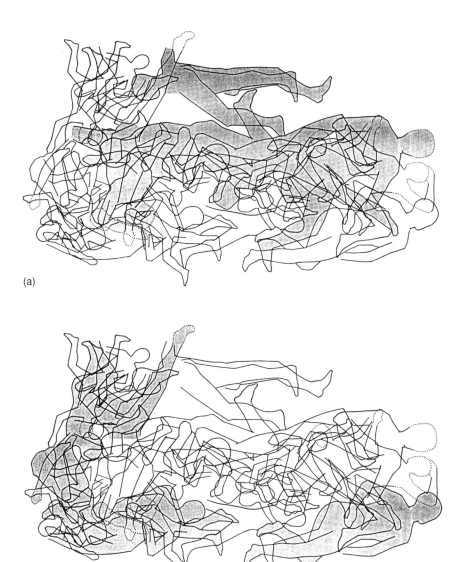

(a)

(b)

Figure 20 Talheim (Baden-Württemberg, Germany). Communal grave dating from the Neolithic, ca. 5000 BCE. The shaded figures show the position of the bodies: (a) males; (b) females; (c) children. After Wahl and König, 1987.

have enabled an assessment to be made of the impacts inflicted upon each body, including the force and angle of the blows received, the point of impact and penetration, and the weapons used to inflict these fatal wounds. In certain cases, the relative positions of the attacker and victim could also be

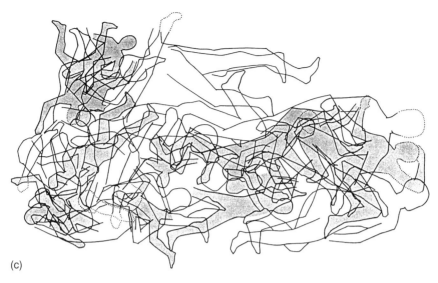

(c)

Figure 20   (*cont'd*)

determined. In general, it seems to be the case that the majority of the victims were attacked from behind as they were standing, presumably as they tried to protect themselves or flee. Having already been struck, many individuals were then hit again as they knelt or even lay on the ground, where they were perhaps already dying. Axes with both thin and thick stone blades (the latter are called "shoe-last" adzes) were primarily used in these attacks (figure 21). Injuries inflicted by arrows are rare, indicating that the bow played an inferior role in this attack. It is possible that clubs were also used to strike the victims. Some of the bodies received heavy blows, caused by large implements (tree trunks?); perhaps they were trampled into the ground. The location of the impacts upon the bodies seems to indicate that the attackers, who struck their victims from behind, were right-handed. This conclusion is based upon the positioning of the blows received to the bodies as well as the morphology of the stone blades which struck and shattered the skulls. It would seem that the skull was struck first of all (plates 11 and 12). The victims were struck on the back of the neck and on the dome and sides of the skull. Blows to the face and to the frontal are rare. In addition to the majority of the skulls being smashed, serious injuries were also inflicted upon other parts of the body – the arms, legs, and pelvis. The fact that certain skeletons bear various different types of injury seems to indicate that some individuals were struck by more than one attacker, unless some of the attackers dealt a *coup de grâce* to the dying or dead victims.

1

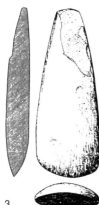

2

3

Figure 21 Types of weapon used in the Talheim massacre of the Neolithic: (1) flint arrowhead; (2) "shoe-last" adze blades; (3) polished axe blade. After Wahl and König, 1987.

As far as the reasons for this attack go, it is only possible to hypothesize. It should be noted that these attackers and their victims may well have belonged to the same "culture": the morphology of some of the axes used (such as the "shoe-last" adzes, mentioned above) are characteristic of the Linear Pottery civilization. If the broken pottery fragments found in the tomb belonged to the group under attack, then it would seem that the two populations involved shared a common cultural background. Clearly, however, such ties did not prevent confrontation from occurring. Was this aggression perhaps triggered by the desire to seize fertile land or livestock? Was the aim of the attack to abduct certain individuals and to kill others? Was it perhaps a vendetta? All this, of course, remains pure speculation. Analyzing the remains of the victims throws up certain lines of enquiry. Of the 18 adults massacred, there were nine males, seven females, and two individuals whose sex could not be determined. The majority of age groups are represented, from children through to mature adults. However, there are no very young children, aged 0–4 years, among the dead. This lack of newborn infants and very young children warrants further scientific investigation. Indeed, anthropologists who have studied these remains claim that they are not representative of a normal population. The population is incomplete, due to the lack of very young children. Were these children perhaps taken away from their parents? Or were they killed elsewhere?

More detailed studies have revealed that these victims shared certain genetic features. More specifically, two groups of individuals could be identified which undoubtedly shared kinship ties. It was even possible to link the children to their parents, also found among these remains.[3] Thus, it seems that the deceased were all related, in one way or another.

Savage killings were evidently carried out within this community in Talheim with its small number of family units, no doubt all of which were part of the same kinship system. It seems likely that this population was completely exterminated – had any relatives survived,

Plate 11 Talheim (Baden-Württemberg, Germany). Neolithic human skull smashed by a stone "shoe-last" adze (individual 83/22 C1). Detail of the injury. Photo Dr. J. Wahl/Dr. H. G. König. Landesdenkmalamt Baden-Württemberg, Archäologische Denkmalpflege, Osteologie.

fled, or been spared, they would surely have given their dead a proper burial, in accordance with the funerary traditions of the day.

Disturbances during the Neolithic

Was Talheim an isolated case? Were other acts of violence carried out during the Early Neolithic with its Linear Pottery culture? The answer to the latter question is yes, although the causes, nature, and consequences of this violence often varied. Another case was discovered during the excavation of a settlement dating from this same period (Later Linear Pottery period, in around 5000 BCE) in Asparn-Schletz (Lower Austria). The site is surrounded by a ditch. Initial excavations revealed 67 bodies among the upper layers of this

Plate 12 Talheim (Baden-Württemberg, Germany). Neolithic human skull struck by an axe with a polished stone blade (individual 83/22 A). Detail of the injury. Photo Dr. J. Wahl/Dr. H. G. König. Landesdenkmalamt Baden-Württemberg, Archäologische Denkmalpflege, Osteologie.

trench, all of which showed signs of violent death. The situation seems similar to that which occurred in Talheim: 39 of the 40 skulls found were smashed and there are signs that multiple strikes and injuries were inflicted. The extremities of the limbs are often missing, having perhaps been gnawed at by canidae.[4] Overall it would seem that, unlike in Baden-Württemberg, no attempts were made here at grouping the bodies in a communal grave following the killings. The remains were simply abandoned where they lay after the massacre.

More recent excavations near to Mannheim (Palatinate) in Germany have confirmed the theory that disturbances did occur during the Early Neolithic. The site in question, Herxheim, covers 5 hectares of land and is surrounded by a double trench. The site once contained dwellings made from wood and earth; the foundations were found to consist of holes where posts would have been inserted. Clay extraction pits were also discovered; the clay was presumably used in the construction of walls and other surfaces. In addition to the rare burials and the remains of dismembered bodies that were found here, numerous skull fragments were also unearthed. Preliminary analysis revealed that they belonged to more than 300 individuals. The majority of these skull fragments (tops of skulls) were found to have been placed, three to five at a time, in the trenches surrounding the site: 32 percent in the outer trench, 64 percent in the inner trench, and 4 percent in the village itself.[5] These skulls show definite signs of deliberate damage: the majority were smashed with a stone or wooden tool; it seems that the aim was to preserve only the top of the skull. Detailed studies of one particular specimen indicate that the individual was struck both across the front and back of the skull. After death the scalp was removed, though not with the usual scalping techniques, instead being removed in strips. The fact that only a few complete skulls were found, whereas the tops of many other skulls were deliberately preserved, requires further investigation. This is especially the case given that the jaws and teeth, which generally preserve very well, are missing – were they perhaps buried elsewhere or simply disposed of? Even more surprising was the discovery of a model of the top of a skull, made from baked earth and resembling the many bone fragments unearthed during the excavations. Of the skulls discovered, many belonged to children. Interpreting the reasons for these killings and the damage subsequently inflicted upon the skulls is far from easy. Perhaps the skulls were war trophies? If this is the case, then the skulls of enemies killed in combat were evidently deliberately damaged. Was this violence perhaps an attempt to abduct and kill a neighboring population, especially its children? This is certainly one possibility. Yet weren't the young victims part of this same community? It is even possible that an internal crisis brought about the decision to eliminate a section of the growing population. If this hypothesis proves correct, then crises and dramas must have occurred within this Neolithic community, with the result that numerous individuals were forcibly killed.

There can be no doubt that research recently carried out in Talheim, Asparn-Schletz, and Herxheim has transformed the traditional view of the first farming communities in temperate Europe. These communities were originally thought to have been calm, united, and fraternal. The new discoveries seem to suggest that they were, in fact, violent, barbaric, and brutal. Rereading archeological literature and reassessing earlier discoveries and the conclusions that were so quickly drawn has brought examples of similar killings to light; the list of this violent behavior keeps on growing. One such example is the "Jungfernhöhle" cave in Tiefenellern (Bavaria, Germany). Here, excavations in 1950 unearthed a layer dating from the Neolithic Linear Pottery culture. Among the discarded items found here (fauna, lithic instruments, broken vases) were the remains of approximately 40 individuals. The majority of these individuals (26) were children and adolescents with almost all of the 15 adults killed being female. Their long bones may well have been intentionally broken.[6] Even the teeth seem to have been removed, perhaps for use as pendants. This is not unlikely, given that a necklace made of human teeth was discovered at a Linear Pottery culture burial ground in Nitra (Slovakia). The bodies of these females and youngsters, the remains of which were found abandoned among the discarded bones of animal kills in Tiefenellern, may actually have been consumed by other individuals within the social group. This may also have occurred at Fontbregoua (France). These are by no means the only examples from this civilization. In Zauschwitz (Brandenburg, Germany), the bones of at least six individuals were unearthed in a small pit, in amongst domestic waste and animal remains. The skulls and long bones had been broken in order to extract the brain and marrow. This may be yet another example of cannibalism.[7] In Fronhofen, at the border between Bavaria and Württemberg (Germany), broken and partially burnt bones were discovered in the cave known as "Hanseles Hohle" and were found to belong to at least five individuals. Similarly, the Hohlestein site in Honetal (Baden-Württemberg, Germany) dates from the Middle Neolithic (Rössen culture). Here, a pit was found to contain the remains of 38 individuals, including many children. The skulls had been broken and long bones deliberately fractured and sometimes burnt. The bones were found scattered among animal remains.[8] This could be yet another case of cannibalism.

These sites, most of which date from an advanced stage of the Early Neolithic in Europe, have proved difficult for archeologists to interpret.

Without wishing to generalize, it is at least possible to identify two distinct scenarios: massacre, which involves a number of people being killed; and killings (and the possible consumption of the body), the reasons for which are less specific and involve behavior which is more difficult to interpret (cannibalism, sacrifice, voluntary killings, etc.). The small-scale survey detailed here indicates that violence was most definitely present in these societies, although the causes are yet to be determined. Some experts are of the opinion that all of these events occurred in around 5000 BCE and have thus attempted to link these examples together in search of a more general explanation for this behavior. Was this violence, in fact, an attempt by the triumphant farming communities to exterminate any last-remaining, resistant hunter-gatherer populations? This is not known for certain. Having inhabited the region for several centuries, the well-established farmers would undoubtedly have been able to deal with any possible pockets of resistance on the part of these Mesolithic hunters. A more likely explanation is that "crises" developed at the heart of Neolithic society, triggering an increase in violent behavior. It is worth considering whether these dramas may in fact have resulted in women and children in particular being targeted as victims, as some of the examples seem to suggest. Perhaps demographic pressures were the cause? Following centuries of stable development, was the balance between the technical-economic system and the population it was intended to feed eventually upset in this Linear Pottery culture? Did internal tensions develop at the heart of these farming communities, bringing about means of "regulation" that were violent, to say the least? And what role did culture, ritual, the need for dramatization and the search for expiatory victims play in the examples cited? If the hypotheses discussed prove to be correct, then a revised, more balanced impression of these first farming societies should emerge.

Fontbregoua (France): Another Case of Cannibalism?

The examples discussed above from Germany seem to indicate that gruesome rituals were carried out at these sites (possibly linked to cannibalism). The issue of cannibalism during the Paleolithic and Mesolithic is still open to debate and remains a topic for discussion where the first farming societies are concerned, as the discoveries made at the Fontbregoua site (Var, France) indicate.

This cave was occupied by the last hunter-gatherer populations of the Mesolithic and then more or less continuously throughout the Neolithic. In strata dating from the Early Neolithic and in particular from the most advanced stage of this era, around 5000 BCE, excavators unearthed several pits or basins, found to contain various discarded items. These somewhat shallow hollows were filled with bones and can be classified into two categories: some (ten) contained animal remains alone, whilst others (three) contained human remains. Some of the pits of faunal remains were found only to contain the remains of wild animals – pits 1, 9, and 10, for example, contained exclusively the remains of wild boar. Others contained the remains of species now extinct. Pit number 3 was found to contain bones from stags, martens, badgers, a roe deer, a wolf, and a fox. In other pits the remains of domestic animals, such as sheep (no. 8) and a cow's skull (no. 2), were discovered.

In addition to these animal remains, three "structures," all with a similar layout, were found to contain human remains. H_3, for example, contained 134 post-cranial bone fragments, belonging to at least six individuals (three adults, two children, and one individual of unknown age). These remains were enclosed in a structure with a small volume of $80 \times 40 \times 15$ cm. It seems they were all buried here following the same incident: the bones of these six individuals had been stripped of their flesh, broken, and discarded at the same time.[9]

H$_1$, another of these structures, was found to contain five incomplete skulls which it was possible to reconstruct, as well as the remains of two other skulls, six jaws, and 34 skeletal fragments. The remains of at least seven individuals (three adults and four children) are thought to have been placed here.

The last pit, H$_2$, contained the remains (20 or so fragments) of an adult.

Detailed analysis of all these remains has revealed that both the human and animal carcasses were firstly dismembered and then discarded in these rubbish pits. In fact, the remains were all treated in a particular way – some of the human bones, for example, are missing from these pits. The parts of the skeleton that are absent may well have been consumed separately or used for other purposes. It has also been noted that only one domestic animal seems to have been targeted at a time; its remains were then placed in a specific pit. Hunted animals, by contrast, were dissected and consumed by several people at a time. The human remains contained in two or three of the pits seem to indicate that these individuals were killed in the same way as the wild animals; they were treated in the same way as animals killed in hunting expeditions.

"Butchering" marks left by flint knives upon both the human and animal bones also indicate that they were treated in the same fashion. Furthermore, it has been established that there was a slight lapse in time between the killings being carried out and the human bodies being dismembered. The human and animal carcasses also share many similarities in terms of the number, location, and nature of the markings left upon the bones once the body had been dismembered and the bones removed. The human skulls, however, differ in certain regards from the animal skulls: they bear very particular kinds of marking caused by the process of stripping the flesh away (figure 22). Were these parallel scrape marks caused by the scalp being stripped away? Was the idea perhaps to retain these skulls for a while as trophies, before discarding them?

Another common feature is that the marrow was extracted from both human and animal bones. In fact, this practice was also carried out by the hunters of the Paleolithic – some of the bones from animals killed in hunting expeditions were either broken in order to extract the marrow or smashed into tiny pieces for use as a fatty substance in some kind of hot broth. Breakage marks on the bones from Fontbregoua give some indication of the kind of tools used to smash the "fresh" bones, shortly after the individual was killed. The same impacts were applied both to the animal and human bones, most notably the femurs and tibias, and caused them to fissure along the length of the bone.[10] It is highly unlikely that such damage was inflicted by carnivores. In fact, calcite tools used in the butchering of these carcasses have also been found. The very fact that these tools were discovered in the

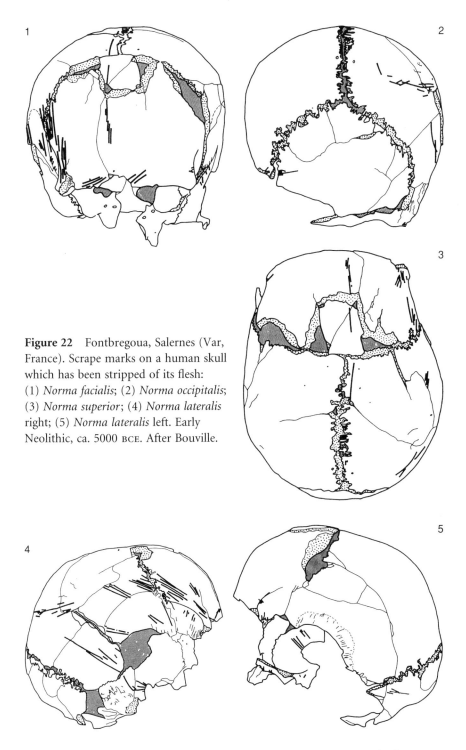

Figure 22 Fontbregoua, Salernes (Var, France). Scrape marks on a human skull which has been stripped of its flesh: (1) *Norma facialis*; (2) *Norma occipitalis*; (3) *Norma superior*; (4) *Norma lateralis* right; (5) *Norma lateralis* left. Early Neolithic, ca. 5000 BCE. After Bouville.

pits and that some of them were still connected to parts of the body also supports the notion that humans were responsible for this butchering.

The experts who carried out these excavations and analyzed the remains have come to favor the theory that this was a case of "nutritional cannibalism." It is thought that these Fontbregoua humans suffered the same fate as wild and domestic animals. Like the animal carcasses, human bodies would firstly have been dismembered and the bones then stripped of their flesh and broken, using the same techniques and for the same purpose. This may also have involved the marrow being eaten. Their remains would then have been discarded in small hollows among the cave-floor sediments.

Cannibalistic Farmers?

The burial of human remains with animal remains is far from unusual.

During our excavations of the Jean-Cros rock shelter site in Labastide-en-Val (Aude, France), we came across human bones lying in amongst faunal remains in a prehistoric layer dating from 5500 BCE. These bones comprised fragments of skulls and mandibles along with various other remains (coxal bone, femur fragment, metacarpus, and metatarsus). They belonged to two individuals (one adult and one adolescent). A newborn baby, known to have died in the perinatal period, has also been identified and linked to these individuals.

In the Gardon cave in Ambérieu-sur-Bugey (Ain, France), some 35 human bones were unearthed, found in amongst food waste;[11] they were scattered randomly amongst the remains of animals. Two adults and a child, aged 9 to 10 years, were identified. Cut marks were identified on some of the bones. This layer of deposits has been dated to 5000–4800 BCE.

These practices were evidently not specific to these first Neolithic communities, neither were they initiated by them. At the Perrats à Agris cave site (Charente, France), signs of similar behavior have been identified in layers of deposits dating from earlier hunter-gatherer populations, from the ninth to the end of the seventh millennia BCE.

The reasons for such similarities in behavior are still unclear. Although in some cases the reasons for cannibalistic behavior are evident, in other cases suggestions are merely speculative. Was this behavior purely an attempt at meeting nutritional needs? In this case, the human body would have been a source of food, just like any other. During the nineteenth century, Morgan claimed that agriculture and stockbreeding, which made their appearance in the Neolithic, had enabled humans to free themselves of the scourge of cannibalism, a practice typical of "savage" behavior (cf. the Paleolithic). In his words:

there are reasons for believing [cannibalism] was practiced universally through-out the period of savagery upon captured enemies and, in time of famine, upon friends and kindred. Cannibalism in war, practiced by war parties in the field, survived among the American aborigines, not only in the Lower, but also in the Middle Status of barbarism [i.e., among the first sedentary farming societies], as, for example, among the Iroquois and the Aztecs; but the general practice had disappeared. This forcibly illustrates the great importance which is exercised by a permanent increase of food in ameliorating the condition of mankind.[12]

According to this theory, Paleolithic man – and perhaps also Neolithic man – did practice cannibalism. Yet, with the exception of a few isolated cases, it has proved very difficult to find archeological evidence to support such theories. Tales of enemies or prisoners being killed and often then eaten are not uncommon in Central and South America and Oceania. The number of victims involved is often high and would seem to suggest that this cannibalism did not serve a "ritualistic" purpose. It is not impossible that, under certain circumstances, human flesh would have been consumed as a means of survival. The consumption of human flesh in the southeast of the United States during stages 2 and 3 of the Pueblo culture (900–1300 BCE) has often been linked to periods of drought, which brought about famine and under-nourishment.[13]

The role of cannibalism as a source of food has been greatly played down or even denied by many writers, who regard this as a taboo subject. Instead, they claim that the consumption of human flesh and blood was an act of war, a means of eliminating enemies, prisoners, or abducted individuals by resorting to extreme practices. Cannibalism is thus often perceived to fulfill a symbolic or magical function. Seen from this perspective, consuming the flesh of an enemy is not a means of nourishment, but rather a way of making that person disappear forever, probably with the aim of acquiring his strength, energy, and resilience in combat. This can be seen as an act of victory and possession which goes so far as to eliminate all trace of the enemy, ensuring his maximum destruction. It is even a means of preserving a part of a hardy enemy within the consumer. This "exocannibalism" can be contrasted with "endocannibalism," which has a ritualistic function and is practiced within a social group. Endocannibalism is a funerary ritual which aims to capture the qualities or spirit of a relative or close acquaintance. In this case, the consumption of the flesh is an expression of an emotional attachment and acknowledges a tie which this ritual seeks to maintain. It goes without saying that, in each of these two cases, the consumption of human flesh is not determined by nutritional requirements or by a particular liking for this flesh. It is purely a matter of dealing with the body of the deceased, taking into account the sentiments this individual once inspired.

It is unclear whether the Fontbregoua victims of cannibalism were enemies (or perceived to be enemies) or were members of the community. Here, the nature of the problem changes: it has often been suggested, based upon anthropological criteria, that there was another population involved, not just the indigenous population.[14] If this was indeed the case, this would have been a massacre of "outsiders." But it is also possible that members of the same group were sacrificed for reasons that are still unknown, for example, to please divinities or to gain favor with supernatural spirits. In both cases, the level of effort afforded in destroying the corpse would have corresponded to the nature of the favor desired. Boulestin and Gomez de Soto focus upon this hypothesis in expressing their reservations about the idea that cannibalism provided a source of food. In fact, they reverse the suggestion that humans were treated like animals and ask whether animals were in fact treated like humans, which they consider to be more likely.[15] Instead of regarding humans as animals, perhaps it would be more useful to consider the role of the animals that were slaughtered. These animals may well have been elevated to the same level as humans, made "sacred" and then ritually sacrificed for the good of the community. By reversing the relationship in this way, the behavior involved can be seen from a different perspective. Humans no longer seem to have been reduced to the role of a common animal. Animals, like humans, perished as victims of sacrifice – one could be substituted for the other.

Seen from this perspective, the theory of cannibalism itself may also be called into question: a funerary ritual such as this, involving the dismembering of the human body and breaking of the bones, may also have been applied to animals for the same purpose. If this was the case, the fact that some of the bones were buried in pits, though it does not eliminate the possibility of the flesh having been consumed, does also introduce other possibilities: ceremonial behavior or mortuary practices are possible explanations. Thus, animals may have been identified with humans. The Neolithic site of Caserna San Pau in Barcelona suggests that this was the case. Here, a human burial ground was also found to contain separate animal graves. The site has been dated to the post-Cardial culture and is thus only slightly more recent in date than the Fontbregoua site.

Before concluding this assessment of whether or not cannibalism occurred within farming communities, it remains to discuss the difficulties faced by archeologists in attempting to decipher the motives behind this behavior (whether warfare, magic, nutrition, funerary rituals, symbolism, punishment, or sacrifice are thought to be responsible – all may be deemed essential to the functioning of society) in addition to the difficulties of finding evidence, discussed above. Highly detailed anthropological studies have shed new light upon the matter of how human bodies were treated after death. But will it be possible to determine the reasons for this behavior and the social climate in which it was carried out? For this, anthropologists must join forces with archeologists to determine why as well as how cannibalism was practiced.

This debate raises an equally complicated issue – that of sacrificial murder. This will be discussed at a later point in the text.

Neolithic Art, a Medium of Violence?

Combat and violent confrontation have always provided individuals with a means of obtaining prestige and respect. Hunting is another equally valid means of achieving this; indeed, the fact that hunting is a means of obtaining food often raises the social stakes. Furthermore, hunting may not necessarily be any less dangerous than confrontation between humans, especially where larger animals, such as aurochs, are concerned. The great strength of and danger posed by these animals meant that they were highly respected and considered to be a symbol of "virility." As a result, humans were frequently driven to track them down and control them. Defeating the bull was, in a manner of speaking, a way of dominating the animal kingdom by attacking its strongest point. This was a triumph over the most fearsome of all savage beasts. It provided a means of celebrating humans' great power (and allowed individuals to celebrate their own power) by regularly acting out a ritual involving victory over nature.[16] Other "noble" animals, such as the stag, also caught the eye of these hunters. This may well explain why the artwork of these Neolithic farmers and shepherds serves no narrative function, i.e., it is lacking scenes of everyday life relating to agriculture and pastoralism. Hunting aurochs, stags, and wild boar was a true test of initiative. Art was thus used to depict highly symbolic activities: hunting and/or war. This was undoubtedly true of certain scenes depicted at the Neolithic site of Çatal Hüyük in Anatolia, dating from the seventh millennium BCE. These are scenes of hunting, amongst other things, and show wild animals (aurochs, cervidae, and wild boar) along with numerous human figures. However, they do not necessarily represent real hunting expeditions. They may, in fact, be scenes from mythical or virtual hunts, intended perhaps to relate imaginary events or to reevoke and retain the memory of a significant past event by placing the image somewhere where it can be seen every day. The number of animals in these representations has been deliberately exaggerated, probably to emphasize the strength and "supernatural" power of the animals, as well as the achievements of those individuals who succeed in controlling them.

Were these hunting scenes? This seems likely since the archers depicted are pointing their weapons toward the animal, often with a raised right

Figure 23 Çatal Hüyük (Turkey). Early Neolithic, ca. 7000–6500 BCE. The scene shows various figures, including archers, adopting different poses as they surround an exhausted bull. After Mellaart, 1967.

arm either to pull the string or to indicate that an arrow has just been fired (figure 23). This scene may be intended to show the animal weakening and becoming physically drained, having been pursued from all angles. This suggestion[17] is based upon the outward appearance of the bull, which has its mouth open and tongue hanging out, as well as upon the number of human figures that surround the animal; these figures seem to be running or moving frantically with raised arms, rather like in the art of the Spanish Levant. Was this a hunt or simply an attempt at bringing a lively animal under control? The scene seems to show violence being inflicted upon the animal, making the animal suffer in order that the most skillful individuals present may increase their social standing. Only the most courageous members of the group participate in this confrontation, from which the humans must emerge victorious.

The most conclusive evidence comes from the Iberian Peninsula. In fact, Mediterranean Spain is home to a particular kind of prehistoric art, referred to as the art of the Levant or "Levante." This area extends from the Piedmont region of the Southern Pyrenees in Catalonia and Aragon (Huesca region) to the Sierra Nevada region to the north and to the Western Betic Mountains to the south. The artwork is limited to the mountainous region, close to the Mediterranean, which forms the easternmost part of the central Meseta. This mountainous region with its limestone eyries and vast, dry plateaus towers over the pleasant neighboring plains of Castellón, Valencia, and Alicante. Only by exploring these wild and harsh expanses is it possible to appreciate the rugged geographical environment that inspired these Levantine artists: the terrain is sometimes bare, sometimes covered with a sparse vegetation, dominated by striking mountain ridges and bare peaks and interspersed with deep and now dry ravines (*barrancos*). The desolate landscapes in evidence here today are not solely the result of human presence, made possible by the dry climatic conditions, and the impact this had upon the vegetation throughout prehistorical and historical times. During the post-glacial era, the environment was actually much greener and wooded but the landscape was still hilly, thus making it just as difficult for populations to spread.

Following the Würmian glacial period, Rupestrian artwork began to appear all across this 600- to 700-km belt of development – numerous paintings now decorate the walls of the rock shelters and small caves which are dotted across this limestone environment. Here, there are no sanctuaries hidden deep within caverns, just scenes painted upon the sloping walls and visible in broad daylight.

Human figures are often rare or even entirely absent from Paleolithic art in the western world. Here, however, they are at the very center of these scenes of hunting, gathering, warfare, and dance. These suggestive and very definite images are also characterized by a continual sense of dynamism throughout and by a particular kind of energy and spontaneity. The highly detailed scenes allow assumptions to be made concerning the lifestyle, behavior, clothing, weaponry, and other such features of this population. The figures are often small in stature and are painted in red, maroon, brown, black, or white. Hunting scenes are the most frequent and most spectacular and reveal the most common animal prey to be wild boar, goats, and cervidae. There are also some scenes of warfare, with which we are more concerned here. Before discussing this in greater detail, it should be noted that these various paintings are more recent than the art of the Paleolithic; they date from a period spanning several thousand years during which Europe's climate became more temperate, not unlike the climate of today.

Battle Scenes in the Sierras of the Spanish Levant

Several of the battle scenes in the art of the Spanish Levant prove highly indicative. They are scenes full of life and movement and show human figures, seemingly full of energy. The battles pictured here capture the same sense of dynamism as is featured in the numerous hunting scenes, also painted by these Levantine artists.[18]

The most famous group of these rock paintings is located in the Gasulla *barranco* in Cingle de la Mola Remigia in Ares del Maestre. Here, there are roughly ten rock shelters in a row, all richly decorated with elaborate images. There are signs that some scenes have been superimposed on top of one

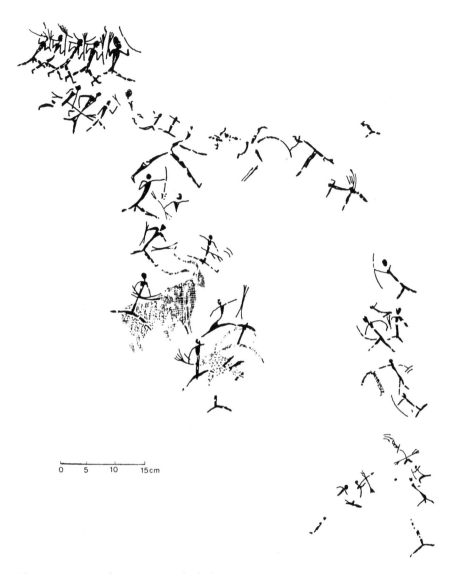

Figure 24 Spanish Levant. Cingle de la Mola Remigia. Rock shelter 9. Archers in battle. After Porcar Ripollès, 1946.

another, making it possible to identify various evolutionary stages in the process. Rock shelter 9 contains one of the most well-known battle scenes in Rupestrian art (figure 24). Archers, painted in black or brown, have in places been superimposed onto images of goats, painted in red at an earlier point in time. Two groups are shown, fighting each other. On the right-hand side

there are 20 or so figures, mostly archers, some of whom seem to have lost
their bows, most probably because
changes were subsequently made to
the picture. One figure seems to be
throwing a lasso-like object, as if to
capture an enemy he has encountered.
On the left-hand side, 15 or so figures
are engaged in battle. Some are throwing projectiles and three figures are
standing back, ready to intervene.
Particularly interesting is a group of
five individuals, separated from the
others in the top left corner of the
picture, who seem to have arrived,

Figure 25 Spanish Levant. Cingle de
la Mola Remigia. Rock shelter 9. Detail
of a group of archers (known as "the
phalanx") arriving at the battle scene.
After Dams, 1984.

determined to assist in the battle (figure 25). The figure leading this
"phalanx" seems to be wearing a hat, unlike his subordinates. These guards
are carrying a bow in one hand and arrows or a quiver in the other.

In this same region and at a similar altitude (800 m), the Los Dogues rock
shelter situated close to the Gasulla *barranco* contains an astonishing battle
scene, only 40 cm or so across (figure 26). There are, at most, 30 figures

0 2 4 6cm

Figure 26 Spanish Levant. Los Dogues rock shelter (Ares del Maestre). Battle
between archers. After Dams, 1984.

involved. The group on the right is slightly greater in numbers and all its members are, more or less, the same. The figures often seem to have their heads decorated with feathers and their legs are wide apart as if running or "sprinting," perhaps even leaping, as they throw their projectiles. Below, at the side, one figure seems to be bent over and is perhaps injured. Their opponents on the left-hand side seem to be advancing less quickly. They are also depicted in greater detail. Four archers are in the front line. One particularly agile figure is shown firing many arrows at one of his enemies. His head, back, and calves are decorated with feathers. This may provide an indication as to how certain Levantine warriors prepared themselves for confronting their enemy. In the top left-hand corner of the picture are five guards who seem only marginally involved in the operation. They may well be carrying out certain preparations (perhaps a ritual of sorts) before joining the battle. They, too, have their heads decorated with feathers or horns.

A similar example is the painting in the Molino de las Fuentes rock shelter (sometimes named the Sautuola shelter after the man who first investigated the Altamira cave site) in Nerpio in the Albacete Province, at an altitude of 1,100 m (figure 27). This painting shows a battle between two groups, or perhaps even two different populations since each side has such a different style and way of behaving. On the right-hand side, 16 figures of small stature are bent over, each holding a taut bow in the stereotypical fashion. Some seem to have a kind of tail attached (possibly feathers). These archers may be crouched down or camouflaged. Perhaps they hoped to launch a surprise attack? Their enemy seem to have taken fewer precautions – they are upright and taller and seem less organized. One of these figures, a man (his penis clearly visible), seems to be wearing a hat or headdress of some sort and has a pointed chin (a beard perhaps). He may well be the leader of this group, since he is shown to be much more robust than his men in the painting. All of these warriors are drawn in black, although a raised section of the wall behind the second group has been emphasized with red paint as if to define a natural or artificial boundary. On the other side, four or five armed figures are guarding this boundary.

The most important Levantine work of art is the large fresco painting in the Minateda rock shelter (Albacete) which shows more than 500 figures. Animals and humans are depicted in a wide variety of scenarios. These paintings are not all from the same period – experts have identified several phases. A battle scene with a very particular style has been singled out from this mass of images (figure 28). There are at least seven attacking figures shown, loosely divided into two groups, all of which are heading in the same direction. Enemy lines have been broken down. An enemy trying to put up resistance

0	5	10cm	

Figure 27 Spanish Levant. Molino de las Fuentes (Nerpio). Battle between two groups of archers. After Garcia Guinea, 1963.

is shown riddled with arrows. All of the attacking figures have vertical stripes running down their bodies which may be tattoos or body paintings, presumably the markings of war. Furthermore, almost all of the figures are wearing rings or jewels around their ankles. Some of the bows in use have a

Figure 28 Spanish Levant. Minateda rock shelter (Albacete). Archers attack an enemy, whose body is riddled with arrows. After Hernandez Pacheco, 1918, and Dams, 1984.

double or triple curvature, which may be characteristic of a particular group or of specialist warriors. One of the attackers has also been struck by several arrows, just like the figure who is putting up resistance.

Battle scenes have also been identified in the rock shelters of Torcal de las Bojadillas in Nerpio (Albacete), most notably in shelters 3 and 6. In the latter case, two bands of archers, each with fewer than ten members, are confronting each other though there seems to be no sense of fury or haste. At the Fuente del Sabuco I site (Moraralla, Murcia), two groups are also shown in confrontation. Similarly, many of the scenes depicted in shelter 3 at the El Civil site in Tirig in the Valltorta ravine (Castellón) have a war theme. On the left-hand side, eight archers are shown charging forward, one of whom seems to be holding a quiver. A short distance away, two figures (or possibly more) are being targeted by a large group led by two of its members. Further to the right is a scene which proves more difficult to interpret. This image gives the impression of a rather confused scuffle. The warriors involved are naked (no signs of any decoration or clothing) and are equipped either with bows or with pikes or other projectiles. The artist may have wanted to create the impression of a sort of collective battle with everyone fighting everyone else. It is also possible that some of the warriors were waiting away from the fighting, preparing to join in. Porcar Ripollès, an artist himself who has conducted detailed studies of these paintings, considers these adjacent scenes from Cueva del Civil to have all been part of the same, large-scale battle scene in which two distinct communities came head to head (figure 29). Unfortunately, the wall has suffered some damage over time leaving the

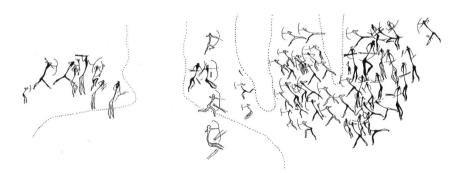

Figure 29 Spanish Levant. Cueva del Civil (la Valltorta) in Tirig (Castellón). Attempted reconstruction of a battle between two communities. Erosion of the wall may be responsible for dividing this painting into several different battle scenes. After Porcar Ripollès, 1946.

image somewhat diminished. Attempts at partially reconstructing this battle scene would seem to suggest that there were at least 22 members of the group on the right. This group may also include the figures "in reserve" to their right, so perhaps another additional 25 members. On the left-hand side, there are only 13 warriors, though damage to the picture suggests that there may have been more. It is also interesting to note that the archers on the right are equipped with small weapons, whilst those on the left are carrying large bows.

Another highly dramatic battle scene can be found in Roure in Morella la Vella (Teruel) (figure 30). Here, eight archers are shown in battle. They seem

Figure 30 Spanish Levant. Roure rock shelter in Morella la Vella (Teruel). Archers in battle. After Hernandez Pacheco, 1918.

highly energetic and are firing arrows and running at the same time. Their slender stature serves to emphasize their agility. The positioning of the archers would seem to suggest that three archers on the right are fighting against four enemy figures on the left. There is also an eighth figure above the scene who seems to be part of the group on the left. He is targeting one particular archer, who is himself busy attacking a possible central figure. Another possible interpretation of this scene is that the central figure (wearing feathers on his head) is the main target here, though this seems unlikely. The fact that this is such a lively scene, along with its stylization, suggests that this may have been a ritual battle, a parody of war.

At the El Cerrao site in Obón (Teruel), two groups of archers are shown confronting each other. All except one of the figures, who is motionless, are running.

Other scenes are less dramatic. A painting in the Cova del Mansano rock shelter in Jalon, La Marina Alta, seems to show a group of seven archers in confrontation with two warriors, also armed with bows. One of these two figures is of small stature, perhaps an adolescent. But it is not impossible that this may have been a hunting scene and that the prey was once depicted but has now disappeared.[19]

In shelter 6 at the Famorca ravine site in Santa Maria, two figures are shown engaged in confrontation. One is about to strike his enemy with a triangular-pointed spear. His intended victim is attempting to stop this by obstructing his enemy's right arm. Again the significance of this dispute is a matter for debate: is this a portrayal of real or disguised violence? A merciless duel or a parody of combat?[20]

Injuries and Capital Executions

As mentioned above, the Minateda rock shelter contains a scene of two figures, one of which is an archer and has been struck by numerous arrows. In fact, there are many examples of warriors being struck and injured by arrows in Levantine art. In shelter 1 in Cueva Remigia, one figure is shown collapsing, after having been struck by several arrows (figure 31). It has been proposed that the spears, painted in brown, were painted onto the red figure later, suggesting that this was a slow death or perhaps even a fierce attack upon a dead body.

In shelter 12 in Saltadora (Cuevas de Vinroma, Castellón), an archer painted in red with a headdress of feathers or ribbons and wearing a flowing loincloth is shown down on one knee. He has been struck by five arrows: once in the back and four times on his legs. In shelter 6 at the Bojadillas site in Nerpio

(Albacete), one tall archer painted in black and carrying a bow and quiver is shown falling, having been struck by an arrow the color of blood. It is possible that this arrow was fired by the short, red warriors surrounding the figure. The difference in height between the tall, defeated figure and shorter surrounding figures indicates either that these were two different populations or that there was a lapse in time between the two being painted. If the latter hypothesis is correct, the arrow striking the tall archer may have been added later, after the small red figures were drawn in.

As has already been mentioned, the figures are shown to be very energetic as they engage in combat. The artists undoubtedly sought to capture both the energy and courage of these combatants – they are depicted dying, at the height of the action, from their numerous injuries. These portrayals seem to comprise two separate chronological stages: the sense of movement demonstrates a certain vigor associated with the most exceptional warriors, whilst the arrows which have struck these warriors portray violent death in the midst of all the action. One such example is the figure from Minateda who is shown to be resisting attack and has been struck from head to toe with numerous arrows. Similarly, one of his attackers has been struck by spears during the battle.

In the Polvorín rock shelter in La Cenia (Castellón), a figure wearing a horned (or feathered?) headdress is shown being struck by arrows from all sides. His rigid posture suggests that he may have had his hands and feet bound before being executed. A tall archer standing nearby was probably charged with this task. Individuals are shown collapsing, their arms raised in pain, at the Cingle de la Mola Remigia and Minateda sites. In other scenes, figures have adopted different positions as they endure their suffering: in rock shelter 3 at the Remigia site, one figure is falling backwards, struck from head to toe by spears which have caused his death. Another figure in Remigia has been struck in the upper and lower back and is shown falling head first to the ground.

These battle scenes, which show certain individuals meeting a violent death as they are struck by projectiles, at times signify something even more tragic: organized execution carried out by a group of archers. Capital punishment of this nature may have been inflicted upon captured enemies, outcasts, and even members of the community during sacrifice. Cave 5 at the Remigia site contains three capital punishment scenes. In one scene, ten archers are shown holding their bows above their heads after having inflicted the punishment: a few steps away, the body of the victim is shown lying on the ground, covered with arrows (figure 32). Close by, five archers are shown having just executed a figure who is lying on the ground with arms outstretched and one leg bent. He has been struck by at least four projectiles from his head to his lower back (figure 33). Fourteen members of another group, all very rangy figures, are shown standing close to an individual who is stretched out on the ground, his arms and legs spread wide. It seems as though the group wishes to disassociate itself from this figure (figure 34). There are no arrows in this picture, just a bow placed horizontally above the group. This scene may represent a sacrifice or some kind of exclusion. In the Los Trepadores rock shelter in the Mortero gully (Alacón, Teruel Province), seven figures are grouped together and seem to be holding up their bows with their victim lying at their feet following his execution. It is also possible that this group is beating its victim with sticks (figure 35).

These scenes seem to indicate a definite distinction between the "squad," comprising a group of individuals who are united, determined, and show definite signs of social cohesion, and the victim, who is isolated and always alone (there are no examples of several individuals being executed together). In this context, the power of the group is indispensable – the individual alone counts for very little. Whether the individual in

Figure 31 Spanish Levant. Figures injured by projectiles: (1) Cueva Remigia 1; (2) Saltadora; (3), (4), (9) Minateda; (5) Polvorin; (6), (7) Cueva Remigia 3; (8) Cingle de la Mola Remigia; (10) Los Dogues; (11) Reboso del Chorillo. After Dams, 1984.

Figure 32 Spanish Levant. Cave 5 at the Mola Remigia site. Execution scene. Group of archers holding up their bows after firing. In the foreground, the victim's body is shown covered with arrows. After Obermaier, 1937.

Figure 33 Spanish Levant. Cave 5 at the Mola Remigia site. Execution scene. Group of five archers and the executed victim. After Dams, 1984.

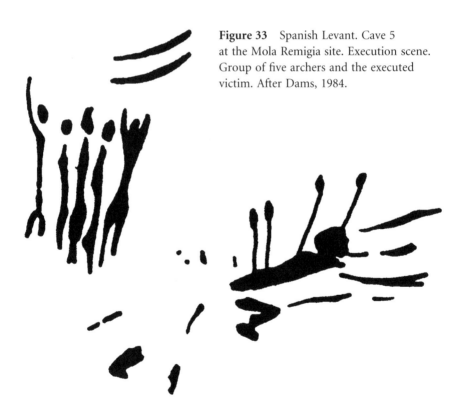

Figure 34 Spanish Levant. Cave 5 at the Mola Remigia site. Scene showing an individual being "excluded." After Dams, 1984.

Figure 35 Spanish Levant. Los Trepadores rock shelter (Alacón, Teruel). Execution scene. After Ortego, 1948.

question is an enemy, outcast, or sacrificial victim, his "social influence" is negligible.

Causes for Quarrel

The art of the Levant comprises several scenes of violence including both group combat and the killing or execution of certain individuals. The battle scenes show a limited number of individuals coming head to head. The largest bands contain some 15 or so members. However according to Porcar Ripollès, one of the groups from a scene at the Mola

Remigia site could have totaled approximately 25 members. A comparable number of individuals may have formed one of the groups in El Civil. Indeed, if the similar number of "reserve" figures is also included, the total could be much greater. These numbers are highly indicative. If the community is dependent upon 25 active warriors, in general the young males, then by adding on the numbers of older men as well as the women and children, an idea of the overall size of the community can be obtained. Thus, a community may typically have comprised approximately 100 individuals. If Porcar Ripollès's suggestion regarding El Civil is correct (that there were approximately 50 active and reserve warriors in total), then this figure may be doubled. Even if the first hypothesis is deemed correct (25 archers), these were no longer bands comparable with those of the Paleolithic and Epipaleolithic, unless the grouping together of several units to combat another population is acknowledged as a possibility. It seems more likely that these were agricultural communities, i.e., Neolithic communities. The chronology of the Levantine art is, again, relevant here – this complicated issue will be dealt with later. The status of the various communities involved in such combat is also an important matter to address. If these were hunter-gatherer communities, which rarely exceed a population of 50, then the total number of active males in the group would be approximately 15, in addition to a similar number of females, along with the children and some ascendants.

If these individuals were members of agricultural communities, the situation becomes even more complex. It is likely that at the beginning of the Neolithic (Cardial period), agricultural communities were still few and far between with limited populations. This seems to be confirmed by their flimsy open-air dwellings (although this flimsiness may have been caused by conditions and may not be representative), many of which are clustered upon and around littoral and fertile plains. Neolithization, i.e., the advent of agriculture and animal farming, is known to have developed upon the Mediterranean slopes of the Iberian Peninsula in at least two ways: the arrival of small groups by sea, armed with new knowledge and spreading out gradually from Italy and the south of France; and acculturation at the very heart of the indigenous populations, following contact with newcomers. Spanish experts have tended to assume that low-lying areas were quickly colonized by populations which brought with them agriculture and animal breeding, with the hunter-gatherer lifestyle continuing to prevail in the nearby austere, wooded mountainous regions. Initially, hunter-gatherers modified their traditional lifestyle only slightly, yet greater adjustments were made later both to the culture and to the economy, which began to incorporate domestic animals. If this process is indeed assumed to date from the early stages of the Neolithic (sixth and start of the fifth millennia BCE), much of the Levantine art must be attributable to these indigenous populations, which would still have been concerned primarily with hunting at this time. Agriculture, although already present in Iberian coastal regions, had made little impact upon the neighboring mainland areas at this stage.

However, it goes without saying that if this art is more recent in date and originates from the more "productive" populations that inhabited stable village settlements and only ventured into the mountainous regions during hunting expeditions, the figures pictured fighting in battle must have been carefully selected as the community's best archers, rather like hunting and, if need be, war "specialists." It is essential to determine the economic status of the communities involved in these confrontations in order to pinpoint the significance of these interactions more precisely.

As has already been discussed, the artists often distinguished one population from another by emphasizing differences in style, behavior, dress, and group size. There are also variations in the morphology of the bows, headdresses, body paintings, ankle rings, feathers, and other such decorations upon the head, torso, rear, and calves.

A central figure is often featured, usually in greater detail than the others. Such subtleties could signify a hierarchy or perhaps an exceptional warrior, "covered" or protected by his guardsmen.

The notion of strategy does not seem to have been completely alien to these warriors. It would be too easy to jump to the conclusion that these were disorganized confrontations, characteristic of primitive warfare. However, the "phalanx" scene from Cingle de la Mola Remigia seems to confirm that the concept of "reserve" was put to use, i.e., impeccably organized reinforcements arriving later to help out at the forefront of battle. The contingent shown on the right-hand side of the picture at the El Civil cave site may well have served a similar purpose. Similarly, the spatial distribution of the warriors in the Los Dogues "battlefield" scene clearly reveals a sophisticated battle formation (figure 36): the group on the left forms an attacking line which includes the chief with "reserve" fighters behind, preparing to join in; the group on the right appears to have adopted a more sophisticated formation – its front line has adopted a triangular formation with four archers at the front; there is a second line flanked by additional fighters below, and finally another triangular formation at the back. Several lines of fighters can also be identified in the scene from the Molino de las Fuentes rock shelter site in Nerpio. All of this suggests that there was an element of discipline in place,[21] an idea confirmed by the presence of "execution squads."

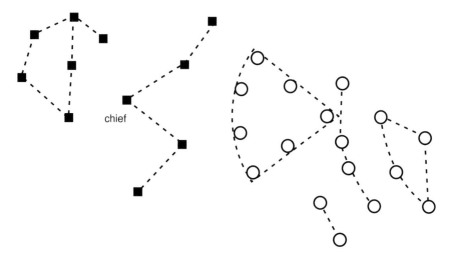

chief

Figure 36 Spanish Levant. Los Dogues rock shelter (Ares del Maestre). Distribution of the various fighters in the combat scene. Clearly visible are: on the left, the front line containing the chief; in the background, several reserve fighters preparing to take part; on the right, successive lines of warriors. After Porcar Ripollès, 1946.

Of course, it is always possible to speculate about the purpose of these battles: did they serve as a regular outlet for violence between populations frequently in dispute due to their close proximity to one another? Or were they instead cases of ritual warfare intended to settle such disputes? In the case of ritual warfare, a wide range of behaviors may be employed to avoid widespread confrontation including exclamations, shouting, threats, simulated battles, and confrontations involving only the best fighters from each side. Among the aborigines of Tasmania, for example, there are documented cases whereby the fighting stops as soon as the first injury has been inflicted – at the first sight of blood – rather like in certain duels.

Thus, the question comes down to whether these were ritual or more violent wars. In several cases, images of figures being struck by arrows suggest that enemies were often killed, thus ruling out the possibility of mock battle in such instances. Other examples show one individual being killed by one or two archers. It is possible that such scenes represent a settling of scores or an ambush attack directed solely at one person. Any hunter from another community found wondering alone in an area of highly coveted land may well have been killed outright.

This raises the question of why these conflicts arose in the first place. It would seem that raids to obtain livestock or fertile land were not the primary concern here. Scenes relating to agriculture are present in Levantine art but are rare. Hunting, by contrast, is a pervading theme. Cervidae and wild goats were the favorite target of these archers. Wild boar are less commonly depicted. Aurochs and equidae also feature in some scenes. The majority of these images seem to portray "tales of hunting" and provide a material and symbolic representation of important hunting events. It therefore comes as no surprise that, in this context, inter-community disputes would have arisen in response to disagreements over hunting territories and the management of the most sought-after areas. Boundaries presumably played an essential part in this particularly rugged physical environment where natural boundaries (mountain peaks, steep cliffs, and deep gullies) divide up the land. Crossing these boundaries, for example in the pursuit of prey, may have sparked frequent quarrels. Tensions surrounding boundaries may have been aggravated at times by populations identifying themselves with a particular piece of land, a landscape, or particular landmarks (rocks, trees), which are often held to mark boundaries. Even this untamed environment may have carried cultural significance and evoked feelings of familiarity in its inhabitants.

This notion is clearly expressed in many of the paintings, which use the topography of the walls or painted ceilings for concrete definition. Protrusions on the rock face, calcite deposits, and areas of moisture are all used to represent natural boundaries which, once crossed, would have sparked tension.

As far as the nature of these confrontations is concerned, the Levantine archers seem to have put just as much energy into getting rid of their enemies as they put into killing wild animals. However, it would be wrong to assume that all Levantine populations lived in largely warring communities.[22]

Hunters and/or Farmers in Confrontation

As has already been discussed, the status of populations involved in dispute is highly significant in determining the reasons behind conflict. Were these "Mesolithic" confrontations, i.e., taking place between hunter-gatherer populations, or were they "Neolithic" populations already engaged in agricultural production and thus only turning to hunting as a subsidiary activity, as and when required? In the first case, the population would have been made up of mobile bands with an economy based upon hunting and gathering. Thus, the paintings could represent these essential strategies for obtaining food. In the second case, production would have been based upon agriculture and animal farming: the hunting scenes could therefore portray a subsidiary economic activity, yet an activity with great symbolic importance given that the artists chose to make hunting a main theme in their artwork. In an agricultural context, such references to hunting would therefore fulfill a symbolic function. Scenes of violence (mostly showing hunting but also battles, executions, and archers ready for attack) are certainly the predominant theme in these paintings. Scenes relating to agricultural production (working the ground, collecting honey) are much less common and there are hardly any pastoral scenes, for example of a shepherd and his flock, apart from a few equidae complete with halters. Similarly, there are far fewer clear depictions of women than of "archer-warriors," although where they do occur, they tend to be highly detailed. There are, however, many asexual figures that could be female; if so, this would cast some doubt upon the claims made above. Yet even if these figures were intended to be female, in which case many of the archers could not be assumed to be either sex in particular, the crux of the issue remains the same: hunting scenes feature heavily in the artwork.

These various considerations have made the artwork difficult to date. The problems are further aggravated by the fact that, in Spain, other more abstract forms of art dating from recent prehistory (schematic art, "macroschematic" art) are also difficult to date and situate chronologically, relative to the Levantine art. The internal chronology of the Levantine art must also be ascertained, since this artwork does not date from one specific point in time; it spans a period of time, the boundaries of which need to be determined. Breuil identifies certain similarities between some of the various animals featured in the art of the Upper Paleolithic and those featured in the Levantine art. Thus, he proposes that the art of the Cantabrian mountains and of the Mediterranean mountainous regions followed a parallel course. The majority of experts in Spain initially rejected this theory, basing their arguments upon specific stylistic features, and claimed the art of the Levant to be "post-glacial" in origin, i.e., to have evolved in an environment characterized by a temperate climate. The scenes were therefore generally considered to date from the age of "Mesolithic" hunter-gatherers, although the later stages were thought to have coincided with the first farming communities (Neolithic) or even the start of the Bronze Age. If this was the case, then Levantine art and schematic art (generally considered to be more recent in date) would have existed simultaneously for a time. This perspective, based upon duration, accounts for all of the economic activities featured in the Levantine artwork: hunting only initially, then agriculture, and finally the beginnings of metallurgy.

The recent discovery of a new form of art – macroschematic art – has led to a complete overhaul of this theory.[23] The main feature of this artwork (highly abstract silhouettes of tall figures, their arms in an "orant" pose) has rightly been compared to identical images featured upon ceramics dating from the Early Neolithic period in Iberia ("Cardial": sixth millennium BCE). The fact that this macroschematic art is likely to have coincided with the Early Neolithic period has also led to observations being made concerning some of the more elaborate paintings where Levantine type art has clearly been superimposed onto "macroschematic" style art, making the former more recent in date. This seems to suggest that the entire Levantine art period postdates the Cardial period or that both existed simultaneously. Given that the art of the Levant spanned a reasonable period of time characterized by increasing levels of activity, the artwork is likely to have been completed throughout the Neolithic and Copper Age, i.e., from the fifth (or possibly even the sixth) to the third millennia BCE. This means that the artwork was definitely produced by agricultural civilizations. Of course, it is not impossible that isolated pockets of hunters continued to inhabit the austere mountain regions at this time. However, such a lifestyle does seem rather incompatible with that of the sprawling Neolithic civilizations, with their increasing levels of development. With agriculture centered upon the most fertile areas of land, those areas which could not be cultivated would have been put to use as pasture land or ranges. The Neolithic economy was extensive, using each and every bit of the land according to its individual potential.

If the art of the Spanish Levant does, indeed, originate from the Neolithic, hunting and to a lesser extent warfare must have played an important role socially. Through hunting and warfare, individuals were able to increase their social standing and exert their influence directly upon the community. Aside from the routine tasks of agriculture and pastoralism, hunting and warfare provided one of the only means of ensuring promotion and increased social standing. It is interesting to note that a great variety of arrowheads, all made during the Final Neolithic and Copper Age (fourth and third millennia BCE), can be linked to this behavior. In other words, at a time when hunting played only a minor role in the economy, its social and symbolic role continued to grow. It therefore comes as no surprise that the production of arrowheads was an intense operation, often resulting in surplus. Making these projectiles was a highly specialized activity. They were used for show, for social display purposes, as well as in attack or defense, and would often accompany the body in the tomb. The arrows also held a symbolic function in the form of protection, order, and dissuasion and gave strength to groups during hunting expeditions or armed raids. Seen from this perspective, the art of the Levant is more than just a simple narrative; it reflects those mechanisms which enabled this society to function.

We will end this chapter with another look at the massacres that took place during the Neolithic.

Studying the age and sex of those killed or sacrificed in the various events of the Neolithic for which there is archeological evidence reveals most of the victims to have been women and children. In Talheim, for example, 50 percent of the dead were children, with women accounting for up to half of the adult victims. The Herxheim victims were also largely children. In Tiefeneller, almost all of the victims were either women or young. Children were also among the victims in Honetal and Fontbregoua. Even though it is not possible to make generalizations, given the small number of cases in question, it is still interesting to note these consistencies. Those individuals who were less able to defend themselves physically would have been killed more easily. Some inter-community conflicts would probably have involved women and children being abducted and then eliminated through massacre. It is however possible that, within a given community, ritual may have influenced the choice of sacrificial victim in terms of age and sex. Perhaps they chose to kill the weakest or most disadvantaged members of the group? In the fortified village settlement of Cesavy near Blucina in Moravia, 700 cranial fragments were found abandoned in a pit, along with other human and animal bones. They are thought to be more recent, dating from the Early Bronze Age at the beginning of the second millennium BCE. These skull fragments are primarily the remains of children. Some of these remains bear cut marks, suggesting that the flesh of some of these individuals may have been consumed.[24]

More disturbing behavior has been associated with some of the Neolithic villages in Romania, dating from the fifth and fourth millennia BCE. It has been suggested that foundation rituals may have taken place here to mark the construction of a new district or building. These rituals may have involved human sacrifice, with the bodies being buried in pits beneath the dwellings. There is nothing original in this; violence, of course, forms part of sacrificial rituals. However, at the Harsova site, a tell in the Lower Danube region, two children were killed as part of such a ritual. With their hands and feet bound, they were placed in a basket. Excrement found in the basket reveals one of the two children to have been highly traumatized. Anthropological studies have shown that these sacrificial victims were either disabled or deformed.[25] Thus, it seems that these children were specifically selected and killed as a result of their physical abnormalities. This eugenics-like practice seems to have formed part of a ritual in which physically disfigured individuals were discriminated against, to a certain extent. Yet at the same time, these disfigurements did not prevent sacrifice, held to be beneficial, from being carried out. Indeed, they may have provided a means of preserving the custom through eliminating any "abnormal" individuals. If these explanations are correct, this form of "regulation" certainly raises many questions.

Chapter 3

Humans as Targets: 4,000 to 8,000 Years Ago

Let us now return to the 4,000- to 8,000-year-old (6000–2000 BCE) tombs in France, including individual, multiple, and collective tombs, where arrow-inflicted wounds have been identified. Far from being a new topic of investigation, this evidence was first properly assessed during the nineteenth century when flint arrowheads were found embedded in human bones in collective tombs (e.g., a Lozerian burial site in Baumes-Chaudes and hypogea in Arles and Marne). This led archeologists to speculate as to whether violence was indeed practiced by prehistoric populations – previously it had always been assumed that such populations led an idyllic existence. Evidence began to mount with each new discovery, giving rise to numerous amendments and reinterpretations.[1] The most up-to-date list of sites available at the time of writing, compiled by Naudet and Vidal at our request, reveals that some 50 sites in France are relevant to this debate.

The Contrasting Geography of Violence

Evidence relating to this violence seems to be limited to specific areas of France and to specific periods of time. The map of the documented evidence reveals there to be a very uneven spatial distribution (figure 37). There are a few isolated examples in the regions of Alsace, Brittany, Vendée, Champagne, and the Massif Central and a few examples clustered around Paris. The majority of sites are based in the south of France (Causses, Languedoc,

Figure 37   (*opposite*) Geographical distribution of the remains of humans killed or injured by arrows during the Neolithic or Chalcolithic in France.

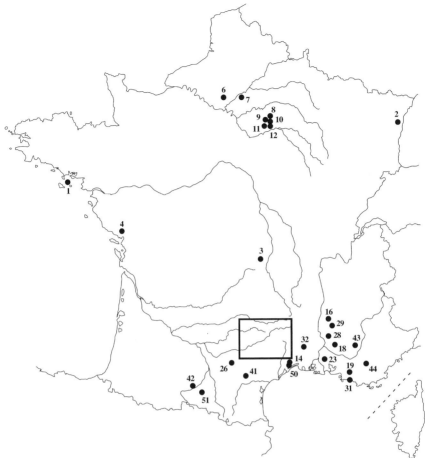

List of sites

1 L'Îlot, Téviec (Morbihan) (Mesolithic)
2 Quatzenheim (Bas-Rhin)
3 Pontcharraud, Clermont-Ferrand (Puy-de-Dôme)
4 Les Châtelliers-du-Vieil-Auzay, Auzay (Vendée)
5 Les Treilles, Saint-Jean-Saint-Paul (Aveyron)
6 La Ferme Duport, Guiry-en-Vexin (Val-d'Oise)
7 La Pierre Plate, Presles (Val-d'Oise)
8 Razet, Coizard (Marne)
9 La Pierre Michelot, Villevenard (Marne)
10 Hypogeum II, Villevenard (Marne)
11 Hypogeum 1, Oyes (Marne)
12 Hypogeum 2, Oyes (Marne)
13 Le Pas-de-Joulié, Trèves (Gard)
14 Suquet-Coucolières, Les Matelles (Hérault)
15 Le Crespin, Marvejols (Lozère)
16 Le Capitaine, Grillon (Vaucluse)
17 Fontcagarelle, Comus (Aveyron)
18 La Lave, Saint-Saturnin-d'Apt (Vaucluse)
19 Saint-Clair, Gémenos (Bouches-du-Rhône)
20 Maymac, Bertholène (Aveyron)
21 Le Sot-de-Lavogne, Montbrun (Lozère)
22 Saint-Énimie (Lozère)
23 Le Castellet, Fontvieille (Bouches-du-Rhône)
24 Puechcamp, Sébazac-Concourès (Aveyron)

25 Prévinquières, Cornus (Aveyron)
26 Mauray, Gijounet (Tarn)
27 Aragon, Le Massegros (Lozère)
28 Les Boileau, Sarrians (Vaucluse)
29 Les Crottes, Roaix (Vaucluse)
30 L'Aumède, Chanac (Lozère)
31 Terrevaine, La Ciotat (Bouches-du-Rhône)
32 Le Chemin-de-Fer, Boucoiran (Gard)
33 Les Caïres, Laissac (Aveyron)
34 Font-Rial, Saint-Rome-de-Tarn (Aveyron)
35 Les Cascades, Creissels (Aveyron)
36 Les Gâches, Veyrau (Aveyron)
37 Sargel, Saint-Rome-de-Cemon (Aveyron)
38 Les Baumes-Chaudes, Saint-Georges-de-Lèvejac (Lozère)
39 Almières, Saint-Rome-de-Dolan (Lozère)
40 Le Monna, Millau (Aveyron)
41 Rec de las Balmos, Félines-Minervois (Hérault)
42 La Tourasse, Saint-Martory (Haute-Garonne)
43 La Fare, Forcalquier (Alpes-de-Haute-Provence)
44 Tumulus du Gendarme, Plan-d'Aups (Var)
50 Castelnau-le-Lez (Hérault)
51 Montfort-sur-Lizier (Ariège) (Paleolithic)

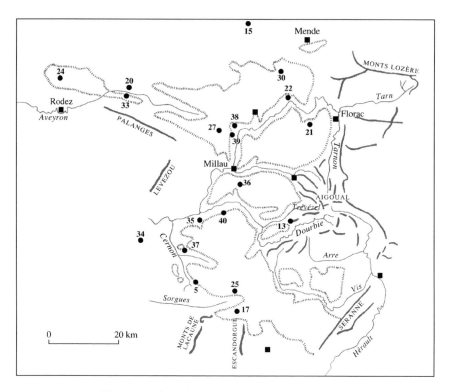

Figure 37 (*cont'd*) Detail of the limestone plateau regions of Aveyron and Lozère.

Provence, and, to a lesser extent, the Pyrenees). In other regions of France, very little relevant evidence has been identified.

This spatial distribution of evidence can undoubtedly be explained by natural, cultural, and historical factors. A system of collective tombs was in widespread use in the south of France during the fourth and third millennia BCE. These were communal tombs and were used over a long period of time (dolmens, "cave tombs," hypogea). Although only 30 or so tombs have been found cut into the rock, there are more than 3,000 megalithic tombs. It is claimed that several hundred caves were also used as tombs, although the precise figure is not known. In these limestone areas, even the smallest crevices (caves, swallow holes, potholes, gaps at the foot of cliffs) were used as tombs throughout the Neolithic and Bronze Age. As with megalithic tombs, there were also probably several thousand caves that "functioned" as a place to bury the dead during prehistory. These sites, both those which have already been investigated and those still to be studied, have great archeological potential. Since the nineteenth century there has been a great deal of emphasis on excavation, i.e., "overly excavating," yet the quality of the observations made has, at times, been overlooked. There have been cases where megalithic and cave tombs have been "emptied," with no attention paid to the human remains inside. Illegal excavators and local amateurs are often only interested in material artifacts, such as arrows, knives, daggers, ornate vases, or delicate jewelry. Even distinguished archeologists have been known to carry out rather rushed investigations, which are no better. Luckily, there have always been excellent excavators among these archeologists, who have been scrupulous and have paid meticulous attention to every last detail. It is thanks to them that the crucial initial observations on violent behavior have been made. However, these various factors have resulted in evidence from the south being abundant, yet at the same time badly organized.

The Champagne hypogea as well as the covered passageways in the Paris region are also relevant to this topic. These structures date from the same period as the collective tombs in the south. Aside from these two clusters, evidence from other areas is patchy and rare. Natural processes are sometimes partly responsible for this. In Armorica, for example, where there are a great many megalithic tombs, the primary rock substrata have often been partly responsible for damage to the human bones, destroying important evidence. There are many other reasons as to why a particular area may be lacking evidence: research may only have begun recently in other areas; there may simply be fewer archeological sites than in the south of France; and agriculture-induced erosion during historic times may be responsible for the disappearance of tombs made of wood or earth, etc. The provisional map available today will become more even and complete through further research, extensive salvage operations, and a more balanced geographical approach to the investigation of sites from recent prehistory.

A Progressive Intensification of Conflict?

After this brief overview outlining the geographical distribution of the sites, time should also be taken into account as a factor. Since the Neolithic (the era associated with the first farming communities) lasted some 3,000 to 4,000 years in France (roughly from 6000 to 2000 BCE, which includes the first stages of metalworking, in this case copper), it is easy to see why evidence from this lengthy period is so varied. After all, this era lasted twice the time from the Gaul period to the present day. During these 4,000 or so years of "Neolithic history," the economic, social, cultural, and ideological makeup of society underwent many alterations, subtle transformations, and abrupt changes. The vast majority of human remains bearing projectile-inflicted injuries date from the later stages of the Neolithic, between 3000 and 2000 BCE.

Does this indicate that violence increased over time? It would certainly be easy to jump to this conclusion, given that more human remains date from this advanced phase of the Neolithic than from the previous phase, from 6000 to 3500 BCE: this would seem to indicate that the population also increased over this same period. However, this observation defies in-depth interpretation since any attempt at drawing comparisons would be biased from the outset. Why are there so many human remains dating from 3500 to 2000 BCE and yet so few have been found to date from 6000 to 3500 BCE? The reason for these disparities and differences is undoubtedly linked to the way in which the body was dealt with – whether the funerary rituals sought to preserve or destroy the corpse. A lack of evidence relating to the earliest agricultural communities makes it impossible to draw reliable comparisons between the two periods. There is also no evidence to prove that a smaller population is associated with lower levels of violent behavior. The Talheim massacre of 5000 BCE is a case in point. Thus, speculation concerning the beginning of the Neolithic is still overly dependent upon qualitative and not quantitative factors.

The Breton site of Téviec (Morbihan) will be left to one side for now. This site is thought to date from the time of the last hunter-gatherers and has been associated with evidence from the Mesolithic, despite its later date (mid to second half of the sixth millennium BCE). Traces of violence have been associated with France's first two agricultural communities (the Neolithic characterized by Cardial Impressed pottery in the Mediterranean region and the "Danubian" Neolithic with its Linear Pottery culture, found in Alsace, Lorraine, and the Paris Basin). As has already been discussed, evidence suggests that some bodies were dismembered in the Mediterranean region. As for the Danubian Neolithic, a burial ground in Alsace (Quatzenheim, Bas-Rhin) was found to contain the remains of two individuals, both of whom had been struck by arrows: one, an adult, had been hit on the right hip (tomb 10); the skull of the other individual had also been struck by a projectile (tomb 11).

The lack of evidence relating to the Middle Neolithic should also be noted. One example, however, is the Pontcharaud burial place in Clermont-Ferrand (Puy-de-Dôme). Here, one grave was found to contain seven bodies: five adult males and two children. At least one of these individuals was killed: a flint arrowhead was embedded in the spinal column. Explaining the presence of the other six bodies in this grave is more difficult. It would seem that they were probably buried here at the same time as the murdered individual and that the grave was then partially covered over with limestone slabs. Perhaps these individuals were also killed during a confrontation, or perhaps they were executed? In proposing such a hypothesis, it is important to note that, if these individuals did indeed die a violent death, interpreting this aggressive behavior is a much more complex matter. Other causes of death are also possible (accidents, illness). However the fact that seven individuals were buried here at the same time, at least one of whom was killed, casts some doubt upon the suggestion that the others died a natural death.[2]

Similar questions may be asked of certain burials discovered along the Rhône dating from around 4000 BCE. Bodies were placed either in graves or in reused silos. Such tombs have been found in the towns of Moulins in Saint-Paul-Trois-Châteaux and Gournier in Montélimar.[3] Each tomb contained from three to four bodies, all of which were buried at the same time (in one case, burials were made in two separate stages within the same grave). In each of these tombs, one individual seems to have received special, privileged treatment, having been buried at the very center of the grave. The other individuals accompany the central figure. This again raises the question of whether they died a natural, accidental, or more violent death.

Determining the significance of these multiple burials, i.e., where several bodies are buried together at the same time, is a rather delicate matter: were these deaths the result of famine or a mysterious illness? Or were these individuals the victims of killings? The question of sacrifice is also raised in any case such as this where one individual accompanies another in a grave, with the grave being permanently sealed after burial. Three tombs from Châtelliers-du-Vieil-Auzay (Vendée) are highly indicative. Each of these graves, dating from around 3500 BCE, was found to contain two males: one adult and one younger male. In tomb 3, the two bodies had been placed top to tail: the grave contained a tall adolescent aged 20 years or so and a young adult (plate 13). These two individuals were both very tall, 1 m 70 and 1 m 90, respectively. The adult had been struck by a sharp arrow, embedded in the fourth lumbar vertebra, which would have caused a quick death. Yet

Plate 13 Les Châtelliers-du-Vieil-Auzay (France). Tomb 3. Grave containing two males: an adult with an arrow wound to the vertebral column and blows to the face, and an adolescent with blows to the head and a chest injury caused by a projectile, fourth millennium BCE. Photo P. Birocheau/J. M. Large.

this individual also received a violent blow to the face which resulted in broken teeth and a broken chin. Blows to the left parietal and to the frontal were also inflicted upon his young companion. A sharp arrow, found level with the adolescent's ribcage, is thought to have penetrated his chest.

Tomb 1 is similar, containing two individuals: one young adult and one adolescent, roughly 20 years old. Both bodies were buried with their limbs bent, their lower limbs placed close together. The adult had been struck on the head several times, possibly with an axe. The younger individual may also have sustained several injuries.

Likewise, tomb 2 contained two bodies, lying side by side on their left sides, their legs bent: one young adult and one adolescent aged 16 to 18 years old. The adult had received several blows to the head, one of which caused a fragment 2 cm in diameter to break away. His companion had also sustained several blows to the head.

Excavators and anthropologists alike have both noted the similar positioning of the injuries upon these six bodies. All have sustained blows to the head, with the two individuals in tomb 3 also being struck by projectiles. The positioning of the bodies in the tombs and the fact that they have been grouped in pairs is indicative of ritualization or dramatization; sacrifice or some other kind of ceremonial "out of the ordinary" burial may have taken place here.[4]

War upon the Plateaus of Southern France?

Although there is little evidence of arrow-inflicted injury from the first half of the Neolithic, as of 3500 BCE there was a sharp increase in the number of projectile-inflicted injuries. Such evidence has been found in megalithic tombs, hypogea, and caves used as tombs, primarily in the south of France. Of course, the Marne hypogea also contained their fair share of victims of such violence. These tombs were used for a good thousand years or so by the so-called "Seine-Oise-Marne" civilizations (between 3400 and 2800 BCE), and then by the "Gourd" populations (between 2800 and 2400 BCE). However, there can be no doubt that the majority of evidence of such injuries dating from the fourth and third millennia BCE comes from the southern limestone regions of Aveyron and Lozère, and the immediate surrounding area (Tarn and the garrigues of Hérault and Gard) (plates 14, 15, 16, and 17). Arnal classified all of these populations as part of the same culture, which he described as "Rodezian." This cultural group was later renamed the "Treilles group" after a cave in Saint-Jean-Saint-Paul in Aveyron. Arnal considered these populations to be particularly fierce, with no hesitation in leaving their

Plate 14 (*left*) Cascades cave, Creissels (Aveyron, France), third millennium BCE. Metatarsal bone, pierced by a flint arrow. Millau Museum, France. Photo G. Costantini.

Plate 15 (*right*) Cascades cave, Creissels (Aveyron, France), third millennium BCE. Tibia, pierced by a flint spear. Millau Museum, France. Photo G. Costantini.

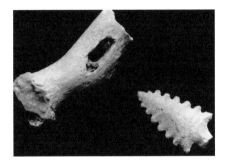

Plate 16 Cascades cave, Creissels (Aveyron, France), third millennium BCE. Radius injured during impact. Alongside, a crenulate ("pine tree") arrowhead, of the type discovered in Aveyron. Millau Museum, France. Photo G. Costantini.

high plateaus to raid communities settled at lower altitudes. These formidable archers armed with arrows, their arrowheads fashioned from chert and characterized by crenulate ("pine tree") edges, were also pillagers, prone to carrying out raids, and would periodically descend upon any surrounding settlements. Thus, the Suquet-Coucolière cave in Les Matelles (Hérault) may have contained the bodies of victims struck by these crenulate arrows.

Many experts have noted that trepanation was often practiced during this same period in the limestone regions of the south. Without wishing to propose that a systematic relationship exists between conflict and early forms of surgery, an issue that will be addressed later, it is nevertheless worth emphasizing that these populations did indeed inflict injury upon humans, either through warfare, medical procedures, or rituals. This region of France has yielded a great deal of evidence, dating from the third millennium BCE: pierced and scarred skulls, various skeletal injuries, and bones bearing projectile-inflicted injuries.

Evidence from the south of France peaks around the mid-Copper Age; there are fewer cases of injury dating from the later stages of this era, a period characterized by the spread of the Beaker culture. The scarcity of individual

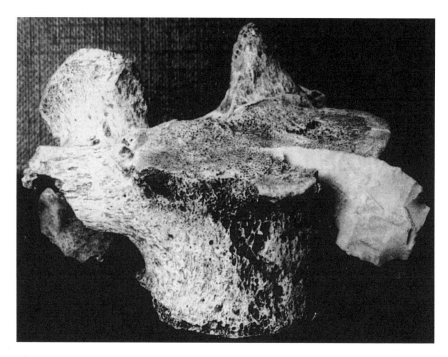

Plate 17   Mauray cave sinkhole in Gijounet (Tarn, France). Flint arrow embedded in a lumbar vertebra, third millennium BCE. Photo G. Costantini.

tombs from the caliciform ware "civilization" in France makes it difficult to draw comparisons with any previous or contemporaneous cultural groups. The Beaker populations, however, continued to bury their dead in the large collective tombs used by their predecessors. The fact that the dead from different eras were buried together in this way makes it virtually impossible to determine for certain which bodies belonged to which period. In view of this, the individual tomb in La Fare in Forcalquier (Alpes-de-Haute-Provence), which was found to contain a body accompanied by a classic caliciform vase, is of particular interest: a flint object was implanted in the ulna, level with the elbow. It seems that the wound caused by this object and its violent impact did not result in death, since signs of scarring have been identified.[5] Similarly, another individual was found with a leaf-shaped arrow lodged in one of the femur bones. This body was buried in a barrow tomb in Plan d'Aups (Var), known as the "Gendarme" tumulus, along with a decorated beaker. Interestingly, the Rec de las Balmas cave near to Caunes-Minervois (Aude) contained an ulna (which had been struck by a stemmed arrow with "ailerons") and, amongst other things, some fragments of beakers (ca. 2500–2200 BCE). The body of an individual found in a cave in La Tourasse in Saint-Martory (Haute-Garonne) had also been struck in one of the vertebrae by a sharp arrow, complete with "ailerons." This incident may well have occurred during the Beaker culture period, given that several examples of this pottery were discovered in the cave.[6]

The Difficulties of Making an Assessment

Individuals injured by arrows, where the arrowhead penetrated part of the skeleton, account for only a small minority of the deaths studied. Of the approximately 74 bodies found in the Treilles cave in Saint-Jean-Saint-Paul (Aveyron), only four had sustained injuries. In the Cascades cave in Creissels (Aveyron), it is just three out of the 79 bodies; two out of 40 in the Nojarède dolmen in Chanac (Lozère); three out of 66 in the Lave cave in Saint-Saturnin-d'Apt (Vaucluse); two out of 150 to 200 in the Capitaine hypogeum in Grillon (Vaucluse); three out of roughly 200 in the Crottes hypogeum in Roaix (Vaucluse); one out of 100 in the Pierre-Plate dolmen in Presles (Val-d'Oise); and one out of 100 in the Castellet hypogeum in Fontvieille (Bouches-du-Rhône). And there are many more examples. Furthermore, it is far from clear whether or not these injuries were responsible for the death of the individual in question; in some cases, the wound evidently healed, indicated by the continued calcification of the bones. Prunières points to several probable examples of healed wounds from remains discovered in Baumes-Chaudes in Lozère.

A survey of 48 sites concluded that roughly 75 bodies, out of the approximately 2,000 to 3,000 bodies buried in the tombs, were injured. This total is only very approximate since the number of bodies in certain tombs, such as the Marne hypogea, cannot be ascertained for certain. Thus, it is possible that less than 4 percent of the estimated total were injured (or even 3 percent, based upon the higher estimated total). This figure is little more than a rough indication; it does not differentiate between the fatal injuries and those injuries which later healed. Other factors must also be taken into account.

This approach does not, for example, take account of the time scale. It focuses upon populations buried over the course of an entire millennium which it is often impossible to date any more precisely. Furthermore, the bones unearthed by archeologists may not be representative of the local population: it is possible that being buried in a megalithic tomb was a privilege not bestowed upon everyone. These tombs were also periodically emptied in order to remove the oldest remains and make room for new bodies. The average number of injured victims given is also rather low and thus may not be entirely reliable. Perhaps it should be recalculated? There are several arguments in favor of this, outlined below.

It is likely that some of those killed in combat or in ambush attacks, or even those who disappeared during expeditions to faraway places, would have been buried or even abandoned where they fell. This hypothesis has been applied, in particular, to a burial ground in Varna (Bulgaria) dating from the fifth millennium BCE – the tombs found here did not contain any bodies. These mock tombs served to mark the memory of the dead in cases where there was no body to bury. However, this privilege may have been restricted to certain individuals only; those of a lower social status who died or disappeared far away from the community may not have been remembered in this way. If this was indeed the case, the number of individuals injured/not injured and buried in the collective tombs must have been disproportionately weighted toward those who died a violent death within the community. Similaun man, who died high up in the mountains far away from his people, is one example of a community losing track of its dead.

There is also the matter of injury to the soft tissue (skin, muscle, intestines) which was, in some cases, a cause of death. The fact that the soft tissue is not preserved makes it impossible to know, or even roughly estimate, what percentage of deaths fall into this category. However, many authors nevertheless claim that arrows (possibly poisoned arrows?) did penetrate the muscular tissue of some individuals. Many arrowheads have been discovered in the large communal tombs in the Paris Basin (covered passageways, hypogea in Marne) and the south (hypogea in Vaucluse and Arles, various different megalithic chamber structures). These arrows are generally thought to have been placed in the tombs either to accompany their owner or as a sort of offering to the dead (in some cases these items are striking, though not functional). However, it is entirely possible that some of the arrowheads are the remains of arrows that struck and penetrated the flesh of the victims buried in these tombs. It may therefore be more appropriate to scale up the percentage of deaths attributed to fatal injury.

A more extensive investigation of some of the collective tombs seems to support this theory. In the Lave cave in Saint-Saturnin-d'Apt (Vaucluse), for example, the remains of three individuals were buried, all of whom had been struck by arrows. Two individuals had suffered cranial injuries to the frontal (perhaps inflicted by a catapult?); some of the other bones also show signs of violent injury.[7] Catapulting projectiles and throwing stones may have been just as effective as the bow and arrow in inter-community conflicts. It is therefore clear that, even though the number of flint arrows embedded in human bones is statistically rather low, this does not mean that attacks were rare or that the number of victims was low. Indeed, striking the head was a common way of attacking and killing an enemy. In addition to the Talheim cases, there are other examples of this type of injury dating from the Neolithic in France (Châtelliers-du-Vieil-Auzay in Vendée, the Boileau hypogeum in Vaucluse).

Effective Weapons of Death

The projectiles fired by the archers of the Neolithic were arrows with a wooden shaft. The mummified remains of "Similaun man" (more informally known as "Ötzi" after the Ötzal glacier which formed his resting place for thousands of years before he was discovered and moved to a refrigerated cell in the Bolzano Museum in Northeast Italy) were also accompanied by 14 wooden arrows in a quiver; the majority of the arrows were still unfinished. Flint arrowheads, which were fixed to the shaft using pitch, are often the only remaining evidence of these weapons. The morphology of the arrowheads varies according to the culture in question and the level of technological development. The body of an individual discovered in Auzay (Vendée) had been struck by an arrowhead with a transverse cutting edge that sliced into the body of its victim. The majority of arrowheads found in France which can be linked to Neolithic human remains are of the piercing type, i.e., they penetrate the bone with a sharp point. Numerous varieties of piercing arrow have been identified (triangular, asymmetrical, leaf-shaped, amygdaloid, and those with "ailerons" and stems), most of which date from the fourth millennium BCE onwards. A study of 63 arrowheads embedded in human bones revealed 11 to have a sharp cutting edge and to date from the start of the Neolithic right up to the end of the fourth millennium BCE (Seine-Oise-Marne culture); 42 were of the piercing type, dating from 3500 to 2000 BCE in particular; the morphology of the remaining ten could not be identified for definite.[8]

Other deadly weapons may also have been put to use. Two cases of injury identified in the Champagne hypogea were caused by thin knife blades (plate 18). In one of these cases, from the Razet hypogeum I in Coizard (Marne), the weapon had cut into the side of a vertebra. In the other example, in hypogeum II in Villevenard (Marne), a knife blade was found to have penetrated one of the vertebra after having first cut through the intestines, causing a fatal injury. Baye notes that arrowheads may have been attached to these flint blades. However, the idea that these were knife or dagger blades, used to inflict direct injury, cannot be ruled out. Yet this does seem unlikely in the case of the smaller blades, since part of the blade would have to be

Plate 18   Thin flint blades lodged in human vertebrae. Marne hypogeum (France): (a) Coizard; (b) Villevenard, third millennium BCE. Museum of National Antiquities, Saint-Germain-en-Laye, France. © J. G. Berizzi/RMN.

concealed by the handle. Longer blades or flint daggers fixed to a wooden or bone handle would, however, have been more effective in the event of squabbles breaking out. One victim of such a stabbing was found in the Pas-de-Joulié cave in Trèves (Gard) with the copper blade of a dagger lodged in the vertebral column (plate 19). Similarly, a metal blade was discovered among the remains of an individual in the Baumes-Chaudes cave (Lozère).

It seems that almost all parts of the body were targets for the archers of the Neolithic. A study into the populations of France's recent prehistory revealed that the head (sockets, zygomatic arches, right and left parietal bones), thorax, and pelvis (coxal and sacrum bones) were all targets. The arms, especially the humerus and radius, were also often struck (figure 38). Injuries to the radius may well have been caused as victims tried to protect themselves, their lives

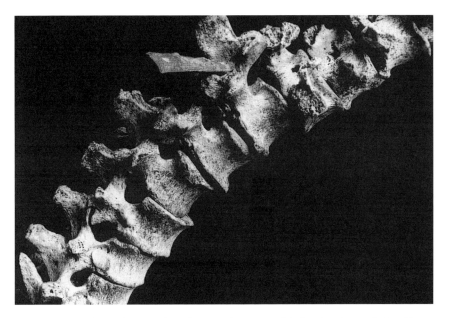

Plate 19   Pas-de-Joulié cave (Gard, France). Copper blade of a dagger lodged in a vertebra, third millennium BCE. Millau Museum, France. Photo G. Costantini.

in danger. However, most of the projectiles were lodged in the vertebrae. It is often difficult to determine which vertebrae these are, although dorsal and lumbar vertebrae are the most frequently cited in reports and other such publications. There are also cases of injury to the legs (the femur and even more commonly the tibia, although rarely the fibula) and feet (the talus bone in particular is often injured). The hands are not usually affected although damaged metacarpal bones were found at two sites in Aveyron: the Puechcamp dolmen in Sébazac-Concourès and the Treilles cave in Saint-Jean-Saint-Paul. This brief overview is based upon 60 localized impacts (figure 39). They can be summarized in table 1 (p. 143), which divides the injuries into those affecting the top and those affecting the bottom parts of the body. The victims were fired upon from the front, back, and side. Projectiles were fired upwards, the attacker being positioned at a lower level (kneeling?), or downwards with the attacker in a dominant position. The ballistic movement is often difficult to determine. In the case of the Mauray swallow hole victim from Gijounet (Tarn), the individual may have been struck at point-blank range while lying on the ground.

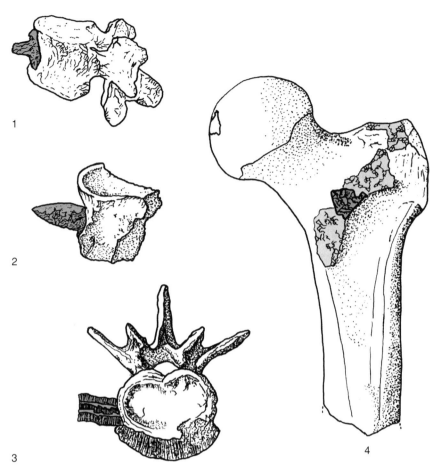

Figure 38   Arrows and flint blades embedded in human bones (vertebrae and femur) in France. Neolithic and Chalcolithic period: (1) Tourasse cave in Saint-Martory (Haute-Garonne), after Cartailhac. (2) Castellet hypogeum in Fontvieille (Bouches-du-Rhône), after Cazalis de Fondouce, 1873, 1978. (3) Razet hypogeum I in Coizard (Marne), after Baye. (4) Prévinquières dolmen (Aveyron), after Azémar, 1989.

Figure 39   (*opposite*) Diagrams showing the point of arrow impact upon various individuals from the Neolithic and Chalcolithic periods in France (numbers in square brackets refer to the list in the appendix). After Naudet and Vidal.

138   *Humans as Targets*

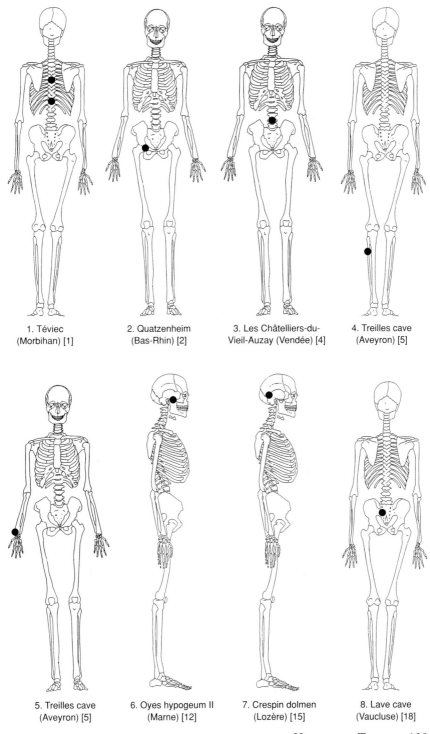

1. Téviec
(Morbihan) [1]

2. Quatzenheim
(Bas-Rhin) [2]

3. Les Châtelliers-du-
Vieil-Auzay (Vendée) [4]

4. Treilles cave
(Aveyron) [5]

5. Treilles cave
(Aveyron) [5]

6. Oyes hypogeum II
(Marne) [12]

7. Crespin dolmen
(Lozère) [15]

8. Lave cave
(Vaucluse) [18]

Humans as Targets 139

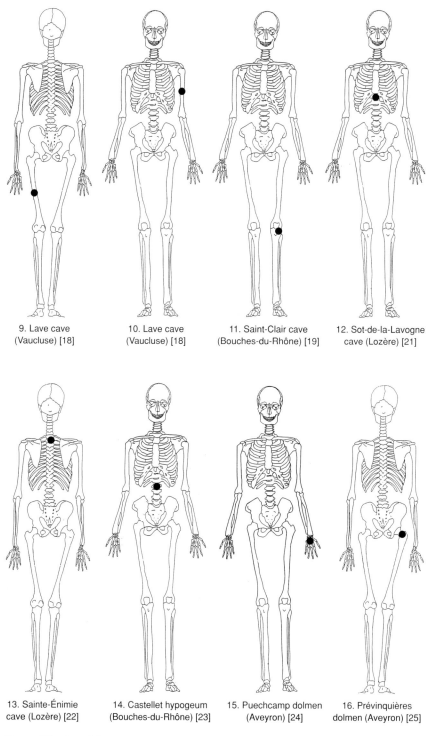

9. Lave cave
(Vaucluse) [18]

10. Lave cave
(Vaucluse) [18]

11. Saint-Clair cave
(Bouches-du-Rhône) [19]

12. Sot-de-la-Lavogne
cave (Lozère) [21]

13. Sainte-Énimie
cave (Lozère) [22]

14. Castellet hypogeum
(Bouches-du-Rhône) [23]

15. Puechcamp dolmen
(Aveyron) [24]

16. Prévinquières
dolmen (Aveyron) [25]

Figure 39   (cont'd)

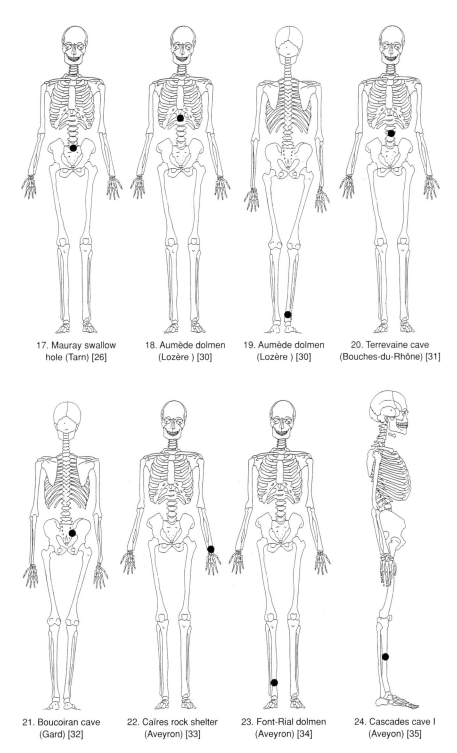

17. Mauray swallow hole (Tarn) [26]

18. Aumède dolmen (Lozère) [30]

19. Aumède dolmen (Lozère) [30]

20. Terrevaine cave (Bouches-du-Rhône) [31]

21. Boucoiran cave (Gard) [32]

22. Caïres rock shelter (Aveyron) [33]

23. Font-Rial dolmen (Aveyron) [34]

24. Cascades cave I (Aveyon) [35]

Figure 39 *(cont'd)*

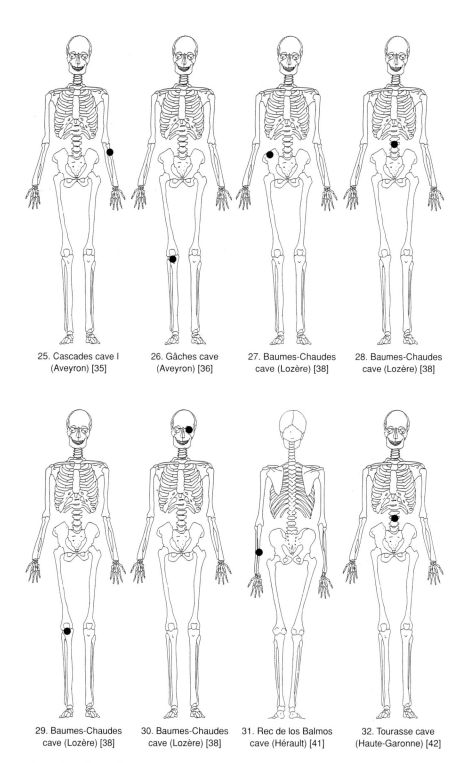

25. Cascades cave I (Aveyron) [35]

26. Gâches cave (Aveyron) [36]

27. Baumes-Chaudes cave (Lozère) [38]

28. Baumes-Chaudes cave (Lozère) [38]

29. Baumes-Chaudes cave (Lozère) [38]

30. Baumes-Chaudes cave (Lozère) [38]

31. Rec de los Balmos cave (Hérault) [41]

32. Tourasse cave (Haute-Garonne) [42]

Figure 39 (*cont'd*)

Table 1 Location of injuries

Top part of the body		Bottom part of the body	
Non-lumbar vertebra	5	Lumbar vertebra	13
Skull	5	Coxal bone	4
Humerus	3	Sacrum	3
Radius	4	Femur	5
Ulna	1	Tibia	7
Metacarpus	2	Fibula	1
Ribs	2	Patella	1
		Talus	3
		Metatarsus	1
Total	**22**		**38**

Injury and Trepanation

The Baumes-Chaudes cave in Lozère was found to contain more cases of arrow-inflicted injury than any other site in France – these remains date from the third millennium BCE. Of a population estimated to total some 300 to 400 people, 17 individuals were found to have been injured by arrows. A thorax was also discovered in which the copper blade of a dagger was embedded. In the southern limestone regions of France, trepanation was a common practice at this time. At the Baumes-Chaudes site, more than 60 individuals were found to have undergone trepanation, a proportion of one person in every five or six. In addition, signs of injury are present upon many other bones and have been noted by the various anthropologists who have examined the remains of this population. These injuries include fractures which have often reset, to the coxal bone, femur, tibia, and fibula; healed fractures to the ulna; pathological injuries to the femur, tibia, and sternum; fractured and healed ribs; ankylosis where the lower tibia meets the calcaneum and talus, and so on. These observations have generally led to the conclusion that these populations lived a difficult existence, plagued by regular confrontation between communities. Many experts have established a cause–effect relationship between the practice of trepanation and the warring behavior of these populations (plate 20). The French regions of Lozère and Aveyron have certainly provided much of the evidence of Neolithic-age trepanation in Europe – approximately one-quarter of the individuals known to have undergone trepanation during the Neolithic in Europe (170 from a total of

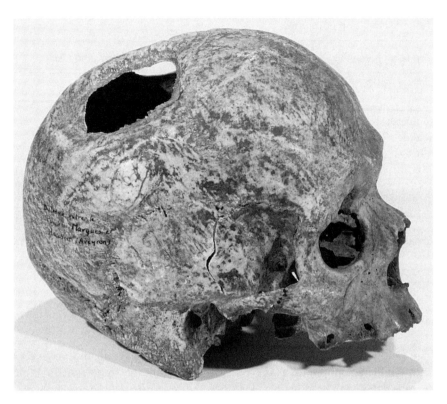

Plate 20   Puech dolmen, between Puech-Marguès and Maubert, Montpellier-le-Vieux (Aveyron, France). Skull bearing healed, biparietal holes (one is visible here), third millennium BCE. Nîmes Museum, France. Photo A. Aigoin.

ca. 600).[9] Can this increase in trepanation be linked to inter-community conflict? It should be noted that trepanation is not a Neolithic "invention." Evidence of trepanation being performed dates back to the last hunter-gatherer populations, having been identified in the Taforalt cave (Morocco) and at burial sites in Muge (Portugal) and Vasilevka II and Vovnigskii II (Ukraine).

Trepanation is thought to have first emerged during the sixth to fifth millennia BCE at the time of the first agricultural communities: cases have been identified in Vedrovice (Czech Republic), Ensisheim (Alsace, France), and Trasano (Italy).

However, it is certainly true that there was a sharp increase in cases of trepanation during the late stages of the Neolithic, coinciding with an increase in the number of arrow-inflicted injuries. Furthermore, half the cases of arrow-inflicted injuries in France were discovered in the southern limestone regions, the same areas which yielded a high number of trepanation cases. Is it possible to establish a relationship between warfare and cranial surgery? Could the latter be a medical consequence of the former? Certain authors have claimed that this was the case.[10] Yet why did the number of cases of trepanation in France fall rapidly from the start of the Bronze Age, i.e., from 2200/2000 BCE? These same writers have attributed this decline to the invention of the helmet: by protecting the heads of those engaged in battle, there would have been fewer injuries to this part of the body. However, this argument is not entirely convincing. Hardly any metal helmets have been found dating from before the end of the Bronze Age or even before the beginning of the Iron Age, i.e., before 1000 BCE. Even then, they are very rare. There is, therefore, no relationship between the notable fall in the number of trepanation cases and the use of helmets. It is, however, possible that helmets were made from other materials during the Early to Middle Bronze Age, for example, from strengthened skins or leather, or even from material lined with a more solid substance. The Myceneans notably attached the canines of wild boar to their headwear for extra protection.

The decline in cases of trepanation was neither widespread nor systematic. Cases of trepanation have been found scattered across Italy, the Netherlands, and Central Europe. Several examples dating from the Iron Age have been identified in Germany. However, there were no more "centers of surgery" like the vast limestone plateaus of Southern France and the Petit-Morin valley at the end of the Neolithic. A second line of argument is that very few cases establish a definite relationship between injury and trepanation.

With this in mind, interpreting the available evidence becomes even more of a delicate matter. There is no evidence from the limestone regions of Southern France to suggest that more males than females underwent trepanation.[11] If trepanation is assumed to have affected primarily those engaged in "combat," then women too must have formed part of the available contingent. Indeed, of 31 cases of trepanation, where the age of the individual in question could be estimated, 71 percent (22 individuals) were young or slightly older adults who would have been capable of fighting. However of these individuals, eight underwent trepanation before reaching adulthood with the wounds healing later. This discovery, in fact, reverses the proportions with the total number of trepanation cases being composed of 45 percent adults and 55 percent children and adolescents. The fact that trepanation was practiced on young individuals who died several years later casts serious doubt upon the theory that trepanation can be linked to warfare.

Evidence from the south of France seems to suggest that no preference was given to either side of the body in trepanation: 37.2 percent of cases affected the left-hand side, 41.9 percent the right, and 20.9 percent the center.[12]

However, these results do not reflect evidence from other areas of France which reveals the left side to have been greatly favored over the right: here, the left-hand side was chosen in two-thirds of cases.

Of the trepanation cases identified in Provence, 12 were performed upon the left side of the head, nine upon the right, and four upon the sagittal area.[13] It is therefore impossible to draw any significant conclusions from this evidence, since the location of the trepanation injuries seems to vary. The notion that the left frontal and left parietal would have been most commonly affected by this therapeutic practice, since injuries to the skull were mostly inflicted by right-handed warriors, is not confirmed by the evidence either from the limestone plateaus of the south or from Provence. The theory is, in fact, based upon the idea that those in battle faced one another, rather like in a duel. However, Neolithic confrontations could certainly have taken another form, such as ambush or surprise attacks.

Few reliable assumptions regarding the relationship between prehistoric warfare and trepanation can be made, based upon these observations. Thus, discussions of trepanation have tended to resort to the same few classic interpretations: that this was either a therapeutic practice designed to rid the body of certain pathological illnesses (headaches, convulsions, etc.) or a "ritual" (initiation, propitiatory rituals, etc.), the latter being more hypothetical.

It is estimated that at least 70 percent of those who underwent trepanation survived the surgery (some even claim the figure to be as high as 90 percent).[14] These figures speak volumes about the skill of these surgeons who, some 5,000 years ago, bored holes into their comrades' skulls using only flint scalpels.

Did Collective Burial Sites Sometimes Serve as Communal Graves?

Tombs containing the remains of individuals killed or injured by arrows date right back through prehistory, showing that acts of violence were not uncommon. The bodies of those who suffered and/or died as a result of these injuries reveal nothing of the motives behind this aggression: all-out "external" warfare, ritual warfare, internal warfare, individuals settling scores, vendettas, sacrifice, and so on. But does the tomb itself reveal anything about the existence of conflict? The collective burial sites of the fourth and third millennia BCE are of particular interest here. These burial grounds were often used for several centuries at a time; a large number of corpses were deposited here over this period. The fact that these burial grounds were used to store so many bodies required the space to be managed periodically: remains were compressed, regrouped, selected, removed, and so on. These tombs, in which bodies were placed regularly during times of peace, may well have been used during conflict to store the bodies of warriors killed in combat or those massacred by the enemy. Thus, the community in question may have rearranged its dead, storing their remains in a collective tomb. During wartime, the use of tombs would have differed from the normal, long-term usage: typically, tombs would be opened occasionally to deposit a body and would be cleaned and reorganized at the same time. During war, bodies would have been deposited here *en masse*; a large number of bodies would have been stored and arranged within a small area, with very little time being devoted to this activity. What was once a tomb opened only periodically and then with great care would have become a sort of communal tomb for a short period of time.

Is it possible for archeologists to differentiate between those bodies placed in the tombs one by one over a long period of time and those deposited here quickly, *en masse*, following a dramatic event? Such a distinction has been attempted with regard to several collective tombs in France and Spain, in particular the Roaix hypogeum (Vaucluse, France) and the ossuary in San Juan Ante Portam Latinam (Alava, Spain).

The Roaix hypogeum in Vaucluse, like the majority of tombs cut into the molasse sediments of the region, was only partially preserved when it was discovered. The ceiling had collapsed and the walls had partly disappeared: the walls remained only around an area of 6 m by 6 m. This tomb was excavated in 1965−6 and was found to contain the remains of some 200 individuals and would undoubtedly have contained more originally, given that part of the tomb was damaged through erosion.[15] However, the bodies were not evenly distributed across the various layers in the tomb. In the deepest layers, the bodies were found to be only partially intact, since the remains had been rearranged over time as new bodies were deposited here. This is "normal" procedure for a collective burial.

Following a period of disuse, a large number of bodies were then deposited here, stacked on top of one another in four or five layers, facing different directions. The corpses had been placed on their backs and were still intact, indicating that they had not undergone the usual rearrangements characteristic of collective tombs (plate 21). Thus during the excavations, the impression emerged that these bodies were deposited here quickly, following a one-off event.

By the last of these upper layers, the tomb seems to have resumed its previous slow pace – opened periodically and occasionally cleaned and reordered. Few of the skeletons from these layers remained intact and numerous skulls were removed and stacked up against the back wall.[16]

Plate 21 Roaix hypogeum (Vaucluse, France). Layer 2. Mass burial of human remains; the skeletons have remained intact ("war layer"), third millennium BCE. Photo J. Courtin.

Thus, it seems that this tomb experienced two periods of use which involved bodies being frequently deposited and rearranged. In between these two periods was a brief stage during which at least 34 (or perhaps as many as 50) bodies were buried here quickly. How can this event be interpreted? The fact that this was such a brief phase suggests that these deaths all occurred at the same time and thus the most convincing hypothesis seems to be that of a collective killing. The theory that these individuals died either in combat or as a result of a population being partly decimated (females are found among the dead) seems all the more likely given that three arrows were discovered lodged in several bones, having caused fatal injuries to their victims: the first had struck a mastoid apophysis, the second was embedded in one of the vertebrae, and the third in the side of the ilium. The label "war layer" has been widely applied and accepted in describing this period of the Roaix hypogeum. However, the possibility that an epidemic was responsible for this apparent drama has not been fully eliminated. It was many years before new excavations and investigations, based on detailed observations, opened the debate on this interpretive model.[17]

Evidence of injury, both fatal and non-fatal, has emerged with the discovery of several arrows lodged in human bones in the collective tombs of Southern France, dating from the end of the Neolithic. This is a fairly common phenomenon, even though the number of individuals concerned is always very low. Thus, such evidence is not particularly indicative in itself. It suggests only that violent behavior leading to death did occur at this time.

Observations from other hypogea of the same period in Vaucluse and the south of the Drôme region are of greater interest here. In fact, there are several artificial tombs like the one at Roaix which have been found to contain a particularly large number of bodies: approximately 150 in the case of the Capitaine hypogeum in Grillon, more than 300 at the Boileau site in Sarrians, and 70 in the small but well-preserved Fourneaux hypogeum in Mours-Saint-Eusèbe. The remains contained within these tombs often share similar features with the Roaix site: the skeletons are often still intact and are either stretched out or placed with their legs bent; the accumulation of skeletons in this way suggests that these individuals were all buried over a short space of time and that the tomb was not subsequently reorganized. But there are also differences: preventing the bodies piling up was clearly a particular concern in the Capitaine hypogeum. The Boileau hypogeum, which was particularly full of remains, contained very few cases of injury: just one individual struck by an arrow in the vertebral column and a smashed skull, possibly caused by an axe blow. It is always possible that there were more injuries to the flesh, of which there would be no trace in terms of archeological evidence; bodies buried in tombs following some kind of killing would certainly have suffered many injuries.

At the Boileau site, sediments were also found to have penetrated the gaps between the bodies. In order for these fine layers of sediment to have developed and settled, a sedimentation process, however slight, must have occurred between each of the various stages of bodies being deposited here.

It has also been noted that, of the bodies initially buried in the tomb, some of the bones had moved from their original locations by the time new bodies were added: skulls, for example, became detached from the body and toppled over. This would not have occurred had the bodies been more closely stored together, forming a tightly packed space. Some of the bodies had begun to decompose by the time others were placed here with skulls becoming separated from the vertebral column. Bones were also deliberately detached from other parts of the skeleton, indicating that the earliest bodies deposited here were, at times, rearranged. Parts of skeletons stored at the top of these mounds of human remains were most frequently affected.

These observations from the Boileau hypogeum indicate that, despite being overcrowded with bodies, many of which were still intact, this mass grave was not quickly filled up with human remains, all deposited at once. In fact the tomb was gradually filled over time, over the course of several centuries. Thus, its seems that the "war layers" hypothesis cannot be applied in this case.

At the Roaix site, disconnected bones were also found in the layer containing complete skeletons, raising the difficult issue of how the two are related. Could these dislocated bones originate from later burials or from earlier burials, the skeletons having been rearranged before the subsequent mass deposit of remains? Some of the skeletons are largely incomplete: perhaps some of the bones were removed or selected to be buried elsewhere? Taking this additional evidence into account, the number of bodies buried in the upper section can be placed at a minimum of 136,[18] 58 percent of which were adults, the rest being children and adolescents. However, this does not rule out the possibility that many bodies were deposited here at once: this is thought to apply to roughly 50 bodies, both male and female, a large quantity for a village community in Mediterranean France of this period. It should also be remembered that this evidence is incomplete: initially, there may have been many more bodies buried here.

The very fact that these hypogea in Vaucluse contained so many bodies, both intact and with bones removed, is a matter of interest in itself. It is still not yet clear what social factors determined the "recruitment" of so many collective burial sites in the south of France. In fact, the tombs themselves are very diverse. Some are very large and could potentially contain a large number of bodies, like some of the megalithic tombs in Aude. Others are small (like the dolmens of the southern limestone plateaus and small caves) – these smaller spaces had to be managed if they were to be used frequently (by reducing the number of bodies buried here or emptying the tomb altogether, etc.). The time factor should also be taken into account when examining all of this evidence concerning the space available. Some of these tombs were used over very long periods of time, sometimes as long as 1,500 years (between 3300 and 1800 BCE). Others were only in use for a short period and were then permanently sealed. Any attempts at drawing comparisons must, therefore, take account of these differences. A more complex matter concerns access to the collective tombs. Did all members of the community (men and women, adults and children) have the "credit" required to be buried in a megalithic tomb or hypogeum after death? In fact, little is known about this and discussion is limited to speculation. However, there are so many different cases that one single model seems unlikely. Social relationships, kinship systems, both biological and symbolic, and group identities may well have varied from place to place over time. Rituals and traditions surrounding the social function of death may also have varied according to the culture in question. Briefly, two extreme cases can be identified, giving rise to two hypotheses.

The first hypothesis claims that the remains discovered in some of the tombs far from represent the total population which inhabited the surrounding area from roughly 3500/3300 BCE over many centuries. The difference in numbers may be due to the tombs being periodically emptied: remains may have been removed in order to "make room" for new corpses. However, the temporary removal of bones would not have been solely responsible for this lack of bodies when compared to the total population assumed to have lived in each area. Thus, it may well be that a selective recruitment process was in operation, determining which individuals were buried in the tombs. Could it be, for example, that only those from certain lineages were buried in the tombs, being perhaps descended from either real or mythical founding ancestors? It is also possible that the young or very young were excluded – certainly, they are notably absent from some (though not all) of the tombs.

Another theory is that the remains contained in some of the tombs are representative of the original population. In this case, rules governing selection would have played very little part in determining which bodies were buried in the tombs. The human remains found in a particular collective tomb would, according to this theory, reflect the composition of the community in question, as well as its demographic evolution throughout the duration of the tomb's usage.

Thus, there are at least two explanations for the use of these tombs: one is based upon selection, i.e., reflects differences in social standing between lineages or families. The other is more collegial or "democratic," stressing solidarity within the community. In both cases, the group is the essential factor because each individual, on being buried in the collective tomb, is depersonalized for the benefit of those left behind, who organize these burials. In the first case, tombs containing numerous corpses can be seen to reflect the extent of the power held by certain notable individuals (cf. leaders) whose relatives and allies would be granted the right to burial in the communal tomb. Those tombs that were found to contain fewer bodies could thus be indicative of families with lesser social influence. According to the second theory, these human remains could provide an idea of the population size for a certain area over a particular time span, despite certain alterations to the tombs over time.

In fact, it is possible that both theories contain an element of truth. It seems likely that there were a great many factors determining which individuals were buried in these tombs, depending upon the rules operating in the society concerned at a given point in time. In fact, any particular tomb may well have been affected by different rules of recruitment, depending upon circumstances, over the course of its long "life." This flexibility may well explain why some of the tombs from the third millennium BCE are so overcrowded whilst others are much emptier, without of course ruling out the possibility of remains being periodically removed.

At some point during the history of the Roaix hypogeum, a number of bodies (male and female) were deposited here at the same time – the cause of death is still unknown. A massacre has often been suggested, yet the supposed victims do not show signs of injury of the type observed in Talheim. Killings tend to leave obvious signs of blows or other damage to the bodies of those who die. The matter is therefore still open to speculation: Epidemics? Food poisoning? "Sacrifices" (during which individuals would be drugged and "invited' to follow someone into the tomb)? The killing of "reprobates" by various methods? Other reasons? This debate, one of the main reasons for the ongoing interest in the site, is far from over.

Lessons from the San Juan Ante Portam Latinam Burial Site (Alava, Spain)

The issue of the so-called "war layers" was recently readdressed during research into a site in the Alavan Rioja region of Northwest Spain: the collective burial site of San Juan Ante Portam Latinam in Laguardia. The site consists of a rock shelter which was completely hidden from view for a long time, since the vault of the cave had partly collapsed down onto the layers of human remains. In fact this ancient cave, which served as a tomb, was only discovered during work to widen a road using a mechanical digger. Some 300 bodies were found here,[19] either stacked on top of one another or jumbled up. The presence of skeletons that are still intact, i.e., "complete" – of which there are roughly 50 – has given support to the "war layer" theory, which stipulates that the population was massacred and then buried here following this catastrophic event. Although the possibility that these deaths were the result of an epidemic has not been ruled out, the favored theory is that this entire community was brutally destroyed. There are many reasons for this, not least the fact that many bodies seem to have been placed hurriedly in the tomb or even thrown in like parcels; the tomb itself shows no sign of having being subsequently disturbed. Limbs belonging to different bodies were occasionally intermingled, which may well confirm the theory that the remains were deposited here in haste. There are also nine cases of arrows embedded in various human bones, providing another strong argument in favor of the warfare theory. Fractures to several ulna bones provide further evidence – these injuries occur at the point where the victims would be struck if trying to protect themselves with their forearms. It seems that some individuals were also struck over the head. Many arrowheads were discovered at this burial site: 55 in total, accounting for 50 percent of the lithic material discovered here. The fact that so many arrowheads were discovered here suggests that some are likely to have struck the soft tissue of their victims and were not offerings: they were discovered lying in amongst the human remains. Many were chipped, which would also seem to confirm the notion that they were used to strike a target.

Five megalithic tombs have been identified in the area immediately surrounding this site. If these tombs are all assumed to have been used during the same period, with megalithic tombs being the most common form of burial in the region at this time, then the differences between megalithic tombs and the rock shelter tomb are evident: the shelter site was found to contain many human remains, unlike the five dolmens; the latter also had specific architectural features. The shelter site seems to have been used by a different population which placed its dead in this simple, natural cave. The size of the cave was perhaps such that no further organization of the site was required.

Analysis of the evidence has not disproved the notion that this was a "catastrophe tomb," i.e., a sort of communal grave which would have been filled quickly following some kind of drama involving widespread killing. Those in favor of this theory back up their viewpoint with logical argumentation.

However, the discovery of this cave tomb immediately raised the question of when these 300 bodies were actually placed here. It is hard to imagine how such a large number of people could have disappeared all at the same time from a small Neolithic agricultural community; such communities rarely totaled more than 100 to 200 members each. Although there is no doubt that certain individuals were killed at the site and died a violent death, it still seems unlikely that an entire population would have been massacred and buried at the same time: such killings normally leave more brutal signs of damage upon the victims, such as the Talheim injuries.

The bodies which show definite signs of fatal injury are exclusively male. Furthermore, although five out of the eight cases of injuries were probably fatal, this still means that, in the other three cases, the victim recovered and healed. After having survived their injuries (the duration of their survival is unknown), these three individuals were deposited at this same burial site after death. This seems to suggest that there was a lapse in time between the various remains being placed here, which directly contradicts the theory of all-out massacre, unless these individuals already bore the scars of previous injuries on the day of the catastrophe.[20] Studies of the human remains deposited here have revealed that this tomb was, at times, emptied; bodies were removed and skulls stacked up together, all of which are features character-istic of a tomb used and managed over a long period of time.

Radiocarbon dating, in particular, has pointed to the long-term usage of this collective tomb. Ten datings revealed a range of dates spanning more or less 1,000 years, from 3800 to 2800 BCE.[21] Thus, it seems likely that this natural cave was used over a long period of time with bodies being placed here one by one, not *en masse*. It is not impossible that certain tragic circum-stances occasionally led to a number of bodies being deposited here at once. There were probably many reasons for such group burials – warfare or confrontation, perhaps.

Ballistic Accuracy

At the San Juan Ante Portam Latinam site, nine individuals are known to have been struck by projectiles (the majority of whom most likely died as a result) (figure 40). Eight were studied as part of a fascinating ballistic analysis.[22] The location of each of the wounds can be described as follows:

- arrow lodged in the interior of the hip (right coxal bone); the projectile most likely struck the individual from behind, directed upwards and from left to right;
- arrowhead embedded in the central section of the first lumbar vertebra; the arrow struck the individual in the right side on a slightly ascending trajectory;
- arrow lodged in the edge the ilium crest, having been fired upwards, from left to right;
- arrowhead embedded in an intercostal space of the right hemithorax; the individual did not survive, having been struck in the lung; he was struck from behind, the arrow being fired from right to left;
- arrow lodged in the left shoulder blade at a right angle, having been fired on an ascending trajectory;
- arrowhead planted in the lower part of the skull (occipital bone); the projectile was fired from behind, from left to right and on a slightly ascending trajectory; the individual survived with the point becoming encysted in the healed bone;
- arrow lodged in one of the dorsal vertebrae, having passed through the right hemithorax; the arrow struck from front to back and from right to left; death would have been quick;
- arrowhead embedded in the arm (right radius); the healing of the bone also affected the adjacent ulna.

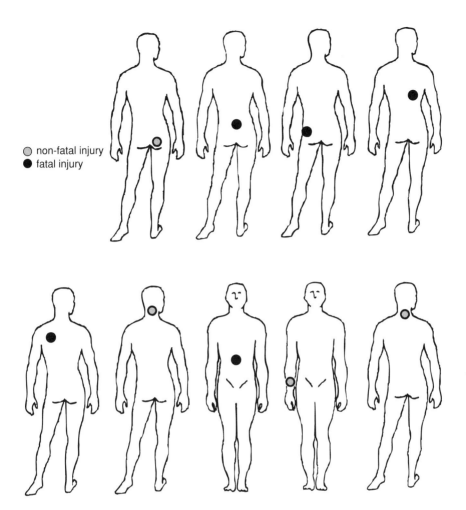

Figure 40 San Juan Ante Portam Latinam ossuary in Laguardia (Alava, Spain). Diagrams show the location of arrow wounds to the nine bodies placed here. After Vegas.

There are also several more doubtful cases of injury, such as arrows found in skulls and an arrow propped against the cervical vertebrae of an individual struck on the hip.

The fact that so many arrows were found embedded in various parts of the body seems to rule out the theory that these injuries were the result of hunting accidents. Except in a few rare cases, these individuals were struck from behind and were almost certainly fired at by archers who were crouched or bent down. The arrows, fired upwards, may well have hit individuals as they tried to flee. Although the tomb contained the bodies of men, women, and children, it seems that only the adult males were struck by the arrows, a sign perhaps of brutal confrontations having taken place between communities. It should also be noted that many arrows were discovered in this tomb, as is often the case when a tomb contains many bodies: were these personal items, placed in the tomb with their owners, or arrowheads that were once embedded in the flesh of some of the bodies? Equally interesting is the Longar hypogeum (Navarre, Spain): four injuries, of which three were fatal, were identified among the 112 bodies counted.

For the time being, these are the only known examples from the Iberian Peninsula. Cases from the Neolithic are rare. Two examples will be discussed here of individuals being struck and killed by projectiles in around 4000/3500 BCE (i.e., earlier than the cases from the Basque burial site). These cases are from a culture of "grave burials" specific to the Barcelona region. The first case concerns the Bovila Madurell burial site in Sant Quirze del Vallès. Here, a grave was found to contain two bodies still intact, yet with skulls smashed. An arrowhead was lodged in a lumbar vertebra of one of the two individuals.[23] This arrow passed through the abdomen, causing death. The second example is from the Can Grau burial site in La Roca del Vallès. Here, a well was found to lead into a subcircular burial chamber. Two bodies were contained in this tomb, placed on their backs and accompanied by a small number of items. The end of a flint point was lodged in the arch of a dorsal vertebra belonging to one of the individuals.[24] This wound seems to have healed over, indicating that death occurred some time after the accident.

The other cases are all more recent and date from the period spanning the end of the Neolithic to the beginning of the Bronze Age: a flint arrowhead lodged in the condyle of a femur from the Las Cascaras cave (Cantabres); a metal arrow in the left occipital area of a body found in the Collet Sú dolmen (Lerida); a bronze arrow embedded in the left of the jawbone belonging to an individual at the Arboli cave H (Tarragona). In the collective tomb in Atalayuela close to Logroño (Navarre), dating from the Beaker culture, a stemmed arrowhead with "ailerons" was found embedded in the back of a skull. Injuries have also been identified at other tomb sites: Cueva de las Cabras (Burgos), Cartuja de les Fuentes, Venta del Griso (Ebre basin), Les Llometes (Alcoy), Cueva del Barranco de la Higuera (Baños), and Valencia de la Concepción (Seville).

All of the examples discussed in this chapter taken from France and Spain concern archeological evidence of either conflict or killings throughout the Neolithic; cases from the most recent stages of this era (fourth to third millennia BCE) are slightly more common. However, this evidence provides no indication of the reasons for or climate underlying these collective confrontations and isolated acts of violence. These general theories concerning Neolithic and Copper Age society must, therefore, be developed further in order that these events can be placed within the context of the period.

Chapter 4

The Warrior: An Ideological Construction

The increase in violent activity that characterized the Neolithic in the West, as confirmed by the archeological evidence discussed thus far, can only be explained through a more detailed examination of the social organization of the day.

Analyzing the content of the large collective tombs (megalithic funeral chambers, hypogea, cave tombs) has proved useful. The items found in these tombs have one thing in common, whether they were placed here to accompany the individual in death or as offerings dedicated to the ancestral community thought to reside here: they provide an insight into the ideological makeup of the community in question. Indeed, the aesthetic quality of these objects, the rare and exotic nature of the materials used, and the highly skilled work and length of time that went into their manufacture reveal that these were status-enhancing products. The items, found lying among human remains, often included "luxury" or "cultural" ceramics, jewels varying in quality and found in far greater quantity here than elsewhere, and weapons – most notably arrowheads and daggers. Yet few elements in the tombs were indicative of day-to-day life or the substance of daily work, despite these being farming societies, deriving their food from agriculture and stockbreeding. Instead the emphasis was placed upon social standing, distinctions, and appearances. Of these items, the weapons – both hunting and war weapons – were always placed in a prime position. They served to glorify those activities involving strength, dexterity, and danger that would have enabled an individual to gain prestige and social standing. It seems to be those activities that were not economically profitable in terms of food which indicated the status of individuals. At this time hunting, although carried out everywhere, was generally only a secondary economic activity, except in a few specific areas. However, hunting played a strong social role. Warfare (or physical confrontation) was a means of seizing produce and land, although as a method it was rarely in continual use and was therefore only a minor activity in terms of assuring subsistence. In other words, in these agricultural societies the symbolic value of the wild existence (hunting) or the abnormal (warfare) took precedence, ideologically speaking, over domestic life and daily routine. For this reason, the distinction between weapons and tools is ambiguous: axes can be used to chop wood but also to attack a potential enemy; arrows may be fired at stags and wild boar but could also be targeted at humans. Displaying or wielding these arms/weapons would undoubtedly have allowed individuals to assert their personality and establish their status as individuals. On a more general level, these instruments provided a means of defining and positively identifying the masculine domain in contrast to the female domain. These points all require further investigation.

The Importance of the Male

As has already been discussed, during the fourth and third millennia BCE when hunting as an economic activity was fast losing ground to agriculture and stockbreeding, the symbolic power of weapons (both for hunting and fighting) continued to increase. They became important social markers. Three weapons played an essential part: the bow and quiver of arrows, the dagger, and the axe. This tripartite bow/dagger/axe combination formed the basis and visible expression of the symbolic masculine domain. A few examples will serve to illustrate this point.

As discussed earlier, one individual dating from 3200 BCE died while attempting to cross the Similaun pass in the Tyrol Alps, his body becoming buried beneath the snow and then embedded within the ice. It is entirely possible that this unfortunate victim did not perish from the cold, as has long been thought, but died as a result of violence inflicted by people pursuing him. Recent X-rays have revealed the tip of an arrow to be lodged in his left shoulder. Whatever the case, these mummified remains were discovered in 1991. The warm clothes the individual had worn to venture into the mountains were preserved. Of particular interest from an archeological perspective are the tools the individual was carrying in order to obtain food and to defend himself in the event of a dangerous encounter with other humans or animals. His yew-wood bow and quiver containing viburnum arrows are prime examples. These arrows were unfinished, though could presumably have been rendered useable in no time at all, if the need arose. "Ötzi," as the media nicknamed him, was also carrying a flint dagger or knife and an axe with a copper blade.[1] These are the main items a man would have required in going about his daily activities. On a more symbolic level, they also defined an individual's attributions and domain, whether they were tools used to enhance force and skill or weapons for hunting and fighting. It should be noted that these artifacts served different purposes in different situations, sometimes being used to obtain food and manage vegetation, animals, and minerals, and at other times being employed in attack or defense in the event of danger. At the same time, they also served as emblems, defining the male domain and prerogatives, perhaps even its monopoly, within the framework of hunting, confrontation, and other such energetic endeavors.

Male preeminence first became established throughout the majority of areas in the West toward the end of the Neolithic, as techniques became more specialized. Indeed, ever since Paleolithic times, weapons of bloodshed were used by men only, with women being excluded. By contrast, women have generally been attributed the role of managing the vegetation: during the Paleolithic this involved gathering vegetation, whereas during the Neolithic it required cultivating, harvesting, and tending to cereals and other domestic plants. Women were also responsible for making ceramics, basketwork, and weaving: in fact, all activities concerning the inside of the house. It could be argued, with reference to certain myths, that the women of the Amazon were involved in fighting and even used bows, which, if true, would disprove this theory. This is, however, purely fictional. In fact, even in this legend these courageous women were forced to have one breast removed, i.e., to become more masculine, in order to fire their projectiles.

As various ethnographic examples indicate, the dichotomy between masculine and feminine "functions" has never been so rigidly defined. Although everything is dependent upon the time and the culture in question, the trend is nevertheless valid on a global scale. During the course of the fourth millennium BCE, the swing plow became more widely used in the fields. This device had to be towed and thus required a certain degree of physical strength. This enabled men to lay greater claim to this domain – cultivated land – where they had previously played a lesser role, except for carrying out deforestation and working the soil. If the hoe also remained in use, women would have had to share this economic sector which was previously their own. Over time, the gradual refinement of craftsmanship and specialized techniques would have limited, if not reduced, the economic and symbolic role of women. Metallurgy, the invention of the potter's wheel (in the East), and later the transition from the sickle to the scythe in harvesting are developments which all, in turn, enhanced male supremacy. Copper metallurgy provided a means of producing tools for men (axes, daggers) – the new metal served the male domain. However, jewelry too was often made from these precious metals and served to increase the social standing of both the male and female elite. Thus, this first metal led to segregation: on the one hand, it increased the number of male activities, whilst on the other it denoted differences in status between the privileged minority and the rest of the group. The new technique was a catalyst for social division.

It is hardly surprising, therefore, that iconography from this so-called "Copper Age" or "Chalcolithic," characterized in the West by the first instances of metalworking, reflects a global increase in masculine and even war-related symbols. The steles and menhir-statues discovered in the area from the Lower Danube to the Iberian Peninsula frequently represent this ideology. Depictions of the human form showing particular anatomical features or attributes have often made it possible to identify gender (figure 41).[2] Female figures tend to have breasts and may also be wearing jewelry, in particular a necklace. Male figures usually bear weapons: a bow, arrows, an axe, and, more often than not,

Figure 41 Menhir-statues from Lunigiana (Italy): (1) Ponteveccio; (2) Moncigoli. On the left is a statue of a male (the copper dagger denotes the male sex). On the right is a statue of a female (breasts denote the female sex). After Anati, 1979.

a dagger which symbolizes male duties. These figures are occasionally endowed with items of symbolic value or signs of transcendence, in particular with what appears to be a crook or triangular "object" with a rounded plate or loop at one end. These are imaginary items that denote the exceptional status (i.e., outside of the material and day-to-day world) of those represented: gods, heroes, and ancestors. Interestingly, the genitalia are never featured and thus cannot be used to determine the gender of these figures. Instead, a contrast illustrates the distinction. Females are characterized by their breasts, i.e., by anatomical and biological features. Weapons identify males. Thus, natural characteristics represent females and cultural innovations represent males. This distinction is far from accidental: the sculptors of these objects have cast women in a nurturing role and have associated men with technical innovations (weapons, metals), control, and physical and moral domination. This artwork served as an ideological vector and reveals certain divisions in social behavior.

Accompanying a Man in Death

The Copper Age in Italy has provided several significant examples of man being "equipped" with weapons and holding a superior social status. One particular example is the tomb of the "widow" discovered in Ponte San Pietro close to Viterbo. This tomb is from the Rinaldone culture, which dates from 3200 to 2500 BCE in Tuscany and Latium. The period was characterized by the development of copperworking, using minerals extracted from the Colline Metallifere (Metalliferous Hills) in early attempts at mining. There is little evidence of settlement. Most of the evidence available is from burial sites. Tombs were generally cut into the rock (hypogea) forming small burial chambers. These usually contained the remains of several individuals. The items placed in these graves to accompany the deceased were often of high quality: metal daggers and halberds, flat axes or axes with slightly raised edges, polished flasks made of baked earth, maces fashioned from polished stone which would originally have been attached to a handle for easier control, prestige axes made of stone with a vertical handle often called "battle axes," and so forth. The highly technical nature of these innovations as well as their supposed role has sparked a mass of (largely speculation-based) literature about the Rinaldone culture, which is perceived to have been a patriarchal and aristocratic society combining animal husbandry and warfare. This explains why these populations have often been categorized as Indo-European, since they seem to share many distinctive features of this category.

However, it is the "widow's tomb" which casts most light upon the rituals of the Rinaldone people (figure 42).[3] In this tomb, carved into the tufa, an

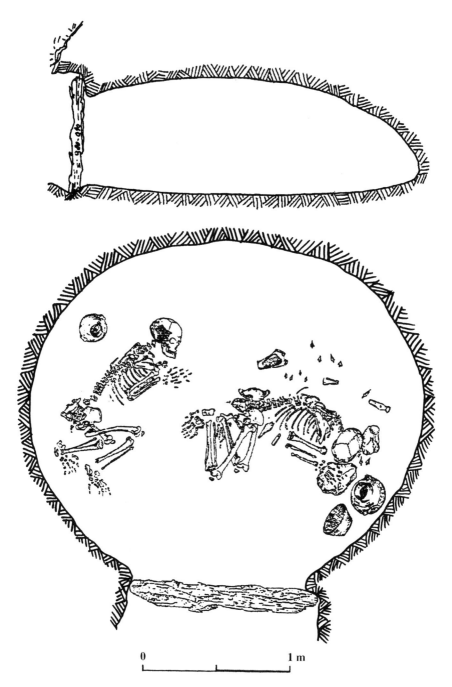

Figure 42 Ponte San Pietro hypogeum, Ischia di Castro, near Viterbo (Italy). Cross-section and plan. Double burial containing a male along with numerous funerary items and a female with a broken skull, thought to have been sacrificed. After Cardini, in Miari, 1994.

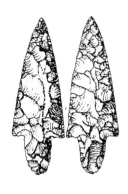

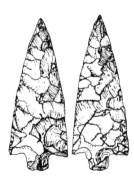

adult male of roughly 30 years old was found lying in the center. His head had been smeared with ocher as if to further his regenerative energy. His bowl and drinking goblet had been placed next to him. His weapons, too, were present: a copper-bladed dagger, 15 arrowheads in a case made from stag antler, possibly a bow, though this no longer remains, a battle axe made from polished stone, and a metal-bladed axe. The body of a young female with a broken skull was found buried at his feet, as if to leave as much space as possible for the man and his notable belongings. This female was certainly not of low social standing: a copper awl and three pendants made of antimony denote her status. However, she was sacrificed when her "master" died in order to accompany him in his new life. If this double burial does indeed reflect a "patriarchal" ideology, this analysis can be taken one step further. While the male has been buried with two containers, the female only has a simple bottle. However, it is the range of weapons and quality of materials used that really emphasizes this difference in status and the superior ranking of the male. The tripartite combination of a quiver of arrows, a copper-bladed dagger, and axes is again present. This male even had two axes: a copper axe "classic" of this period and a highly sophisticated stone axe, which would have fulfilled more of a ceremonial function. This warrior was certainly an important figure given that he was buried with those items that represent his masculinity and denote his status and social function: his weapons. His companion, sacrificed to her master, was remarkably lacking in such items. Her awl and three items of jewelry were used respectively in a domestic role and for seduction purposes.

A similar burial of a "leader" or notable person dating from the same period was identified at a site in Tursi, close to Matera in Southern Italy (figure 43). At a time when collective tombs in the form of hypogea were in widespread use, this individual was placed in a coffin made from thick flagstones of conglomerate rock. Food containers accompanied him in his grave: two pots, a bowl, and a goblet. The body was also decorated with a necklace strung with almost 300 brown steatite beads. His status is reflected partly by his weapons – a copper dagger and a quiver containing eight arrows with impeccably carved flint arrowheads – as well as by a kind of scepter sculpted from sandstone, 40 cm in length and with a loop at one end. No battle axe was present. Instead, he was accompanied by this ceremonial scepter-like object, which in outline rather resembles the mysterious "objects" depicted on the menhir-statues in France, except that these "objects" were smaller in size. However, the sculptors of the fourth and third millennia BCE did not always recreate proportions accurately.

The social standing of certain individuals is thus reflected by their items of prestige (scepters, "battle axes") as well as by their weapons, with metal beginning to be favored over high-quality flint. All of these elements are featured upon the menhir-statues.

Figure 43 Tursi tomb in Matera (Italy). This Copper Age tomb was found to contain several items: flint arrowheads, a "scepter" (40 cm in length), and decorated pottery. After Cremonesi, 1976.

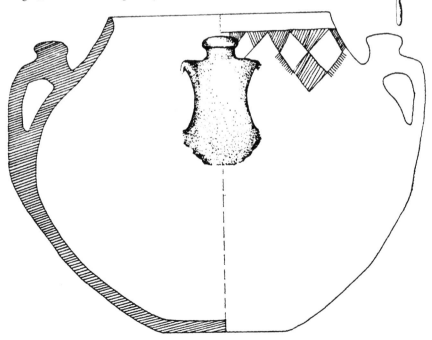

The tombs of these "warriors" and representations of the ancestors and heroes correspond perfectly; these skillful creations and symbolic images both reflect the exact same ideology.

This theory is confirmed by other examples from Europe dating from the third millennium BCE. The Corded Ware culture, which was widespread throughout Central and Northern Europe between 3000 and 2500 BCE, is characterized by individual burials in barrow tombs. The bodies were buried in a flexed position lying east/west. Males were placed on their right sides and females on their left. Males were also buried with a goblet, a perforated battle axe, a flint-bladed dagger, and arrows (figures 44 and 45). This mirroring of the world of the living was also a feature of burials from the Beaker culture, dating from 2500 BCE. In the middle regions of Europe, where this

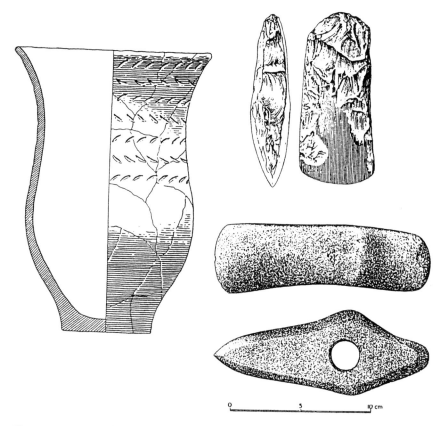

Figure 44 Steenwijkerwold in Steenwijk (Netherlands). Items found in a tomb dating from the Corded Ware culture, ca. 2600 BCE: a goblet, a small flint axe, and a "battle axe." A tertiary flint dagger has also been linked to these finds (see figure 45). After Waterbolk and Glasbergen, 1957.

culture flourished, a similar contrast between those tombs containing males and those containing females has been noted. The status of males was denoted by arrows (and undoubtedly also bows), perforated blocks of stone thought to have been used by archers as armguards, and above all by a copper-bladed dagger placed in the tombs. The tombs of females were found to contain jewelry, buttons perforated in a V-pattern, and other items associated with textiles (spindle whorls, awls). In some cases, daggers were also found in the tombs of females: does this indicate that these women had "masculine" responsibilities? Were they heroines? Whatever the case, it seems that women were not necessarily excluded from the dominant class.

A Full Quiver: For Hunting, for Fighting, or for Show

The role of the bow in Neolithic warfare has already been discussed. Fighting upon the plateaus and in the gorges of the Spanish Levant was performed almost exclusively by archers. In France, those who were injured or killed during the Final Neolithic and buried in collective tombs were found to have been struck by arrows fired with a bow. This weapon, along with a quiver of arrows ready for use, would have been an essential possession of these early farmers.

Throughout the Neolithic, arrows with sharp, cutting arrowheads were the most common type, although piercing points were also used at times; these differ in terms of their morphology and technique. As of 3500 BCE, there was a reversal of this trend, whether this was rapid or gradual. Piercing arrowheads became increasingly common and more varied and are now typically associated with archeological finds from this era. However, somewhat confusingly, hunting began to play a lesser role as a source of food at this time. There may be one of three explanations for this: (1) hunting may have continued to be an important symbolic activity; (2) the defense of a site, territory, or kinship group may have remained an underlying concern due to increasing levels of competition, which may have sparked conflict; (3) individuals may have equipped themselves with weapons in order to affirm their personality and social standing. This last point may well explain why so many arrows were discovered in tombs along with their owners. Knives and axes, which served a more practical purpose, may have been carried for the same reason.

Although these various explanations do not exclude other possibilities, they do highlight certain significant points: the confirmation of an individual's status, an increase in the group's sense of identity, and the more widespread

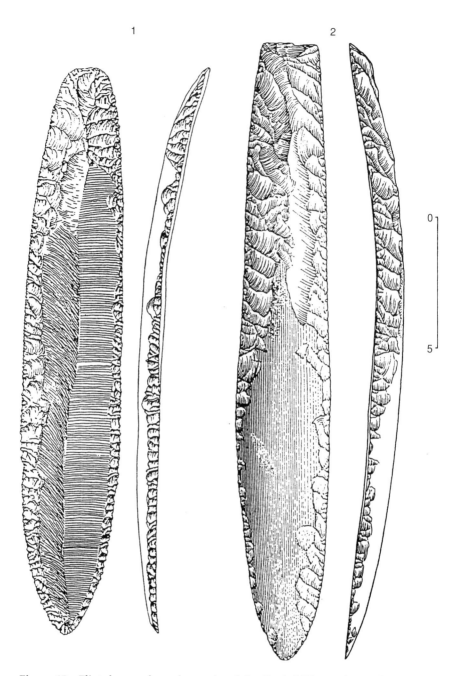

Figure 45 Flint daggers from the tombs of the Corded Ware culture of
Northwestern Europe. (1) Steenwijkerwold in Steenwijk (Overrijssel, Netherlands),
after Waterbolk and Glasbergen. (2) Galgwandenveen III in Eext (Netherlands),
flint from the French site of Grand-Pressigny, after Vlaeminck, 1997. (3) Spahn
(Emsland, Niedersachsen, Germany), flint from the French site of Grand-Pressigny,
after Vlaeminck, 1997.

3

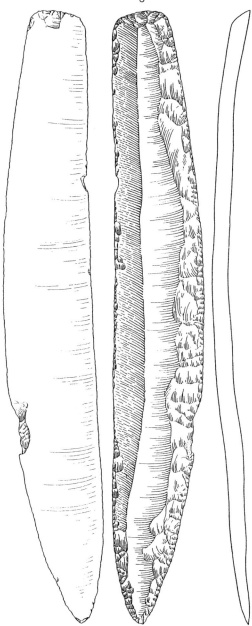

Figure 45 (*cont'd*)

use and social role of the more technical objects. In terms of resourcefulness, this period seems to have combined tradition with innovation. The bow was not a new invention at this time; it had been in use from the end of the Upper Paleolithic, if not earlier. As has already been discussed, the bow also played a sustaining role in the last hunting and fishing societies of Northern Europe. Polished stone axes were introduced by the first agricultural communities that arrived from the Near East in the seventh and sixth millennia BCE. Although blade-knives of a kind had long been in existence, the bifacial "dagger" with a leaf-shaped blade, followed by its copper equivalent, only really began to appear in the West from 3500 BCE. Piercing, bifacial arrowheads began to appear in the fifth millennium BCE. However, it is the increase in these artifacts in around 3500 BCE as well as their diversity and stylistic variation which is of interest here.

From this time onwards, skilled craftsmen produced arrows in greater numbers. Even if this remained a domestic and part-time activity, the arrowheads produced by the most skilled artisans would have required more time and effort and would therefore have been attributed greater material and social "value." In fort 1 which dominates the large-scale Los Millares site (Almeria, Spain), one room seems to have been a workshop where arrowheads were made. Here, blocks and fragments of flint derived from various sites in the region were stored, ready for use. The flint would have been heated in order to make it easier to carve using "pressure flaking." Firstly, bifacial shapes were formed which were then transformed into the final product by applying this technique. The ground was often littered with chippings from the carving process; ditches were often filled with the discarded waste. At the El Malagón site (Cullar Baza) close to Grenada, Spain, two distinct areas also seem to have been used as workshops for carving arrowheads.

These societies from the fourth and third millennia BCE maintained two stages of production: domestic and craftwork activities. The former concerned the simple process of making tools for subsistence. These tools were made quickly and easily and required no great skill. At the same time, the most skilled "flint carvers" produced items of higher quality such as arrowheads, daggers, and long blades, to be used outside the community.[4] These same skilled workers may also have crafted jewelry from various different stones as well as bones or shells to be exchanged. This production process would have been aimed at the external community; with local demands exceeded, a surplus would have built up. This would have enabled the elite to engage in exchange and to form political alliances. These "riches" were essentially intended for local networks. They served to spread, create, and even amplify social dynamics and to emphasize the social role within a system based upon gift giving and reciprocity. Demand for these objects was sustained because many arrowheads and items of jewelry were placed in tombs, along with other funerary items, as if to denote the status or personality of the deceased. Thus, some of the items produced were hoarded in these graves. As a result of these items being regularly "lost," they had to be replaced, thus fueling ongoing production by these skilled craftsmen.

Arrows and Jewels: Masculine/Feminine

Much debate has centered upon the function of these arrowheads. Were they used primarily in hunting or even warfare, or were they merely used for social display, ritual, or symbolic purposes? It is highly likely that the more aesthetic arrowheads, which are far rarer, would not have played a "functional" role like the large axes of the fifth millennium BCE. The superior value of these arrowheads is reflected in the quality and coloring of the materials used, the skill and dexterity that went into their production, and their perfectly carved shape. Once ready for use, arrows could also be distinguished by the evenness of the arrow shaft and color of the feathering: whether these items symbolized prestige or served to draw attention to their owner, they were eventually placed along with the body in both individual and collective tombs. Egyptian daggers from the fourth millennium BCE were also buried in this way. The daggers have impeccably carved blades and sculpted ivory handles. These ceremonial objects served to draw attention to prominent figures and perhaps also to maintain their memory and enhance their standing after death.

However, prestige and symbolism are not the only explanations. There are many ethnographic examples which demonstrate the functional role of such objects, for example, in hunting and possibly also in conflict. Certain regions of France experienced an increase in hunting toward the end of the Neolithic, in particular the less-populated and densely forested areas of the lakes in the plateau regions of the Jura and along the Cévennes side of the Massif Central. Hunting trophies (pierced canine teeth from wild boar or carnivores, pendants made from stag antler) have been discovered as well as many carved arrows. Meat obtained from the natural stock of fauna may still have been a significant food source at this time.

Although the consumption of wild animals subsequently fell, the minor role of hunting as a source of food did not necessarily reflect a decline in the social role of hunting. A similar situation could be said to exist in many villages in France today, although with some obvious differences: hunting is a valued pastime, especially among men, but plays only a very minor role as a source of food.

The role of arrowheads is documented in many ethnographic examples. One study of the Dani of Irian Jaya (Indonesia), for example – a group that cultivates sweet potatoes, sugar cane, bananas, and taro as well as keeping pigs – revealed that these populations distinguish between those arrows used in hunting and those used in warfare.[5] Furthermore, bows and arrows are often passed from one community to another. The arrowheads used in hunting are made quickly and tend to inflict large, deep wounds. Those used in warfare are much more sophisticated. These arrows can be fired accurately from a long distance and are capable of inflicting deep wounds. The arrowheads are tipped with bone, ensuring that the tip stays in the wound so as to continue poisoning the victim. Similarly, spiraled orchid fibers are attached to the tip of the arrow. These fibers penetrate the flesh and remain within the wound in order to prevent healing. Anyone struck by these arrows tends to die several days later, rather than dying on the spot. In short, the Dani go to greater lengths to kill than to hunt.

In one village of New Guinea situated in a primary forest at an altitude of 800 m, i.e., in an area with a very low population density, conflict takes the form of skirmishes and ambush attacks. By contrast, in another village in New Guinea, marked levels of social competition are evident. This village is located in an area of savannah and secondary forest at an altitude of 1,600 m where agriculture is highly developed and hunting plays a lesser role. Here, the quest for prestige is a powerful driving force. The various villages are organized into confederations with battles commonly occurring along the borders between communities. Heider details these disorganized battles with their lack of strategic planning. They tend to take the form of a series of duels in which two enemies face and attack each other using a bow or spear (see plate 3, p. 21).[6]

Two models can be identified here. In densely forested areas with a low population, hunting and conflict are both common. In the more cultivated savannah regions where populations are larger, war is frequent. Pètrequin and Pètrequin conclude that demographic pressure, sedentary lifestyles, and greater control of the natural environment have led to warfare taking precedence over hunting.

It is tempting to compare this situation to the Neolithic in the West. Initially, hunting played a large part in these primarily mobile societies. However, during the course of the fourth millennium BCE, a more sedentary lifestyle was adopted and the environment was opened up to greater exploitation. In turn competition, both internal and external, became a more important feature.[7] The increased number of arrow types as well as their increasingly widespread use could be the result of several different factors: an increase in population, social competition, transformation of the environment, and greater value being attached to items of prestige. The transition from the flint dagger to the copper blade was probably the result of the quest for quality weapons made from exotic materials or from metal, products of an innovative technological development (figures 46 and 47). Competition often resulted in new weapons being produced. At one time, skillfully carved honey flint daggers were commonly made in Grand-Pressigny, France. Their popularity began to fade as soon as red copper daggers appeared on the scene. It is important to note that objects used in hunting and warfare benefited from these technical developments far more than any other tools.

However, the very existence of two distinct sets of items – weapons and jewelry – is the relevant factor here, more so than the debate surrounding their functional or symbolic role, discussed initially. Both handcrafted objects and items placed in tombs point to the existence of two domains; this phenomenon is also reflected in the menhir-statues of the period. Weapons denote the masculine sphere, whilst jewelry represents the feminine sphere. The subsequent increase in the number of potential weapons emphasizes the image of the hunter or warrior, even though confrontation remained a very sporadic and temporary activity.

Menhir-Statues: The First Armed Steles

It is time to turn our attention again to the iconography of the menhir-statues from the Western Mediterranean. The regions that compose this vast area (Adige, Lunigiana, Aosta, Sion, Sardinia, Southern France, the Iberian Peninsula) certainly do not form a homogeneous whole. A common denominator is the fact that most of the statues of male figures are depicted carrying a copper dagger. However, the most significant group of menhir-statues, concentrated in and around the southern limestone regions of France (Saint-Ponais, Tarn, Aveyron), do not feature such daggers. Instead, the dagger is replaced by a mysterious triangular "object": perhaps a pendant hanging from a ring or a scepter with a loop at one end? Or even an imaginary object signifying status? Bows and stone axes are featured on occasion, although they are rare. Why does this group of menhir-statues differ from the others? Menhir-statues of male figures found in France tend to be hunters (ancestors or perhaps heroes who gained their status through hunting). The environmental setting (hunting would have been an important source of food in these often wooded mountainous regions) seems to confirm this view. It is also possible that these statues tend to be older than the other groups of menhir-statues, in which figures are shown holding a triangular-bladed metal dagger with a handle and pommel at one end (Adige, Aosta,

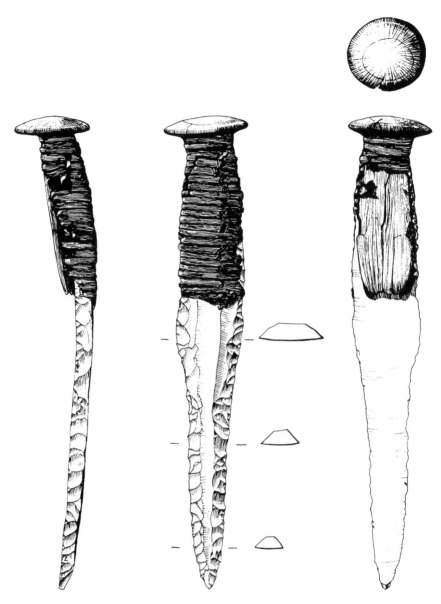

Figure 46 Charavines (Isère, France). Flint daggers from Grand-Pressigny, third millennium BCE. Dagger 1 has a hilt with a pommel at the end, attached to the flint blade by a fir twig wrapped around the hilt. Dagger 2 has a flint blade with a willow twig wrapped around one end, held in place with tar. (Length of dagger 1: 181 mm; length of dagger 2: 190 mm.) After Bocquet, 1975.

2

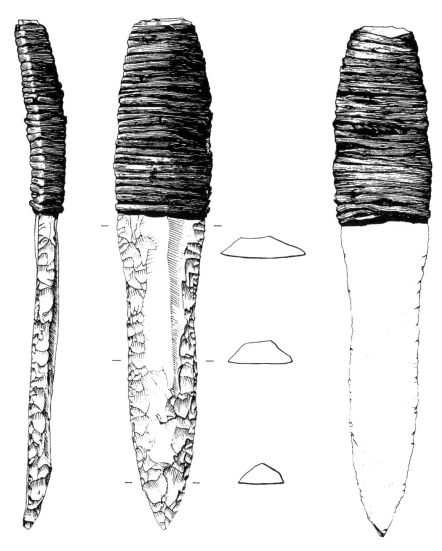

Figure 46 (*cont'd*)

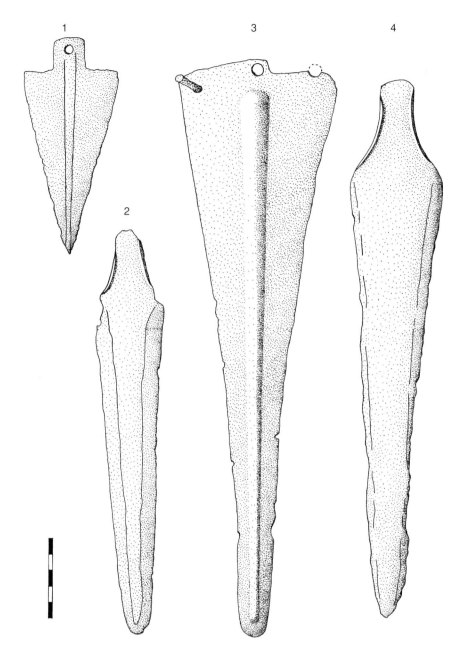

Figure 47 Copper blades from daggers and halberds, third millennium BCE: (1) Remedello burial site, Brescia (Italy); (2) Bounias, Fontvieille (Bouches-du-Rhône, France); (3) Villafranca, Verona (Italy); (4) Le Vernet (Ariège, France). 1 and 3 date from the Italian Remedello culture; 2 and 4 from the Beaker culture.

Lunigiana, Sardinia). Unlike the statues from Southern France, those statues which feature copper daggers may have been carved during the first half of the third millennium BCE by the populations of the Western Alps (Remedello, Sion) or Tuscany region, who were by then familiar with metallurgy.[8] These stone carvings are not hunters but symbolic warriors; perhaps they even symbolize the social value of certain male figures, either real or mythical (figure 48). The "male" represented by these menhir-statues is, in fact, a Bronze Age or Iron Age warrior. Why is this?

One stone sculpture discovered in Europe and dating from the third millennium BCE shows various figures carrying weapons. There may be two or more explanations for this: the spread of populations in which warfare – or at least weapons – played a significant part, or a gradual progression within Neolithic communities toward an increasingly advanced social hierarchy.

Those in favor of the invasion/migration theory point to the archeological evidence which indicates that nomadic populations from the steppe regions of Central Asia and Eastern Europe began to spread toward the West in the third millennium BCE, if not earlier.[9] Horses were widely used within these communities and were undoubtedly domesticated in

Figure 48 Lagundo (Upper Adige, Italy). "Masculine" stele. The figure is carrying nine daggers, 14 axes, and has a battle chariot pulled by oxen. After Arnal, 1976.

the fifth millennium BCE in the steppe region of the Ukraine or perhaps more to the east. These communities were patriarchal and based upon a very definite pyramidal structure. Their mobile economy was based, preferentially, upon animal husbandry. Funerary items from some burial sites in Eastern

Europe clearly reveal that elements from the steppe regions infiltrated the local Neolithic civilizations. Some claim that movements from east to west were not limited solely to forays during which pockets of settlers established themselves at the heart of the indigenous populations. These forays may well have been the first of many large-scale displacements as groups came to invade the territory of Paleolithic farming communities, bringing with them their weapons and belongings. These farming communities had previously lived without any such outside interference for some 3,000 to 4,000 years. It is claimed by some that successive waves of intruders arrived, rather like the barbarian invasions of more recent history. These intruders, often considered to have been pillagers, are thought to have put an end to the preceding centuries of prosperity by subjugating the native population and introducing a new, more rigid social organization based upon male authority. They are also thought to have introduced new vocabulary and new structures of thought. For a good century or so, these invaders were considered to be vectors of "Indo-European" idioms. With the aid of maps showing the distribution of significant archeological finds, attempts have been made to identify the progression and area of expansion associated with these cultures. Certain prehistorians have envisaged a more elaborate scenario, claiming that several waves of invasion took place between the fourth and second millennia BCE.[10] The emergence of cultures occupying a large area (the Baden culture across the entire Balkan region of Europe; the Globular Amphora culture of Northern Europe; the Corded Ware groups of Central and Northwestern Europe; even the Beaker cultures of Western Europe) has been interpreted as evidence of this rapid "Indo-Europeanization" of Europe. Other more limited Mediterranean cultures are also said to show definite signs of Euro-Asiatic influence – certain cultural features are thought to originate from the steppe regions (such as "battle axes" and crutch-shaped pins). The same can be said of Anatolia (Troy), Greece, and Italy (Remedello and Rinaldone cultures). Steles representing "warriors" are distributed from the Crimean Peninsula and Lower Danube as far as Italy, Southern France, and the Iberian Peninsula. This may be another indication that these invasions led to the spread of systems of thought.[11] Such large-scale movements may well have established the male warrior as an admired and respected individual since the warrior's authority was dependent upon the weapons he carried and displayed.

As far as the Indo-Europeanization process is concerned, we shall not endeavor to address the linguistic debate surrounding the search for the original base language. Staying within the field of archeology, it is possible that the armed male statues, which began to appear in the third millennium BCE and have been found from the Black Sea to the Atlantic Ocean, were not in any way linked to the arrival of invaders from the steppe regions. The emergence of these steles in cultures that were technologically, economically, and socially similar may equally be the result of a convergence process. Gradual, small-scale influxes are also a possibility. Within these societies, the hierarchy in place would have enabled those wishing to demonstrate their power to gain status: metal weapons would have become the new symbols of this ideology. However, it should again be noted that these were not just statues of males: females also feature, indicating that females were not excluded from decision-making or from certain influential spheres.

Another argument has been proposed that seems to cast some doubt upon the theory that there was a large-scale expansion from east to west. The argument is based upon the origin of the statues. In many regions, the statues did not make a sudden appearance. Rather, they were the end result of long-standing local tradition spanning several thousand years of the Neolithic. Seen from this perspective, the steles of the third millennium BCE may be an innovation only in terms of their depiction of metal weapons. Nevertheless, the statues seem to provide confirmation of new technological developments (the dagger and metal axe) and of a social structure in which the concept of the male warrior was becoming established. The emergence of charismatic "leaders" during the Neolithic in Europe was, therefore, not a new concept. From the fifth millennium BCE onwards, individuals of high caliber were buried in Varna, on the shores of the Black Sea, with their scepter (proof of their authority), their weapons, and a great many riches – gold jewelry, diadems, and trinkets occupied pride of place. At the other end of the continent in Armorica, powerful figures were buried in monumental burial mounds along with highly "exotic" items: a necklace with variscite beads, long ceremonial axes, and circular tablets of noble stone were discovered. Thus, high-ranking individuals were already a long-standing feature of Europe. As for the first anthropomorphic stone statues, examples have been found to date from well before the Copper Age. In Brittany (France) large steles, frequently decorated with symbols denoting masculinity (crooks/scepters, horns or ox skulls, snakes, axes) often predate dolmenic tombs. Such art forms were sometimes found adorning pillars in certain passage graves (Gavrinis, France). Some early burial monuments (Île Geignog, Finistère, France) also contain anthropomorphic steles. Human figures with a "head" were subsequently depicted in artwork within corridor dolmens (figures with an "apical rostrum") as well as being incorporated into the morphology of certain menhirs. These carved stones with their ogival morphology and often distinct "head" are notably found in Vendée, France (within the confines of Avrillé), in Switzerland (Yverdon), in the south of France, and in Malta and can all be dated to before the third millennium BCE from their archeological context. In the south of France, anthropomorphic steles were found to pre-date the classic menhir-statues, such as the Trets-type steles from Provence. Indeed, it seems likely that the vast majority of these stone-carved figures were created before the Copper Age began in full, which suggests that this was a highly technical era. Small, human-like statues upon the Iberian Peninsula, for example, at the Parxubeira site in Galicia, predate the menhir-statues. In Sardinia, some steles were found to have been created before the "double dagger" statues of the third millennium BCE. In Corsica, a long tradition of anthropomorphic stones has been identified which predates the large and armed Bronze Age statues.

There are, therefore, many examples that deserve a mention. Indeed, a long tradition in anthropomorphic menhirs has been identified in several areas where Europe's first "armed" statues flourished. However, steles and menhir-statues are often very rare, if not absent, in many of the vast areas occupied by the first communities of Southeastern Europe, if the migratory hypothesis is assumed to be correct. It is, however, possible that wooden sculptures may once have existed here.

Consequently, it is perhaps preferable to consider two possible explanations, rather than attributing the emergence of these "armed male menhir-statues" solely to populations being displaced. One factor may have been the spread of metal-making techniques, since metal enabled new and highly symbolic weapons to be made (copper daggers), thus replacing flint daggers and blades. Progressive social evolution was also a relevant factor and led to either female or male figures being created (the latter represented by their weapons). This process occurred at the heart of rural communities, aided by their century-long Neolithic tradition. In the West, weapons are highly indicative and their evolution can be traced over time: the "ceremonial" stone axe during the fifth and fourth millennia BCE, then the flint dagger, which was subsequently replaced by the copper dagger. In the second millennium BCE, the bronze dagger and later the sword in turn became the symbols of warriors and heroes.

From Mount Bego to the Italian Alps

The Rupestrian engravings discovered in the Alpine regions (Northern Italy, Mount Bego) contain a great many motifs and symbols with masculine connotations.

The Mount Bego artwork features many ox skulls and other horned animals, a theme that symbolizes ardor and vitality (figure 49). It is the strength of the cattle, aurochs, and oxen (be they wild or domesticated), and not their economic value, which sets the tone in these images. Weapons, and in

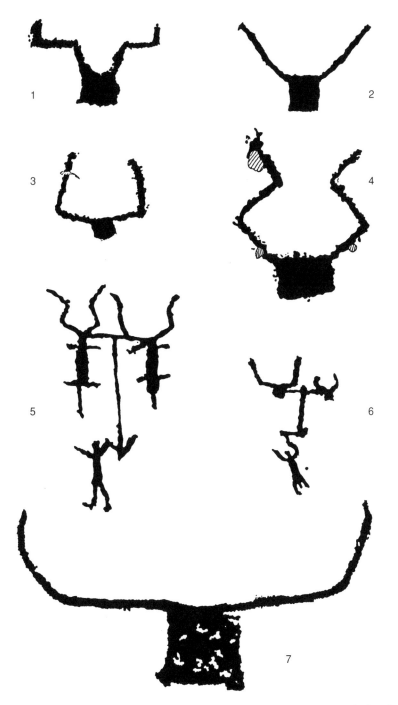

Figure 49 Mount Bego (Tende, Alpes-Maritimes, France). Engravings: skulls of oxen or other horned animals (1 to 4, 7); plowing scenes (5, 6). After de Lumley.

particular metal daggers, were found on Mount Bego and are thought to date from the Copper Age to the beginning of the Bronze Age (from 2800 to 1800 BCE). It was during this period of time more than any other that daggers made of flint, then copper, and then bronze became the male objects *par excellence* and served to establish an individual's "citizenship" (figure 50). Again, the swing plow is depicted in certain scenes. This piece of machinery was primarily towed by men: the male genitalia of the workers are clearly depicted in several of the Mount Bego images. The scenes also feature certain enclosures or areas divided into sections, which are more difficult to interpret; they are generally thought to represent fields or small parcels of land. With the aid of the swing plow, humans were able to mark their presence in these areas.

The overriding theme in these scenes is male superiority, as indicated by the various symbolic images discussed here. Women are absent. Even one supposedly female figure who has adopted an "orant" pose has been depicted with two horns emerging from her head. Thus, even this individual is part male and takes the form of a hybrid – part human, part bull.

The site itself is distant, raised, and difficult to reach and seems to have been selected for its remote location. Many theories have sought to interpret the Mount Bego site: the most common is the theory that this was a place of "bull worship" associated with divine powers.[12] A less extreme possibility is that this mountainous region was a place for initiation rituals in which men alone participated. These may have been "rites of passage" marking either entry into a different age group, acquisition of a superior social status, or integration into a particular social group. Mountains have always been the exclusive domain of males, usually hunters or shepherds. Here, in these remote areas hidden among the mountain summits and far away from the world below, knowledge would have been exchanged during the course of these ceremonious and often mysterious rituals. It is no coincidence that these practices took place in a "wild" environment, away from areas tamed and domesticated by human intervention. Exceptional settings would have been selected for exceptional events. These locations were reserved solely for the use of men; women would have been kept at a distance, in the same way as they were distanced from weapons.

On Mount Bego, these ceremonies may have been recorded in a "written" documentation of each event: "signs" of masculinity such as daggers and ox skulls were carved into the rock. Upon entering into the adult world, individuals may have been permitted to carry weapons or may perhaps, according to another theory, have been admitted into a closed group with a strict set of rules. Carrying a dagger certainly formed part of male behavior during the Copper Age. The dagger symbolized an individual's status, character, and

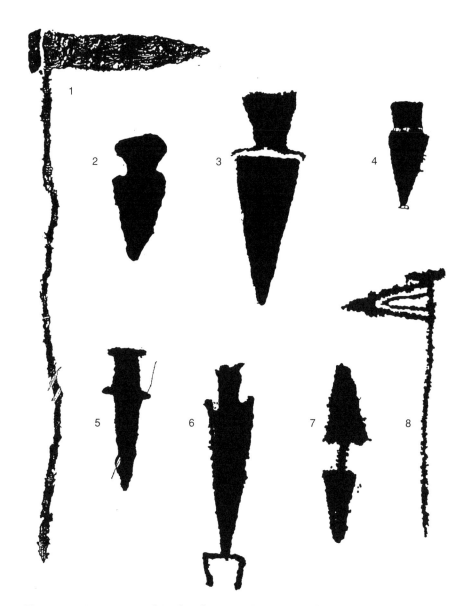

Figure 50 Mount Bego (Tende, Alpes-Maritimes, France). Engravings: halberds (1, 8) and metal daggers (2 to 7). After de Lumley.

even the respect owed to him and was often buried with its owner in the tomb. Flint daggers from Grand-Pressigny in France and other such noteworthy villages also fulfilled this role; manufactured during the third millennium BCE, they were buried in individual tombs in Northwestern Europe to accompany the dead of the Corded Ware culture. Flint and copper daggers fulfilled this same function among Copper Age populations in Italy (Remedello, Rinaldone). The daggers commonly carried by males in the Beaker culture may also have held this same symbolic significance. As far as Mount Bego is concerned, this explanation certainly does not rule out other possibilities. Indeed, several interpretations may be simultaneously applicable. These sites can all be seen as open-air sanctuaries. Our hypothesis is plausible in that it accounts for the repetition of many of the same signs, such as the bull's head and the dagger, at various different locations.

The overall aim may have been to use ritual as a means of giving concrete expression to an increase in social standing (a "rise in rank") awarded to certain individuals. It is not known for certain whether the individuals involved were specially selected or whether all members of a community or indeed members of several surrounding localities participated. It is largely irrelevant to this discussion whether these ceremonies, directed by "leaders" or "priests," were restricted solely to adolescents, adults, or even individuals of exceptional standing, such as warriors or hunters. The aim would have been to give prominence to specific male activities: an individual's ability to defend himself, the possibility of fighting and challenging one another with the aid of weapons, and the use of the swing plow to penetrate and gain control of fertile land, rather like a sexual act of fertilization. Thus, the objects that formed a part of these ceremonies were ideological rather than banal and prosaic: the dagger was not just a commonplace knife; halberds were ceremonial weapons; yokes were much more than mere objects in simple plowing scenes. These scenes would undoubtedly have acquired a certain mythical value and would have been associated with epic tales recounted to initiates.

Rupestrian engravings from the Italian Alps give the same impression. As has already been discussed, metal weapons are featured upon male statues from Lunigiana, Aosta, and Upper Adige from the third millennium BCE. In some cases, the figure is shown holding a whole range of weapons in place of a dagger. This accumulation of weapons may indicate that the "character" or individual represented was of superior status (figure 51). One particularly striking example is the stele statue from Arco I (Trento, Italy) that shows the "hero" wearing a necklace and holding three halberds, three axes, seven daggers, and an object which resembles a battle axe (plate 22).[13] Other monuments depict the relationship between weapons and the sun. However, the spirit of this society, in which symbols of masculinity played a prominent role, is not just imprinted upon the steles. Motifs denoting masculine activities are also dotted across landscapes, in particular certain mountainous areas. Weapons – most notably daggers and halberds – feature prominently. Wild animals (stags, deer, chamois, ibices, cervidae) were also depicted on rocks and walls throughout the third millennium BCE: they are references either to ardor or to nobility. Thus, these scenes reveal that wild animals were greatly admired. Human figures, too, are occasionally glorified and scenes of ritual plowing are a prevalent theme. Despite the slight chronological and cultural differences, the importance attributed to nature/wild animals/masculinity/strength dominates the ideology featured upon the monuments and rock art.

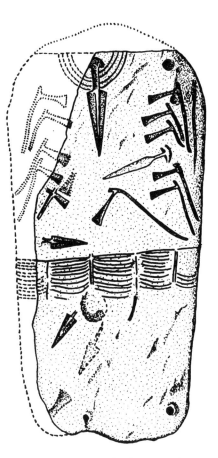

Masculinity/ Femininity: Reversing the Symbols

Figure 51 Lagundo (Upper Adige, Italy). Male statue: necklace, axes, daggers, and belt. After Arnal, 1976.

From 3500 to 2000 BCE, the male image and male domain, both real and ideological, gradually became established. The male domain contrasts structurally with the female domain, which centers upon the home, family, and reproduction. Warriors were equipped primarily with either a flint or a metal dagger, which were the most popular weapons of the era. They also carried a bow, arrows, and an axe, the latter being the legacy of a former era. However, technical innovation had made its mark: arrows were produced with a greater degree of perfection than ever before and copper axes had replaced stone blades. The archeological evidence reflects the warrior's ever-increasing status over time. Statues of male figures (Europe's first statues) are shown to be equipped with weapons. At the same time, more and more fortifications were being constructed to protect

Plate 22   Arco statue-stele (Trento, Italy). The figure is wearing a necklace and carrying seven daggers, three axes, three halberds, and a battle axe. Photo Elena Munerati, Archivo Ufficio Beni Archeologici. Provenca Autonoma di Trento.

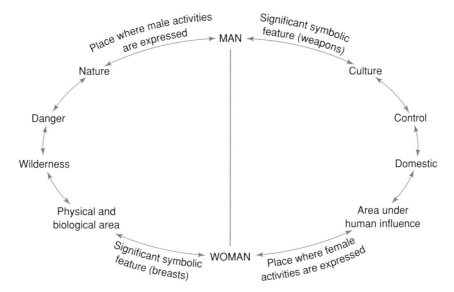

Figure 52   Diagram showing the contrast between male and female symbols. Males are denoted by cultural attributes (weapons) and occupy the "wild" domain. Females are represented by natural, biological attributes (breasts) and occupy the domestic domain.

settlements. Arrows (and thus bows as well) became more widely used than ever before. Most notably of all, symbols of masculinity began to appear in even the most remote of areas: rock engravings of weapons and stag-hunting scenes appeared upon high mountain summits and in deep forests.

However, a certain contradiction in the use of these symbols should be noted (figure 52). Whenever venturing into untamed territory or making their mark upon areas of wilderness, men always had their weapons to hand, i.e., relatively sophisticated technical innovations in the form of cultural artifacts. Weapons aided man's taming of nature, with specific symbols representing man himself.

Conversely, women were valued for their biological role: the female menhir-statues focus primarily upon anatomy, in particular the breasts, which are a symbol of maternal and nurturing behavior. Due to their reproductive and nurturing role, women have always been associated with nature. Since the beginning of the Neolithic or perhaps even earlier, their favored domain has been the home, dwelling place, and fields, i.e., areas that have been greatly influenced by human activity and transformed by society – in short, the most cultural domains. The contrast between the male and female domains reached its limit at this point in time though continued to exist for a long time afterwards. With the aid of cultural tools, men were able to gain control of those areas less influenced by human activity, i.e., peripheral regions, forests, unexplored territory, and open wilderness where they were able to freely express their masculinity and accomplishments. Women, on the other hand, were defined primarily by their natural and spontaneous role and were associated with the domestic sphere, a closed domain heavily influenced by human activity. A complete contrast is evident here: men either began or continued to tame areas of wilderness; women, still defined by their natural, emotional, and spontaneous roles, occupied areas more heavily dominated by human activity.

Open Villages and Fortified Settlements

Although a climate of conflict is often assumed to have existed during Neolithic and protohistoric times – an assumption based upon the existence of weapons, defended settlements, and signs of fatal injury upon human remains – very little attention has been devoted to studying the layout of villages and, in particular, the contrast between open villages and fortified sites. The use and consciousness of the territory in question as well as the concept of territoriality are relevant here.[14] It is certainly true that the "majesty" of a particular fortification can increase a site's grandeur as well as enhancing its role, importance, and status, adding value even in the eyes of the archeologist. For this reason, fortified sites have often been the focus of attention among excavators: archeologists themselves gain greater prestige by excavating defenses or fortresses than by investigating peaceful, unfortified hamlet sites. Archeology has suffered greatly as a result of this bias. By selecting certain types of settlement in this way and focusing upon their specific characteristics, theories on the overall distribution and organization of the population as well as on the complementary relationship between sites of different status have become confused and, at times, superficial.

The Southeastern Iberian Peninsula is a particularly revealing example. In this region of Europe, fortified sites dating from the third and end of the fourth millennium BCE were identified early on. It was initially thought that these sites, which are protected by solid walls flanked by semicircular bastions, were built by engineers from the Aegean region where similar lines of defense are commonly found.[15] Later, these fortified sites were thought to have been constructed by local workers: the increase in population that occurred here during early agricultural times may have led communities to defend themselves, perhaps developing specific architectural features for this purpose

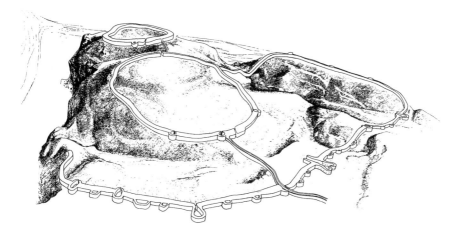

Figure 53 Los Millares (Santa Fe de Mondujar, Almeira, Spain). Sketch of the site's fortifications during phase 2b. Enclosed area, ca. 7 hectares. Courtesy of F. Molina.

(figure 53).[16] Thus, another explanation was proposed, replacing the theory that external influences (migratory movements or invasions) were responsible. Instead, it was suggested that the indigenous society evolved over time, resulting in gradual changes being made at a social and material level: these changes were reflected in the layout of the site, the status of settlements relative to one another, social hierarchies, and the construction of important, fortified sites. This evolutionary process may have taken several forms. Two criteria seem to have played an important part: population density on the one hand and, on the other, the local geography and, in particular, the relative proportions of plains and mountains. In both cases, access to local resources (water, land, raw materials) would have been a crucial factor. In the more remote regions where groups lived a more isolated existence, population densities remained low and there were few grounds for conflict. Local resources could be exploited by several communities at a time without any great degree of competition arising between them. It is even possible that groups may have regularly cooperated with one another on certain occasions. Here, there was no need for sites to be defended or protected.

By contrast, the more exposed areas (valleys, plains, heavily used tracks, highly sought-after land where sediments are deposited) were characterized by greater levels of competition with proximity to water, arable land, river confluences, and raised areas determining which land was suitable for agriculture. In these areas, population density increased rapidly. Several settlements quickly sprang up in the same area, in close proximity to one another. It was here, among these various neighboring settlements, that certain groups became more wary and began, wisely, to protect their territory behind solid walls. Thus, high population densities in Almeira as well as Grenada (Spain) led to fortified settlements being developed; these were soon distinguished from open sites.

The role played by environmental constraints is also evident.[17] Very few settlements were established in the harsher environmental regions. Thus, a small number of settlements were able to dominate any areas of open space, enabling a wide range of subsistence strategies to be maintained. Although their population continued to increase, it was easy for settlements to sub-divide: at regular intervals, part of the population of a particular settlement would split away and establish new villages and hamlets without upsetting the economic and social balance across a given expanse. Fortified sites were never required.

It was a different story across lower ground. Fertile areas of land supported numerous settlements while adjacent, less desirable areas (swampland, for example) remained uninhabited. In areas with a high population density, it would have been necessary to assert oneself: exploitation of the land would have been more intense, greater effort would have been required, and the risk of degrading the environment would have been higher. As a result, competition would have become so intense that any dispersion of a population or setting up of a new site would have been impossible due to the high population density of these fertile areas – they became focal points of population as a result of their fundamental economic significance. It was here that the "enrichment" and enlargement process of certain communities first began. These same settlements, often protected by natural defenses alone until this point, began to defend themselves with the aid of ever more sophisticated defense mechanisms. The central sites subsequently began to control the smaller, peripheral sites under a vassalage-like system in which the smaller sites were subject to the political superiority of the central sites. Some of these micro-capitals may even have served as refuges and places of economic surplus on occasion. Their role was certainly more than just protective – everyday village activities also took place here. Furthermore, each of these sites had its own history with ongoing changes being made to the defense systems. The fortified walls at sites in Zambujal (Torres Vedras, Portugal), for example, were continually being altered throughout their occupation (plate 23). The most well-known site is the Los Millares site close to Almeira in Spain, which was surrounded by several lines of defense; the entrance was also protected by a barbican. A dozen or so small forts were built on hills surrounding the site.

Much debate has focused upon the role of these fortified sites, their effect-iveness in protecting against potential intruders, and their actual purpose. It

Plate 23 Zambujal fortress in Torres Vedras (Portugal). View across the barbican, third millennium BCE. Deutsches Archäologisches Institut, Madrid.

has been suggested that they were constructed for show to dissuade intruders or for prestige purposes. It is, however, undeniable that they were probably also constructed to protect the goods and people within. From the beginning of the Neolithic, the social organization of the day sparked the development of specialized or privileged sites surrounded by ditches and stockades, the construction of central squares, the emergence of villages that controlled the production and distribution of specific items, and the construction of crossroads that were managed by the elite. The southern Iberian Peninsula had one of the most successful and imposing fortification systems of the European Copper Age and was based upon stonework construction. Any attempts to penetrate these fortifications are certain to have provoked tension and conflict.

Over the course of the fourth and third millennia BCE, the image and ideology of the warrior gradually began to emerge. Whilst conflicts took the form of "primitive warfare," raids, or ambush attacks between males of neighboring communities, the mentality of the male, equipped with weapons and ready to engage in combat, was reflected in the iconography of the day. It has often been suggested that the concepts of war and the warrior were introduced by the spread of Indo-European populations originating in the steppe regions of Southeastern Europe. This has already been discussed with regard to the menhir-statues. The issue will be readdressed here, though from a more general perspective, with regard to the origins of warfare. The peaceful farming communities of the Neolithic, devoting their time to working the fields, would have been overpowered by these newcomers who were willing to use force to seize the possessions of other groups. Thus, this influx of migrants would have brought groups of outsiders to Central and Western Europe, introducing to the area their patriarchal social structure and stockbreeding economy (rather than the local agriculture-based economy); they would also no doubt have plundered and exploited the native population. In short, a new socioeconomic system of external origin was introduced which put an end to the existing sedentary, agricultural civilizations of the Neolithic with their general lack of social hierarchy and social tensions. Theories propose that the image of the warrior evolved as new populations, with a greater tendency for warfare, arrived on the scene: they suggest that this was not a natural state of affairs, rather it arose through contact with other groups, i.e., invasion and groups splitting away from populations in the East.

However, such theories can be called into question: the "ideological construction of the warrior" prevalent at the time may instead have arisen from the social organization of Western Europe's populations. Indeed, the tensions that characterized these first agricultural societies have already been discussed over the preceding pages. Furthermore, social hierarchies became ever more marked over the course of the fifth and fourth millennia BCE. At a burial site in Varna (Bulgaria) dating from 4500 BCE, a few of the 280 tombs located here seem to contain high-ranking individuals: these individuals have been buried with a scepter, a sign of their strength, along with an array of gold jewelry, copper weaponry, and ceremonial flint knives. Similar "princely" tombs exist in the West, although they do not contain metal objects, which were confined to the Balkan region at this point in time.

During the fourth and third millennia BCE, different forms of hierarchy began to emerge. These hierarchies may have been based upon exchange systems in which prestige or everyday items were circulated following the spread of new technology: the wheel, the wagon, and the use of horses. "Leaders" would have intervened in any decisions or inter-community disputes. These situations would either have been resolved peacefully or would have resulted in war. There is undoubtedly no "standard model" by which to define these dominant individuals – their role would have varied over time and across cultures. Evidence from tombs provides the best indication of the social structures of the day and reveals that Central and Western Europe during the third millennium BCE could be divided into (at least) three cultural zones.

The Western Mediterranean region was characterized by collective tombs (hypogea, megaliths, cave burial chambers) in which numerous bodies were buried over the course of 1,000 years or more. This practice has enabled experts to identify groups (families, clans) rather than individuals. In this context, a "leader's" authority may have been dependent upon his ability to control dependence networks based upon social or kinship ties, with many members of a particular network being buried in a group burial vault.

A similar arrangement seems to have been in place in the Atlantic region, extending from Portugal to Ireland. Here megalithic tombs, a legacy of the Neolithic, were still in widespread use to the extent that populations continued to bury their dead in these large stone burial chambers, despite the arrival of new cultures, such as the Beaker culture.

Throughout Central and Northern Europe, individual tombs in the form of barrows were in widespread use. These tombs emphasize the individual. This was by no means a new practice. Corded Ware populations had been using this burial technique since the first half of the third millennium BCE. The later Beaker societies retained the practice. Indeed, individual tombs have long been a feature of Central Europe and were used here almost throughout the entire duration of the Neolithic, from the sixth to the third millennia BCE. The same can be said of the Alpine regions of Italy where the box tombs associated with the Remedello civilization (in the third millennium BCE) are known to have followed on from similar burial techniques employed by the local Square-Mouthed Vase cultures of the fifth millennium BCE. It is, therefore, evident that there was a certain degree of continuity linking Europe's funerary practices over time, connecting the civilizations of the third millennium BCE with their roots and with previous funerary traditions, creating a kind of "Braudelian" permanence across certain cultural areas.

However, despite the significance of these similarities across the various areas, Europe was changing. Metallurgy (already a feature of Central Europe during the fifth and fourth millennia BCE and of Western Europe from the end of the fourth millennium BCE) was one of the main factors that fueled these changes. With the introduction of metallurgy, the copper dagger replaced the stone axe as an item of prestige, marking the social standing and masculinity of its owner. Drinking goblets also became a common feature in Europe (Baden culture, Corded Ware culture, Beaker culture). These goblets are more than just a reflection of taste; they are an indicator of the cultural practices of the day (drinking bouts? rituals in which drinks were passed round? banquets? drinking as part of an initiation ritual?).[18] Such practices would have brought about the spread of certain ideas. Indeed, they may have been at the heart of behavior associated with the newly emerging social class. This social class sought to employ specific customs for its own purposes: to identify its members and distinguish itself from the other classes. Thus, a "proto-aristocracy" may have emerged. Membership may have been partly hereditary with members being periodically reassessed as a result of internal competition and the flexibility of relationship ties. Power struggles among these hierarchies may well explain why this society never progressed beyond the level of chiefdoms; this situation continued into the Bronze Age.

However, warfare was not a full-time activity for the warriors of this period, despite the fact that the ideology of the western warrior was "created" at this time, and was featured upon steles and large statues. Every man capable of fighting was a virtual warrior, if required to be. This "proto-warrior" would have played an intermediate role falling somewhere between a bold hunter and, when necessary, a warrior ready to invade a neighboring tribe, should the generally good relations between two groups suddenly deteriorate. Confrontation was another form of competition or a test from which prestige and high standing could be gained. This notion is specific to "barbarian" Europe. In the eastern regions of the Mediterranean, the urbanized system that characterized Mesopotamia, Syria, and Egypt at this time (and was just beginning to appear in Palestine and Anatolia) favored the existence of guardsmen, militia, and even troops that even included temporary recruits during specific conflicts. When discussing the "warriors" of the third millennium BCE, it is therefore essential to specify the region in question, given these differences between the various social structures and levels of integration.

At this time when, in the West at least, there was no regular army nor any need for one and when conflicts concerned small groups from neighboring communities and the settling of scores between individuals, the reputable image of the warrior was nevertheless firmly rooted in the mentality of the day. Before warfare began in earnest with all its devastating effects, the image of the male fighter was established in society. Since Paleolithic times, this image has been linked to the image of the hunter. From the third millennium BCE onwards, an impression of the warrior in his own right began to emerge. With conflicts beginning to increase, a new ideological framework developed in which the best warrior acquired greater status: that of the hero.

Chapter 5

The Concept of the Hero Emerges

When discussing conflict and violent behavior during the Bronze Age in the Mediterranean and in Europe (roughly covering the second millennium BCE and the following 200 to 300 years), striking and highly significant differences are immediately evident. Writing had already developed in urban and suburban regions at this time, whilst other village-based areas were still centered upon oral tradition. In the Eastern Mediterranean, in both Mesopotamia and the Upper Euphrates region, fortified towns have existed since the fourth millennium BCE. Shortly after, urbanization spread to the Near East and along the Indus. During the third millennium BCE, Sumerian "city-states" are known to have waged war against one another. This state of ongoing conflict is thought to have sparked the construction of the Akkad empire in around 2300 BCE, following Sargon's conquests. This weak empire extended from Anatolia to the Gulf region. From 3000 BCE, a centralized state emerged in Egypt with cities also developing right along the Nile, although these cities are poorly documented in terms of archeological evidence. Armies were, therefore, in part a product and guardian of these towns and states. On a more general level, this urban civilization would have required militia or permanent guards.

In troubled times, weapons also formed part of this defense strategy. From the third millennium BCE onwards, cities became an increasingly common feature, spreading out toward Anatolia and the Aegean. These cities often served as center points for principalities or governing families, as focal points for the distribution of produce, as craft centers, or as hubs for trade both within the region and further afield. They were often defended behind strong walls: Hittite capitals and Cretan and Mycenean palaces were even built upon the sites of small fortified cities dating from previous centuries.

In the second millennium BCE, eastern imperialism brought about greater tensions. Sovereigns were often driven by the desire to conquer and, as a result, local wars gave way to confrontations on a more "international" scale. Invasions and conflict gave rise to annexations and shifts in the layout of territories. Empires emerged and remained in existence for a while before collapsing, and new centers of authority formed. Between 2000 and 1600 BCE, the first Babylonian empire flourished and then foundered following a Kassite invasion. As of 1600 BCE, the Hittite population of the Anatolian plateau became ever more powerful relative to its neighbors and rivals: Myceneans to the west, Mittanians and Assyrians to the east, and Egyptians to the south. There were regular disputes along the borders with Palestine and Syria; this land was often conquered by the pharaohs and incorporated into their empire. These ongoing battles, in addition to the internal disputes and unsettled periods of migration, brought about a rapid decline in most of the large kingdoms in the East in around 12,000/11,000 BCE: Mycenae, Hittite Anatolia, and Egypt under the rule of its pharaohs. Assyria then reaffirmed its supremacy over the whole of the Near East at the beginning of the first millennium BCE, only to subsequently founder at the hands of the Persians.

This chronological and factual overview does not take account of the fact that no comparable system was in place throughout most parts of Europe at this time: there were no towns and no states. Instead, Europe consisted primarily of hamlets and villages, some of which were evidently of greater importance than others and played a more central role: these may have been home to an elite or to important figures. Whatever the case, these were places where alliances were formed, deals negotiated, collective ceremonies held, and social cohesion strengthened. However, the hierarchies in place remained weak and often gave rise to conflict. Even certain influential lineages were unable to integrate too closely into the system. Those in charge had only limited authority which rarely extended beyond a local or even a regional level. Although this system may have witnessed the emergence of an aristocracy, there were none of the larger-scale principalities that tend to stabilize over time. Indeed, the social hierarchy was periodically challenged. Europe did not adopt the Mycenean or eastern model. Instead, prosperous villages developed but no towns. Rulers often emerge in response to such levels of social competition, yet do not tend to found proper kingdoms. Does this mean that, in contrast to the East, war did not take place here? This is certainly not the case. Across most of the continent, small bands of men from various different local chiefdoms would have been involved in conflict with one another. Such confrontations would have been localized and isolated events. However, war at a regional level would have been rare. Even if the social organization of the day did spark competition, the village-based lifestyle and the need to maintain exchange networks for prestige items, at least on the part of those in charge, would have prevented widespread conflict from developing. Confrontation, whether fueled by a breakdown of alliances, by psychological motivations, or by the need to acquire new land or livestock, was geographically limited.

Archeologists have also sought to determine the scale and nature of Bronze Age battles in Europe. What is clear is that the role of weapons, be it real or symbolic, continued to grow during this period: the armed warrior, until this point more of an idealistic model, became an everyday reality. Socio-economic differences between the West and the East are barely reflected in the weaponry of the day: weapons were, for the most part, just as sophisticated in the West as in the East. It seems that no area was left untouched by long-distance links, ease of communication (demonstrated most notably by the "amber routes" between the Baltic Sea and the Mediterranean), and the fast spread of ideas and techniques. Interactions became a constant way of life. In this context, with cultures filtering into one another, the concept of the warrior gave rise to another figure, defined by his bravery: the hero. The concept of the hero remained through protohistory right up to recent history, where it resided at the heart of society. This shift in scale and perspective will be discussed at length below.

Weapons and their Significance

From the Copper Age onwards, weapons were depicted in many places in the West: upon steles, among the petroglyphs featured on blocks of stone, and upon rock faces at mountain summits. These weapons (arrowheads, flint or copper daggers, metal-bladed axes) varied both in technical quality and in aesthetic appearance. Whatever the case, they all represent the first weapons of war. In the second millennium BCE bronze was first produced (an alloy of copper and tin), creating a more durable metal than copper. This technical development was soon after coupled with an increase in production. It was primarily weapons that benefited from this development. In around 1500 BCE, daggers and swords were the most sophisticated objects created by bronzeworkers. It seems that the bronzesmiths channeled their skills initially into manufacturing weapons, perhaps in response to demand. The most advanced technology of the day was applied in making these weapons. Note that very little changed in this respect in 4,000 years. Furthermore, throughout prehistory these weapons, which were perfected over time and became a source of prestige, were always associated with the masculine domain. Only the men had access to these tools, which were instruments of war, pride, and death. Swords first made their appearance in Europe, with only short two-edged blades being used in the Near East for some time after. In fact, the sword soon replaced the dagger as the warrior's most symbolic weapon. These swords were often beautifully formed pieces of bronze with a long, elaborate blade attached to a solid, decorated hilt with rivets. Initially, in approximately 1500 BCE, these swords were little more than larger versions of the Early Bronze Age daggers with their decorated blades and large handles, typically found in Central Europe and the Western Alps. However, it was not long before a range of sword types emerged, becoming more varied and widely distributed over time. Swords from Saint-Brandan in Armorica (France) and Cheylounet in Haut-Loire (France) all had a hilt – some as an extension of the blade in handle form, others with a separate hilt fixed to the tang of the blade with rivets. Swords from the Nordic regions had ornate handles combining metal with organic materials. Rapiers from Hungary (Hadjusamson) had solid hilts and often an elaborately decorated blade.

Examination of these remarkable objects from the first half of the European Bronze Age (daggers, the first swords, and large axes, thought to be part weapon and part tool) reveals that these items were most frequently concealed, given as offerings to divinities or placed in tombs. Technological developments were advanced to such a degree that highly sophisticated items could be fashioned from metal, making it a worthwhile investment: metal objects served to glorify warriors, satisfy the more affluent individuals, and appease the divinities. However, only very slowly did metal begin to feature in the domestic and day-to-day domain.[1] In fact, excavations of dwellings from this period unearthed the surprising discovery that stone tools, varying in their level of sophistication, were still in use at this time, continuing the long-standing prehistoric tradition. Wood was widely used for agricultural and domestic tools, as indicated by evidence from pile dwelling sites. Thus it seems that two distinct spheres existed, even in the domain of tools, a distinction that was further emphasized by these new technological developments. This was no longer a dichotomy between the masculine and feminine spheres; rather, it was a division between the prestige sphere and the domestic sphere. This was by no means a new distinction and had always existed in one form or another. It was, however, unique in terms of the increasing gap that emerged between the various production techniques. Metallurgy required full-time specialists, whilst materials like wood and flint were used for more commonplace objects that would have been the result of more routine and less intensive labor. Objects were, therefore, coded or assigned a value. Metal objects were the most highly "valued": these included weapons and ceremonial objects and even certain items of jewelry (indicating that women were not excluded from the superior domain).

Thus, it seems that a "two-speed" society was emerging in which those with weapons were accorded greater social standing. From this point onwards, the gap between those engaged in simple production tasks and those able to carry weapons continued to widen. Flint also lost its value, despite its long-standing dual purpose: its domestic role in producing items for everyday use and its prestigious role in producing weapons and other pieces of equipment such as daggers. The most skillful creations belonging to the latter category were the daggers of the pre-dynasty era in Egypt and the Scandinavian daggers. After this point in time, the number of items associated with this category began to fall and eventually disappear altogether. The only stone tools that continued to be produced were ordinary, commonplace objects of "no value."

The Warrior Becomes a Feature of Barbarian Europe

It is no easy task to identify the social categories that characterized the Bronze Age in "Barbarian" Europe in the second millennium BCE and affected most of the continent. On the one hand, different regions may have had very different levels of social organization. On the other, the very length of this period – more than 1,000 years – suggests that any changes that occurred were only gradual. Thus, any proposed hypothesis is bound to be rather simplistic. Although somewhat generalized as a theory, it is possible to say that some degree of basic social division was nevertheless likely. There would probably have been a superior social class responsible for controlling the economics of producing and distributing metal objects. This class would have been entitled or obliged to carry weapons in order to defend the community and its possessions and, if the need arose, would have recruited courageous and competent men to join their sphere of influence. An inferior social class may have been responsible for food production, both crops and livestock. Metalsmiths would probably have formed a class of privileged craftsmen, there to serve the elite, in view of their specialist skills and economic value.

A more "democratic" view could be proposed in place of this brief classification: each and every member of the community may have been entitled and obliged to carry weapons and defend the community whenever the need arose. The situation may well have varied according to the period and region in question. However, it does appear that European society during the Bronze Age was, to a certain extent, structured as a hierarchy, given the society's level of development. These differences in status are reflected in tombs, the elevated location of sites, and a gradual increase in the fortification and scale of such sites, symbolizing an increase in authority over time.[2] The increase in food production, sparked by the growing population, would have enabled more individuals to turn to specialized activities. Although metallurgy may have remained a family-oriented and domestic activity in certain cases, particularly where everyday objects were concerned, producing the heavier and more elaborate pieces would often have required specialized skills. From this point onwards, metal swords, daggers, spears, helmets, shields, and greaves would have been produced by bronzesmiths working full-time.

It is likely that these objects were costly to produce in terms of copper, tin (which was not always locally available and often had to be imported), and time. Only those behind this production process, i.e., those with a certain amount of social influence, would have benefited. The elite classes alone, along with their direct partners or those selected to follow and protect them, were able to make use of these weapons for conquests and defense purposes. Alliance networks of varying size and scale would have dominated society at this time. The status of these privileged individuals was reaffirmed by their charisma, perhaps maintained through feasting and gift giving. Responsible for looking after the interests of the area and community, these individuals were gradually transformed into an armed defense unit. Their role was to protect the human and material capital and as such they became established at the top of the social pyramid. From this point in time onwards, strength and obligation became important factors, in addition to economic influence and prestige: authority gave way to power. Indeed, not only was warfare appealing in economic terms, it also provided enjoyment and an outlet for physical activity.

In this context, the concept of the warrior seems to have become a feature of Bronze Age society, although this would undoubtedly have been a very gradual transformation. Several pieces of evidence seem to confirm this. At the end of the third millennium BCE, for example, individual tombs were developed, though they emerged more quickly in some areas than in others. These tombs reflect an emancipation of the individual: the individual became less constrained by kinship ties and more open to destiny. This greater freedom to act may have aggravated political instability at the time. Although collective tombs, characteristic of the preceding era, were still in occasional use – up until around 1700 BCE in the Mediterranean region (Sardinia, Southern France) – a distinct social pyramid quickly became established in Central Europe and along Europe's Atlantic coast: "leaders" were buried in striking barrows and their remains decorated with jewelry fashioned from precious metals, amber, and glass and accompanied by ever more sophisticated weaponry and high-quality vessels. The princely tombs of Armorica, Wessex, and Saxony were of this type. In Southeastern Spain, the bodies of high-ranking individuals from the El Argar culture were decorated with silver diadems and buried along with weapons and jewelry. These tombs were found to contain Southern Iberia's most precious metal objects. The archeological record indicates that the social pyramid became more marked over time, as is symbolized by the quality and, in some cases, the exotic nature of the objects placed in the tombs. From this, it is evident that aristocracies were beginning to emerge, although their future was, at this stage, uncertain and their membership criteria periodically reassessed.

Was metal responsible for the warrior's increase in status or did the elite classes desire ever more effective weapons, thus fueling developments in metallurgy? It is difficult to distinguish the cause from the effect. Whatever the case, bronze – an alloy of copper and tin – was first used to improve the weapons of war. In addition to the decorative daggers of the Early Bronze Age, which may well have been ceremonial, like the halberd, as well as functional, the sword soon appeared. The sword served as both an item of display and a weapon of violence. The spear, too, was fitted with a metal point from this time onwards and could be used either for attack or for prestige purposes, depending upon the situation. The bow, a more traditional weapon, remained in use for firing over long distances. With bronze metallurgy mastered, technological developments began to focus upon weaponry. The motivations behind this were far from innocent. In fact, this focus upon weaponry indicates that the metalsmiths of the day were greatly influenced by those of superior standing: a number of influential figures channeled early metalworking into producing objects for those entitled to carry weapons.

From the end of the Bronze Age in roughly 1200 BCE right up until the development of iron metallurgy (ca. 800/700 BCE in the West), warriors were an established feature of society, armed with their weapons of attack and defense. Over time, these weapons underwent changes in style, shape, and material. However, these changes were only slight until the development of more sophisticated techniques such as the crossbow and firearms. Thus, the archetype of the western warrior, characteristic of protohistory, antiquity, and medieval times, was established in the second half of the second millennium BCE.

Of course, a permanent army was not always on hand and intercommunity conflicts in the Bronze Age were more like raids than pitched battles and often resulted in women and children being captured or livestock being stolen. However, guarding the social group, seizing goods from neighboring villages, and even challenging others to fight would have become the responsibility of specially selected individuals, skilled in handling weapons. No doubt Iron Age aristocracies would have taken a firm hold in these small-scale "feudal systems" of the Late Bronze Age.[3]

The symbolic role of the sword has already been discussed. Swords were manufactured with great technical skill in Europe and first appeared in the Mid-Bronze Age.[4] Swords with flat tangs were already being produced in Central Europe and Scandinavia in the fifteenth century BCE. They soon spread to the Eastern Mediterranean regions: Greece, Cyprus, and Egypt. From the thirteenth century BCE, the sword was beginning to develop further in Western Europe. A narrow flat tang often enabled the blade to be slotted into the hilt and fixed in place with various different types and shapes of rivet, such as the following, all discovered in France: the Haguenau type (Bas-Rhin), Rixheim type (Haut-Rhin), and Rosnoen type (Finistère). In certain cases, swords had a longer, narrower tang which was covered by the hilt (Monza type, near Milan). The more sophisticated swords were often distinguished by their different hilts: octagonal, ribbed hilts with concave pommels (Möringen type, Switzerland), or pommels with antennae, some of which coiled over to form spirals (Northern Germany, Central Europe), while others were hardly curved at all (Italy). Other swords were distinguished by two holes separating the body of the hilt from the guard (Auvernier type, Switzerland; Tachlovice type, Czech Republic).

Toward the end of the Bronze Age, the blade and area to which the hilt was attached were made of the same piece of metal. The hilt was either fashioned from organic matter, in which case it was not preserved, or from metal and was fixed in place using rivets attached to the guard and grip. The blades were often leaf-shaped and widened slightly close to the tip: these are called pistilliform blades. This original morphological and technological feature was also found in Continental Europe (Hemigkofen type, Germany; Locras and Forel models from Switzerland) as well as along France's Atlantic coast (figure 54). Another sword type, primarily associated with Europe's Atlantic regions (England, France, Iberian Peninsula), was characterized by its parallel edges and sudden narrowing toward the end to form a sharp point: these swords are referred to as "carp's tongue" swords. The hilt was made of organic matter and was separated from the blade by notches. Several types of this sword have been identified, including Boom (Belgium), Vénat (Charente, France), and Monte Sa Idda (Sardinia). Swords from Majorca (Balearic Islands) have been discovered which have a large hilt and disk-shaped pommel, often topped with a spherical button.

The last large bronze swords to be produced in the West date from the beginning of the Iron Age. The Gündlingen type (Baden-Württemberg,

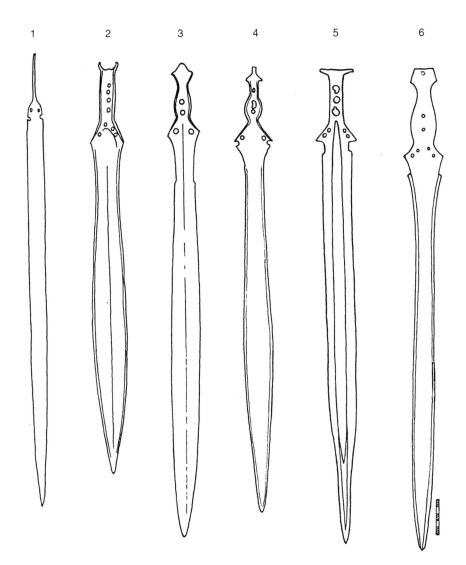

Figure 54   Sword types from the Final Bronze Age in the West: (1) Monza type sword (Chalon-sur-Saône region, France); (2) Hemigkofen type sword (Germany); (3) Locras type sword (Switzerland); (4) Forel type sword (Switzerland); (5) "carp's tongue" type sword (tip from La Hague, Manche, France); (6) Gündlingen type sword (first Iron Age, Germany). After Gaucher and Mohen, 1972.

Germany) is the most common, with swords of this type varying slightly in detail. At the end of the hilt plate is a trapezoidal-shaped section.

In Europe, a great many of these weapons have been found in rivers. It is thought that conflicts between neighboring communities took place along such rivers, which may well have served as boundaries with fords providing contact points. Thus, rivers may have constituted important routes, on land as well as water. Controlling the rivers would have provided a means of establishing economic supremacy over specific areas. Certain sections of these rivers would have been particularly highly sought after, whether they served as natural boundaries or as essential routes. This competition for the control of river routes is similar to that which occurred during the time of the Mesolithic hunters, several thousand years earlier. It is important not to overlook the part played by symbolism: riverbanks may have been a prime location for holding ceremonies that possibly involved the victorious warriors offering their swords to the divinities of the water.

From the middle of the second millennium BCE, the bronze-tipped handheld spear became a common weapon. In fact, the spear was often just as popular as the sword, though did not have the same prestige. The bow was also still used in conflict. A greater variety of arrowheads began to appear (tanged, socketed, with "ailerons," etc.), though arrowheads were made of metal right from the beginning of the Bronze Age. It is likely that some of the more robust arrowheads served as spearheads for throwing.

The Late Bronze Age warrior of Continental Europe is often portrayed fully equipped with weapons and armor (figure 55).[5] In addition to their weapons, warriors were also protected by a helmet, breastplate, greaves, and a shield. The metalsmiths of the day were more than capable of producing these items because they benefited from a long-standing tradition of technical skill, often obtained in workshops attached to the monarchies of the Eastern Mediterranean. These skills subsequently spread throughout Central and then Western Europe. At the same time, slight typological differences signify regional variation.[6] In Europe, for example, the remains of breastplates are rare, indicating that these forms of protection were most likely made from leather or animal hide. Furthermore in Greece, the tradition of wearing large breastplates during the Bronze Age seems to have been

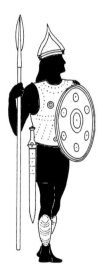

Figure 55
The western warrior and his quipment from the middle of the eighth century BCE. After Brun, 1987.

Figure 56 Parts of the bronze breastplate iscovered in Dendra (Greece), fifteenth century BCE. After Eiroa et al., 1999.

quickly abandoned. One piece of armor discovered in Dendra, Greece, dating from the fifteenth century BCE and resembling a breastplate, was found to be composed of several pieces of metal. However, this type of armor was not found at any later point in time (figure 56). It is thought to have belonged to an infantryman, though it could equally have been used by a warrior riding in a battle chariot given that the armor would have been rather restricting for anyone involved in fighting a battle on the ground. The infantrymen depicted on the "warriors' vase" from Mycenae, Greece, dating from 1200 BCE, are protected by armor only around the trunk, with a short skirt surrounding the pelvis region. Their upper legs are bare and their arms are covered by greaves, perhaps made of metal. The fresco battle painting from Pylos, Greece, shows warriors wearing cnemids for protection. Breastplates found in the West (Marmesse, Haute-Marne, France; Filinges, Haute-Savoie, France) date from the ninth to eighth century BCE.

Shields were also an important means of protection. Various different shapes have been identified. Initially they were long and rectangular (Mycenae is unusually characterized by its "figure of eight" shields), but soon became circular. Round shields are depicted in battle scenes involving the pharaohs. From the twelfth century BCE, various different shield types emerged in Northern Europe (Great Britain, Ireland, Denmark, Germany).

Metal helmets first appeared in Europe around the thirteenth century BCE. In Mycenae, these helmets replaced leather headgear covered with wild boar teeth. In Europe, there were several types of helmet being produced at the end of the Bronze Age. In the East, helmets were bell-shaped with a button on top, a tradition originating in the Aegean region. In Western Europe, helmets with a long, transversal ridge were more common. In Denmark, some of these helmets had horns. Horned helmets were also found in the Mediterranean. Figures featured upon the menhir-statues in Corsica, for example, were wearing horned helmets. It is known that warriors and heroes existed in Sardinia at the beginning of the first millennium BCE thanks to small bronze statues (*bronzetti*) discovered in the island's fortresses, known as nuraghes. These statues show the warriors to be protected by helmets bearing horns and by their round shields. Their weaponry comprised small daggers with a curved guard at one side, spears, bows, and a pole that would undoubtedly have been attached to a mace.[7] A metal figure discovered in Enkomi, Cyprus, thought to date from the Recent Bronze Age (roughly covering the twelfth to eleventh centuries), is depicted holding a spear, with a horned helmet and circular shield for protection. The statue is standing on an oxhide ingot, thus transforming it into a divinity or hero.

Ramparts, Forts, and Citadels

If the warrior did indeed become an important figure in Bronze Age society, political regimes and economic requirements were presumably responsible. In the state system of the Eastern Mediterranean (comprising empires, principalities, or even independent cities, depending on the period and location in question), warriors conquered and defended kingdoms and communities. Garrisons and armies were thus essential and contained those individuals who were proficient in battle, and even some foreign mercenaries. Since the days of the Ancient Empire in Egypt, for example, every nome had a militia with its own leader. Similar armies were also associated with guarding treasure and temples. However, it was not until the Middle Empire that the sovereign acquired his own guards in the form of an elite troop. During the New Empire, pharaohs formed important contingents comprising large numbers of mercenaries from neighboring lands (Nubia, Libya, etc.) as well as Egyptian soldiers. These contingents were composed of troops that varied in terms of both their dress and weapons used.[8]

This situation, in which kingdoms and cities were able to raise an army varying in scale and composition, did not exist in Europe, with the exception of some urbanized areas of the Aegean. In fact at this time, the majority of Europe had not evolved beyond the village or, at most, the proto-urban stage. Even the fortresses in the southeast of the Iberian Peninsula which often covered large areas – 7 hectares in Los Millares – defended only a limited population. Of course, this does not mean that there was no rivalry or conflict, but it does indicate that the number of participants was greatly restricted. As we have seen, ever since the Copper Age or even earlier, those in charge of the largest village settlements obtained their influence in various different ways: from alliance networks of varying size and scale, by controlling the routes used for distributing both common and rare materials, and through establishing kinship or economic-based allegiances with smaller settlements. With the exception of its Eastern Mediterranean fringe, Europe remained a rural continent during the second millennium BCE. However, this situation was no less suited to the gradual emergence of an aristocracy over several hundreds of years. This aristocracy would have developed as dominant families sought to gain favor with locals and exerted influence and economic control over farmers, skilled laborers, and areas of land, however small. In the West, a new stage in the process was reached when one of these aristocrats became known as the "suzerain," whether this situation was imposed upon the people or favored by them. In the sixth century BCE, pressure from exchange systems originating in the Mediterranean led to the development of large fortified sites headed by a prince. This prince would have derived prestige from the status of his village relative to other villages as well as from his authority and charisma.

The gradual emergence of a small-scale aristocracy during the second millennium BCE may also have been linked to the need to protect the population and its possessions. This would have been a particular requirement of any agricultural-based settlement as such communities were often widely dispersed and depended upon the maintenance of good economic and social relations in order to function. Toward the end of the Bronze Age, society gradually became more culturally advanced. This was characterized by an increase in the production of bronze objects, which soon replaced the stone and wood toolmaking tradition inherited from the Neolithic. The downside to these developments was greater instability and pillaging. The fact that so many populations settled together at high altitudes to form villages and that fortifications began to emerge toward the end of the second millennium BCE, both in the Western Mediterranean and in the temperate regions of Europe, is indicative of attempts to combat banditry. The aristocracy and their associates would have been responsible for maintaining social order whilst at the same time being involved in disorder themselves, on occasion. Physical confrontation, armed combat, and sporting interaction remained. In contrast to soldiers in the Eastern Mediterranean armies, the European "warriors" of the advanced Bronze Age were high-ranking individuals with combatants under their control.

Evidence from dwellings also reflects this progressive stratification of society. The trend was slow to develop in Northwestern Europe, though made a much more rapid appearance in Central Europe. As a result, certain tells in the Carpathian Basin became both active commercial centers and small regional capitals. Some even had sophisticated protection systems, such as the Spišsky Sturtók site. Fortifications, which were first developed during this period, gradually spread across the whole of Europe, although not all sites were fortified. Indeed, a network of "open" sites also remained. However, during the ninth to eighth centuries BCE, fortified settlements increased more quickly than at any previous point in time.

In the Western Mediterranean, small fortified villages began to appear during the third millennium BCE, the Iberian Copper Age. Forts and small fortified citadels continued to exist during the Bronze Age. On certain Mediterranean islands, most notably Sardinia, large circular buildings (nuraghes) often formed the heart of small villages (plate 24). These buildings had cyclopean-type walls and were frequently placed at the center of an enclosure, firmly defended by a large wall with corner towers. Small villages with their modest dwellings huddled in between these keep-like structures, which were symbols of political, economic, and ideological power long before keeps as we know them today had been developed.

In the Mediterranean region as well as in Europe, ever more sophisticated fortifications were built around villages, citadels, and, subsequently, urban centers. Several examples are featured in figure 57.

The East: Chariots in Battle

The problems posed by the invention and spread of the wheel and mobile vehicles are, as yet, only partially clear. Images from the Uruk culture, which existed in Mesopotamia between 3500 and 3000 BCE, contain schematic representations of chariots shown to have a caisson or cabin and two wheels along the side (i.e., four in total). In the Black Sea region and in the North Caucasus mountains, bodies have been found buried in vaults, some of which also contained the remains of four-wheeled chariots. Even in Northern Europe, a civilization dating from the fourth millennium BCE (known as the Funnel Beaker culture) produced ceramics bearing images of four-wheeled vehicles. Thus, if chariots were invented in one particular area, the technique seems to have spread quickly. Whatever the case, the existence of the wheel and chariot in Central and Western Europe during the third millennium BCE is well documented, even though actual archeological examples are very rare, given that wood does not preserve well: the only evidence comes from swamps in the Netherlands (De Eese) and the excavation of lakeside towns in Switzerland (Zurich). However, the Baden culture in Hungary has been associated with models of four-wheeled chariots made from baked clay, and in the Alpine regions of Italy rock engravings of chariots have been identified. This, too, is evidence of the spread of this new form of transport.[9] The wheel led to a variety of vehicles being produced: chariots for transport or battle as well as for ceremonial or religious purposes. Only battle chariots are of relevance to this discussion.

Chariots have been used in conflict from the third millennium BCE or perhaps even earlier: the Standard of Ur features heavy, four-wheeled vehicles

Plate 24 Sardinian Bronze Age fortresses, second millennium BCE. Above: Barumini nuraghe; below: inside the Sant Antine nuraghe. Photos J. Guilaine.

Period	Site	Date	Area	Fortification
NEOLITHIC	Jericho (Palestine)	9000 BCE	3 ha	Stone wall, 3 m wide and a tower 9 m high and 11 m in diameter (the excavations were only localized and did not enable the actual scale of these defenses to be ascertained).
	Çatal Hüyük (Turkey)	7000 BCE	12 ha	Terrace-like houses forming a "blind wall" along the outside edge.
	Passo di Corvo (Italy)	5000 BCE	40 ha	Ditch 850 m × 500 m; 6 m wide and 4 m deep at the time of excavation (this would originally have been doubled by a palisade).
	Urmitz (Germany)	4000 BCE	More than 100 ha	Two parallel ditches 10 m wide and a palisade surrounding a large area adjacent to the Rhine.
CHALCOLITHIC	Habasesti (Romania)	4000 BCE	1.2 ha	Two adjacent ditches from 2 to 5 m wide; 2 m deep at the time of excavation. Protected the west side of the site. Along the east and south sides, steep slopes provided natural protection.
BRONZE AGE	Arad (Israel)	2500 BCE	11 ha	Wall 1,176 long and from 2 to 2.5 m wide. Maximum height was 1.6 m at the time of excavation. The lower section is stone. At intervals, there are semicircular towers (it is often claimed that the upper section was brick, though there is no proof of this).
IRON AGE	Biskupin (Poland)	600/500 BCE	3.2 ha	An island-like site. "Breakwater" composed of 35,000 posts intended to protect against the effects of water and glaciers. 463 m rampart, originally 6 m high, constructed from timber and earth. Gateway comprising a portal dominated by a tower.

	Heuneburg (Germany)	600/500 BCE	3 ha	Phase 2 in the Iron Age occupation of the site. Stone base supporting ramparts 3 m wide. Rectangular bastions (raised towers).
	Bibracte (Mont-Beuvray, France)	100/50 BCE	ca. 200 ha (enclosed area of 135 ha, doubled by an outer line)	Successive defense mechanisms. "Murus Gallicus": ramparts with a framework of horizontally and vertically laid timber.
URBAN PHASE	Habuba Kabira (Iraq)	3500/3200 BCE	20 ha (enclosed area)	Wall 3 m wide complete with towers and bastions, in a rectangular layout. Outer wall 5 m beyond the ramparts.
	Uruk (Iraq)	2900/2700 BCE	ca. 400 ha	Ramparts 9.5 km long and flanked by towers at 9 m intervals: 900 towers in all. Ramparts 5 m wide. Bastions are rectangular at first, then semicircular. Wall preserved at a height of 9 m in parts. Outer wall 4 m beyond ramparts and 0.6 m wide.
	Ebla (Syria)	2400/2200 BCE	50 ha	Ramparts with an external stone face, composed of levees 50 m wide at the base. Defenses extend over 2.8 km.
	Babylon (Iraq)	700 BCE	975 ha (area surrounded by the exterior defense)	Town's external defenses, 11.3 km long, comprising two lines of defense: an inner wall built from sun-dried mudbricks, 7 m wide; an external wall constructed from baked bricks, 4 m wide. The "town" was partially surrounded by these defenses and extended beyond the Euphrates. It was also surrounded by rectangular ramparts 6 km long comprising an internal wall 6.5 m wide and an external wall 3.7 m wide. These defenses were flanked by towers. A water-filled ditch ran alongside the defenses.

Figure 57 Examples of fortified sites (Neolithic, "metal ages," Paleo-Urban).

pulled by onagers charging over fallen enemies. In fact, lighter battle chariots with spoked wheels only really became established during the first half of the second millennium BCE. In the Eastern Mediterranean, battles involved exceptional archers riding in chariots with the aim of putting enemy infantrymen to rout. Chariots provided a superior means of attack, given their speed and the fact that they enabled warriors to keep a certain distance from the enemy. One of the first areas to develop battle chariots was Anatolia, in around 1700 BCE.[10] Shortly after, there is evidence that chariots also appeared in the Aegean region. In Egypt, chariots became an essential element in battle during the New Empire. These two-wheeled chariots were pulled by horses, sometimes protected by a cuirass, and had a driver who sat next to an archer. Hittite chariots had three passengers, the third being responsible for protecting the others with a shield. It is thought that the Hittites used spears when attacking from their chariots. Whatever the case, archers were certainly the main means of attack onboard such chariots. Pharaohs are often depicted firing arrows at their terrified enemies from their battle chariots.

Battle chariots quickly became more widespread: archers primarily aimed at the horses that pulled their enemy's chariot in order to scatter their enemy. Thus, each side aimed to have the greater number of chariots as this would give them the upper hand. During the thirteenth century BCE, the armies of the Hittite king and of the pharaoh had several thousand battle wagons at their disposal. The king of Ugarit (a vassal of the Hittite sovereign) had several hundred alone. It is estimated that the palace of Knossos also had between 500 and 1,000 chariots during the Recent Bronze Age.[11] Maintaining the wheels, framework, and horses for these vehicles would have been costly. Furthermore, breastplates to protect the archers and drivers became increasingly necessary. Mycenean warriors also used two-wheeled chariots, although confrontations often finished with one-to-one battles on the ground. A fresco painting from the palace in Pylos depicts what look like "duels" taking place between Myceneans and "barbarians" using two-edged swords (figure 58). Pikes were also used in this encounter.

Horses and chariots were naturally plundered by the enemy. In Megiddo in around 1460 BCE, Thoutmosis III made off with 980 chariots and more than 2,000 horses, taken from the king of Kadesh and a coalition of leaders from Canaan. The most famous battle to have occurred in the East involved Ramses II fighting against Muwattalis II, king of Hatti, and his allies. The battle took place in 1275 BCE in Kadesh and brought warriors riding in chariots and infantrymen face to face. The outcome was undecided, yet Ramses claimed it to be an Egyptian victory in his country. He immortalized the

Figure 58 Pylos fresco (Greece) showing a battle between Greeks and barbarians. After Drews, 1993.

battle in images upon the walls of temples in Abydos, Karnak, Luxor, and Abu-Simbel and upon pylons at the Ramesseum.[12]

The actual role played by chariots has often been cause for debate. Some experts believe that the archers who fired their arrows from these chariots benefited from the speed and mobility of the vehicle in order to break down enemy lines and avoid direct combat. Others consider chariots to have provided a means of transporting the best soldiers onto the battlefield. These soldiers would then have charged into the battle. The driver of the chariot would have been able to rescue any soldier in danger or even transport him quickly to a more crucial battle zone. Chariots would also have been able to pursue an enemy as it withdrew or fled, thus worsening the enemy's defeat.

Figure 59 Ramses II aboard his chariot, besieging a Syrian fortress, Debir. Drawing after Erman and Ranke, 1986.

The infantry also played an important role in battles in the East (figure 59). Troops were composed primarily of infantrymen. The ground battle between Ramses III and the Philistines seems primarily to have involved infantrymen, despite the existence of chariots at this time. It is thought that chariot-based wars were gradually replaced by combatants on horseback or on foot. This would have been revenge of a sort for the poor barbarians against the eastern sovereigns, who were the only ones permitted to have chariots produced and maintained and the only ones entitled to acquire large numbers of horses. Chariots soon after became display vehicles, reserved for ceremonies or victories.

Spoked wheels have existed in Europe since the middle of the second millennium BCE (Mid-Bronze Age), as examples from the Carpathians and Italy (Mercurago) indicate. The famous miniature chariot from Trundhom (Denmark) seems to show that these European vehicles were used more for cultural than for warfare purposes. This chariot had four wheels, like the ceremonial chariots of Western Europe that were found from the Pyrenees right up to the Mid-Rhine region and date from the ninth to eighth centuries BCE.

Another type of combat occurred on water. In Egypt, the Hyksos forced the Egyptians into fighting upon the Nile. The well-known battle between Ramses III and the "Sea Peoples" (a confederation of diverse populations that plundered the Levant) took place on land as well as along the mouths of the Nile in around 1179 BCE. This assault is documented in fresco paintings in the Medinet-Habu temple and shows the Egyptian archers fighting back triumphantly against their pugnacious attackers.

The Development of a Cavalry

In the third millennium BCE, infantrymen and chariots both played a key role upon the battlefields of Mesopotamia, as illustrated by scenes upon the Standard of Ur. From the seventeenth century BCE, chariots became a primary feature of battles. This situation lasted up until the end of the second millennium BCE. The fall of kingdoms and cities in the Eastern Mediterranean that occurred at this time has often been attributed to changes both in weaponry and in war techniques.[13] Bronze Age kings and princes of the East derived their strength from mobile troops, complete with chariots and composite bows; these weapons were greatly feared as a result of their resistance and elasticity. It was therefore of prime importance that combatants were able to move around and keep a distance from their enemy. Conversely, the ever-present infantrymen would have begun to play a more significant part with the arrival of large numbers of warriors from barbarian regions as of 1500 BCE. These masses of warriors were equipped, in particular, with swords and short battle spears and thus engaged in close-range encounters or even fierce hand-to-hand battles. This would have tolled the knell of confrontation between archers.

Even in Greece during Mycenean times, infantrymen played an important role in battle. These battles gave rise to confrontation and duels characterized by ardor, fury, and cruelty. For this reason, the advent of the phalanx in the seventh century BCE (a compact formation, several rows long, of hoplites armed with long spears and protected by helmets and shields) changed the very nature of combat: individual exploits were replaced by collective actions. The archaic warrior became a disciplined soldier. Such military training techniques were greatly superior to any degree of individual success that could be attained without them. However, the weapons of the day (both for attack and defense purposes) do not seem to reflect these strategic changes so strongly. In fact, the archeological record reveals these strategic shifts to be distantly rooted in the weapons of the second millennium BCE.[14]

Speed of movement remained an important tactic in these clashes between infantrymen. It was in this climate at the end of the second millennium BCE that chariots began to play a lesser role, although they did not disappear from the Eastern Mediterranean completely. Some time after, at the height of the Neo-Assyrian era (eighth to seventh centuries BCE), they regained popularity.

It was, in fact, the emergence of a cavalry that led to mobile combat (in which animals played a key role) regaining its significance from the second millennium BCE. At the turn of the first millennium BCE, elite combatants began to take the form of warriors on horseback. During the Iron Age, several populations in the West and in Africa are known to have developed excellent cavalries. During the Roman conquest, the Gauls reputedly fought on horseback, armed with a spear and sword. In fact, it was only the aristocrats and their immediate subordinates who fought in this fashion, whereas the infantrymen were generally peasants conscripted during times of military activity. The Garamantes and Numidians from the Sahara and North Africa also had intrepid cavalrymen, although their monarchies were brought down by Rome.

One of the problems associated with the development of these cavalries is the question of when horses were first mounted. It is thought that horses were first domesticated in the steppe region of Southeastern Europe in around the fifth or fourth millennium BCE. The earliest known remains of domest-icated horses are often claimed to come from the Dereivka site (Ukraine). In addition to skeletal remains, the first bits made from antler tines were also discovered here and provide the earliest indications of harnessing.[15] Some experts believe that the domestication of horses occurred even earlier, more toward the East in the region of the Urals. Whatever the case, domestic horses, although harnessed, were not necessarily ridden. It is often claimed that many of the population shifts that occurred within Europe during the third millennium BCE were due, in part, to such cavalries. One example is groups from the steppe regions that are said to have infiltrated agricultural communities in the areas around the Balkans and Danube. Similar cases are the Corded Ware populations that spread across Central and Northern Europe as far afield as Eastern France and Scandinavia. Or equally the Beaker cultures, which were distributed from Portugal to Poland and from Sicily to Scotland. These populations sometimes buried horses close to members of the community, indicating the familiarity and even affection that linked humans and animals. There is, however, no convincing evidence from this period of horses being mounted, despite certain claims made in archeological literature.

In fact, before the beginning of the first millennium BCE, there is no definite evidence of a cavalry having existed. Again, it is thought that the populations of Southeastern Europe (Cimmerians) or the steppe regions (Scythians) were the first to travel on horseback along the borders of Asia and the Black Sea, perhaps following numerous attempts dating back to the second millennium BCE. Horses quickly became a symbol of leaders and members of the aristo-cracy, who would wield their bronze and later iron swords in battle. The species became ever more prestigious on being adopted by the social elite. In various regions across Europe (Hungary, France, Spain), barrow tombs have been discovered dating from the beginning of the first millennium BCE that contain the bodies of warriors and funerary items along with the remains of the deceased individual's horse. Humans and animals seem to have been indissolubly linked in life as well as in death. In other cases, cavalrymen were buried with parts of the horse's harness. The use of horses would certainly have enabled quicker confrontations to take place in the form of raids, forays, and plundering instead of large-scale, organized attacks. Larger-scale attacks would only have occurred later with the development of a more extensive cavalry equipped with breastplates and subsequently using stirrups.

Tracing the Footsteps of Heroes

What warrior does not dream of becoming a hero? Although certain males and ancestors of the third millennium BCE in Europe may have been branded "heroes" and sculpted in stone bearing weapons, a thousand years later warriors had become prominent figures in society and were only fully satisfied if they managed to carry out activities that would gain them recognition, prestige, and legendary status. These honors were only attainable through competition in the form of battle and a desire for confrontation. Like the legendary combatants of the Trojan war in the thirteenth century BCE, whom Homer praises for their ardor, insatiable persistence, and often cruel behavior, all regions of Europe probably had their heroes who fought in single combat and exerted great fascination over their contemporaries. In the absence of writing, of course, no one was able to record such epics. However, it is likely that the exploits of these warriors would have been passed on by local bards who may have exaggerated details concerning the warriors' courage, merit, and weapons. Two types of archeological evidence remain which relate to these warriors: their graves, which were found to contain quality objects, and steles that denote their hero status.

Without a doubt, these were figures renowned for their charisma and participation in battle who existed well before the great warriors of the end of the Bronze Age and the Iron Age. During the third and beginning of the second millennia BCE in Europe, it is likely that "heroes" were leaders who, for one reason or another, awarded themselves this superior status. They were rather like great ancestors[16] acting to protect a given community. This may be the significance of some of the masculine steles. Breaking these steles, thus making them disappear, would therefore be indicative of ruptures in the hierarchy. Judging by archeological evidence, it would seem that these heroes merged with local dynasties, their personal prestige being underpinned by alliances and distant connections. Some of the kings from the Kurgan culture, which was located between the Caspian Sea and Black Sea during the third millennium BCE, fall into this category. The most famous of these kings was discovered in the city of Maikop in the north of the Caucasus. His body was found lying, sprinkled with ocher, in a timber vault under an 11-m-high mound; two more funerary chambers were located adjacent to the vault, each containing one of the sovereign's servants. A royal canopy had been dismantled and placed in the tomb: the structure was supported by hollow silver tubes of more than 1 m in length which were slotted into small statues of bulls, some gold and some silver. Jewels gilded with gold leaf in the shape of wildcats or oxen as well as beads of rare stone were resting upon the body. Vessels made of precious metal, copper weapons and tools, and gold and silver appliqués were also placed on or around the body. Although less ostentatious, the magnificence of objects buried in the barrow-type princely tombs of Armorica, Wessex, and Saxony-Thuringia in around 2000 BCE should also be noted. In Leubingen (Germany), an 8-m-high barrow tomb was found to contain a funeral chamber made of stone blocks, rather like a reproduction of a house from this period. The body of an elderly male had been placed in line with the room, surrounded by objects of prestige: halberds, daggers, metal axes, a serpentine "battle axe," bronze pins, solid torques, and various pieces of gold jewelry. However, this elderly leader was not buried alone. The body of a young girl had been placed crosswise upon his body, probably sacrificed for the occasion. More famous examples are the Mycenean rock-cut chamber tombs, which were protected by two large circular walls (circles A and B). These tombs contained the remains of the governing families. Between the seventeenth and fifteenth centuries BCE, kings were buried here with an exceptional range of treasures: a gold mask, a sword, the blade and hilt of which were inlaid with gold, silver, and niello, and a number of highly precious jewels. The impressive dome tombs, where members of the leading families were buried during the fourteenth century, are very different structures.

About halfway through the second millennium BCE, tombs containing important figures began to appear in Central Europe, though they were less lavish than the Mycenean tombs and their contents. One such example is the tomb of a warrior discovered in Hagenau, close to Ratisbon (Upper-Palatinate). This warrior was buried with his bronze weapons – a sword, a two-edged sword, a dagger, an axe, a set of four arrows, and a shield. The tomb also contained several distinct signs of his status: four bronze bracelets, some thin and some wide, two gold spiral rings, three awls, 43 pins, a razor, and, most astonishingly of all, a kind of large clothes pin of more than 50 cm in length. Later, during the eleventh and tenth centuries BCE, similar notable figures were buried in Scandinavia beneath imposing mounds. In the Haga valley in Sweden, an individual known as "King Björn" was buried in an oak coffin beneath a mound 45 m in diameter and 8 m high. He was accompanied in his grave by a sword set with gold, a buckle, two razors, tweezers, and other decorative objects. In Korshøj, in the south of the island of Fünen, a high-ranking individual was buried with his sword, various items made of gold, and a bronze bucket. Later, other burial mounds such as those in Lusehøj, Fünen, were found to contain a range of objects impressive in terms of both their variety and their quality (a bronze cauldron and goblets, jewels, toiletry items, a sword, and the remains of a chariot).

Certain tombs of warriors or rulers were also found to contain a ceremonial vehicle in the European Alpine regions (Austria, Southern Germany, Switzerland). The earliest examples date from the thirteenth and twelfth centuries BCE. Along with the body of the deceased, they were also found to contain the remains of a ceremonial chariot, a sword, and a set of drinking goblets. These "heroes" were generally burnt, along with their possessions and chariot, upon a funeral pyre. Aristocrats from the Late Bronze Age were often buried with their sword, toiletry items (razor, tweezers, pins) perhaps to keep their beard kempt, bronze vessels for drinking rituals or banquets, and parts of their horse's harness or indeed parts of the horse itself. These items continued to appear in the tombs of high-ranking figures throughout the Iron Age in Central Europe such that, by the sixth century BCE, they were the most striking feature of these large, princely tombs, along with items imported from the Mediterranean.[17] The most well known is the Hochdorf tomb in the region of Ludwigsburg (Germany) (figure 60). Here, a mound 10 m high and 60 m across was found to contain a funeral chamber, the walls of which were concealed behind funeral hangings. The tomb contained the remains of a prince of athletic build, placed upon a funeral bed on castors topped with bronze figurines. He had been dressed in his ceremonial clothing: a necklace, an armband on his right arm, two buckles, a gold belt holding his dagger, and shoes covered with gold appliqués. Close by was a large cauldron containing 500 liters of mead and his set of funerary vessels. A four-wheeled chariot had been placed against the opposite wall. Upon the chariot were parts from a horse harness and various items of a dinner service. A funerary meal is one possible explanation for this. Similar treasures were discovered in the Vix tomb in Burgundy (France). In this case, however, it seems that the funerary ceremony and exceptional treasures were in honor of a young woman. One of these treasures was the famous bronze crater, imported from Greater Greece, which measured 1.6 m in height and had a capacity of 1,220 l. Thus, it would seem that "heroines" too could be the focus of the group's meticulous hard work in preparing for such high-status funerals.

The awarding of hero status to a leader or prince, marked by a grandiose funeral ceremony (either burial or cremation), was in fact a custom that

Figure 60 Hochdorf tomb (Germany). Attempted reconstruction. The leader is shown lying upon his death bed. In the opposite corner, there is a four-wheeled chariot and dinner service. After Kimmig, 1983.

continued in the Eastern Mediterranean regions up until Hellenistic times, following on over many centuries from the Homeric tradition of awarding outstanding individuals greater status.

Steles: Marking Combatants for Posterity

As has been discussed, during the third millennium BCE steles, despite being rather crude, reflected the superior status of the figure depicted and reaffirmed the attributes associated with this status. During the second millennium BCE, there was a definite change in these attributes (the sword replaced the dagger), yet those individuals made heroes at this time retained their status, having generally been valorous warriors to whom the population was indebted for having provided protection or prosperity or for their successful conquests. With exchange systems becoming more widespread and rare materials being transported over long distances, it would have been all the more necessary to maintain security, to combat banditry and plundering, and to use weapons either to enforce existing rules or to establish new ones. As has been seen, the status of the warrior became ever more valued in this society. Steles from both Corsica and the Iberian Peninsula confirm that this was indeed the case.

Throughout the Neolithic and Copper Age, Corsica developed a long tradition of sculpted stones. Whether these were menhir-statues or steles, the aim was always to represent the human form, however crudely, although specific attributes were never featured. In contrast to the stone statues of neighboring Sardinia and Lunigiana, there was no tradition of identifying these human figures either sexually or socially. As a result, individuals were never honored for any success they may have had in battle. During the course of the second millennium BCE, the situation began to change. As mentioned previously, these changes were not the result of an invasion; it is more likely that they can be attributed both to the evolution of the local society toward greater stratification and to Corsica becoming firmly established within a Mediterranean *koinè* where armed men were able to display their superiority. Thus, it was during the Mid/Recent Bronze Age that war-related attributes began to feature upon certain menhir-statues. Initially, long swords with a cruciform or horned hilt were featured, the best examples of which were found in the Aegean-Mycenaean region. Mycenaean ceramics were often exported as far afield as Southern Italy, Sardinia, and the Iberian Peninsula. Corsica seems to have been excluded from these exchanges within the Southern Mediterranean. However, the shape of the swords featured upon the menhir-statues may well have been influenced by the Aegean region; certainly they seem to share more cultural features with the Mediterranean than the Continental regions. In some cases, a dagger is featured as well as a sword. Leather corset-like garments were also depicted, designed to protect the chest. The horned helmets featured were also common to the Mediterranean, from Sardinia to the Levant. It is possible that these statues were erected in sacred locations where ancestors and heroes belonging to prominent families were worshipped. The breaking of these statues could, therefore, represent a protest against and exclusion of one particular clan, and the acceptance of another.

The southwestern Iberian Peninsula is another good example of a region where warfare-related steles developed in a particular way and, in this case, over a long period of time (figure 61).[18] In fact, toward the middle of the second millennium BCE monuments began to appear in Alentejo and the Algarve that differed from the early Copper Age steles that featured daggers. As times changed, so did the objects portrayed: most frequently depicted were swords with a solid hilt, held in place by a belt or baldric. In some cases, axes were featured along with this sword. A mysterious double-ended,

Figure 61   Steles of "warriors" from the Iberian Peninsula: (1) Heredade de Defesa, Santiago de Cacem (Portugal), Mid-Bronze Age; (2) Assento, Santa Vitoria (Portugal), Mid-Bronze Age; (3) Santa Ana de Trujillo, Cáceres (Spain), Late Bronze Age; (4) Bronzas, Cáceres (Spain), Late Bronze Age; (5) Solana de Cabañas, Logrosán, Cáceres (Spain), First Iron Age; (6) Cabeza de Buey, Badajoz (Spain), Early Iron Age. After M. Almagro Basch.

anchor-shaped object has also been identified, which may be either a scepter or a ceremonial object specific to this region. These steles were, therefore, both functional and prestigious objects that served to glorify certain high-ranking individuals.

During the Late Bronze Age in Extremadura and Western Andalucia, new steles began to appear bearing ever more complex symbols relating directly to the image of the warrior. It should, however, be noted that the majority of these steles were discovered during agricultural work and it is therefore difficult to ascertain whether, or indeed how, they were linked to burial sites without full knowledge of the original context. The simplest of these monuments feature a sword, a spear, and a notched shield. Others also portray more elaborate items: a two- or four-wheeled chariot, a bow, a helmet, a buckle, a mirror, and a lyre (?). These are social markers associated with the increasing role of the aristocracy. The most elaborate steles represent a crude version of a human figure, often wearing a horned helmet and surrounded by the objects already mentioned: weapons, chariots, or prestigious items. These various representations, dating from the transition period between the Bronze and Iron Ages, seem to denote a hierarchical social structure with a clear male leader upon whom were bestowed symbols of power.

The question of how this hierarchy first came about will not be dealt with here, other than to speculate that it was probably the result of local economic progress, the management of food supplies and rare materials, and a gradual increase in the influence of Mediterranean-style societies upon certain rural communities in the West. Some experts see the statues as more than just funerary steles; they may also have served to mark out territories, having been erected along certain routes. These monoliths may equally have conveyed a code or symbolic language associated with the dominant social hierarchy in those areas where they were erected; regional variation may have occurred. Female figures are often featured, adorned with tiaras, which seems to confirm the theory that those portrayed upon the steles were high-ranking individuals.

Multiple Sacrifices

As societies evolved and became more complex during the period of transition between prehistory and history, with hierarchies becoming more marked, the "sovereign's" social control continued to increase. In view of a leader's charismatic influence and position as mediator between "his" people and the supernatural forces, attempts were made to transform the greatest moments of the leadership into "theatrical" events, thus reinforcing the perception of this being a sacred role. Indeed, certain funerals often had a rather empathic dimension to them. Those who were close to or served the sovereign were often sacrificed either by their own choosing or by force. This process is known to have taken place in certain chiefdoms and in dynasties at the beginning of history. It is interesting to note that collective dramas became a necessary means of marking leaders as sacred and enhancing their personal attributes at the point when state societies were first forming or royalty was first becoming established. As a result, the gap between the main figure and the many subordinate figures widened. Sacrificial rituals also added a rather mythical quality to the role and power of the king: the hierarchy on earth continued even after death.

The dynasties of Ur, which existed in Mesopotamia in 2500 BCE, provide a good example of the extravagance that characterized the burial of leaders in history's first sovereignties. These funerals were both dramatic and grandiose and sought to glorify the deceased sovereign as well as to reinforce the exceptional character of the role and the king or queen's status in people's minds. In the royal tombs excavated by Woolley, which were made of stone and brick, the bodies of sovereigns had been buried along with highly treasured objects: copper or gold bowls and daggers and jewelry made of gold, electrum, lazuli, and so on. The entrance to the tomb known as the "king's" grave (RT 789) was found to contain the bodies of 59 servants and 19 women, as well as two chariots and the remains of six oxen. The inner vestibule of tomb 800 (tomb of Queen Puabi) contained the remains of five guards, a sled pulled by two oxen, the remains of 12 women, one of whom had a harp, and four servants. In the burial chamber itself, the queen was found lying beside metal containers and 250 funerary objects; two individuals, adorned with jewels, accompanied her remains. Tomb RT 1237 contained the remains of 68 women and six men at its entrance ("the pit of death"). This was, therefore, the scene of a collective "suicide" where lives were ended; the animals were killed after the humans. It seems likely that the humans were killed by poison. This example demonstrates how, in Ur, sacrificial rituals dedicated to a king or queen took the form of a drama involving those individuals appointed to serve the sovereign (were they slaves, or were members of the elite also executed?)

Similar mass sacrifices occurred in Egypt at an even earlier date. From pre-dynastic times in the fourth millennium BCE, traces of violence identified upon some of the bodies from the Adaima burial site seem to suggest that these individuals were executed. Cut marks upon the cervical vertebrae suggest that their throats were cut; the heads may later have been removed. However, it is not known whether this cruel treatment was ritualistic. "Mass" sacrifices are likely to have taken place during the first dynasty, as the sovereign's tomb was surrounded by the graves of his servants. In Abydos, some 800 of these "subsidiary tombs" surrounded the grave of King Aha (of the first dynasty), with another 500 graves being placed nearby. Steles indicate that these were the graves of courtiers, women of the harem, skilled craftsmen, and affluent individuals. It is, however, not always possible to prove whether or not these deaths all occurred at the same time. Sacrifice is known to have occurred to mark the burial of the sovereigns Qa and Semerkhet, whose graves were placed above those of their servants. Similar sacrifices are thought to have occurred in Saqqara. These sacrifices seem to have stopped at the end of the first dynasty, in around 2800 BCE.[19]

In Sudan, "sacrifice-mania" seems to have swept through the Kerma culture in the third and second millennia BCE. At the beginning of the twentieth century, Reisner identified evidence of sacrifice among graves at a burial site to the east of Kerma: the remains of one individual were surrounded by circles of human remains, each varying in the number of skeletons they contained. Practices did, however, evolve over time. In Early Kerma, the process was in its initial stages: certain tombs were found to contain two bodies, both placed here at the same time, which would indicate that one of the two was killed, probably by force. During the Middle Kerma period, there was a notable increase in the number of human bodies and animal remains placed to the west and south of the main burial site. However, it was during the Classic Kerma period that the real fixation with sacrifice emerged. The remains of several hundred bodies (up to 400 in certain cases) were placed around some of the princely graves. Signs of injury were identified upon the lower parts of some of the vertebral columns found here, between the sixth and seventh cervical vertebrae: it is thought that these individuals were victims of ritual decapitation. Again, the question arises as to whether these victims were slaves or the prince's close acquaintances or even relatives. Anthropological studies were unable to identify any significant morphological differences between the bodies of the sacrificial victims and those of the deceased rulers, thus eliminating the possibility that these were foreign slaves, at least in this case. However, some studies have established a biological link between the victims and the deceased, in whose honor they were sacrificed.[20]

Later, in the fifth century BCE, Herodotus described how the Scythians behaved during the funeral of a leader:

> Then, having laid the dead in the tomb on a couch, they plant spears all round the body and lay across them wooden planks, which they then roof over with hides; in the open space which is left in the tomb they bury, after strangling, one of the king's concubines, his cup-bearer, his cook, his groom, his squire, and his messenger, besides horses, and first-fruits of all else, and golden cups;

for the Scythians make no use of silver or bronze. Having done this, they all build a great barrow of earth, vying zealously with one another to make this as great as may be.

However, this was only the first stage of the ritual.

With the completion of a year they begin a fresh practice. Taking the trustiest of the rest of the king's servants (and these are native-born Scythians, for only those serve the king whom he bids so to do, and none of the Scythians have servants bought by money) they strangle fifty of these squires and fifty of their best horses and empty and cleanse the bellies of all and fill them with chaff. Then they make fast the half of a wheel to two posts, so that it hangs down, and the other half to another pair of posts, till many posts thus furnished are planted in the ground [. . .] Then they take each one of the fifty strangled young men and mount him on the horse; [. . .] So having set horsemen of this fashion round about the tomb they ride away.[21]

Of course, a great deal of time and distance separates the Kerma chiefdoms (dynasties?) of the third millennium BCE from the Scythian chiefdoms of protohistoric times. Despite this, the layout of the tombs where leaders were buried became increasingly similar over time: a central figure, sacrificial victims (humans and animals) arranged in concentric circles, and many funerary objects. It is also important to note that the Scythians strangled their sacrificial victims, whereas injuries were identified upon the cervical vertebrae of the Kerma victims: these acts of violence (either inflicted with bare hands or with a sharp instrument) focused upon the victim's neck region and so avoided too great a mutilation of the body. As a result, the body could be prepared for a more aesthetic burial; bodies were either erected upon the backs of the slaughtered horses (Scythians) or laid upon cowhide in a flexed position (Kerma). These practices thus demonstrate a curious combination of respect for the victim's body and ritual violence.

In the Byci Skala cave in Moravia, Central Europe, the remains of an individual were discovered, dating from protohistoric times, which had been cremated among a number of "treasures." These included the remains of a chariot and two horses (from which the heads and extremities of each limb had been removed), bronze and iron objects, metal, glass, and amber jewelry, animal bones, and the charred remains of cereals. These were surrounded by the remains of more than 40 individuals: 35 women, five men, an adolescent aged between 10 and 12, and a child of only a few years of age. Various items (valuable jewelry and scraps of clothing) were scattered among these peripheral remains. The state of the bodies had often been altered, with some skulls being removed and humerus bones broken. These archeological discoveries, which date from the seventh century BCE, suggest that a collective sacrifice occurred here which sought to glorify the individual cremated.[22]

Those in charge and their entourage were able to influence their dependent subjects both through their charisma and through despotism. Similarly, such influence is responsible for identical patterns of behavior across different areas and over different periods of time. In Oceania in the thirteenth century CE, for example, similar rituals were performed by societies that were still "prehistoric" in the sense that, at this point in time, they had had no contact with the written word. Upon the small island of Retoka, which was found to be uninhabited when Europeans first arrived, "Roy Mata" was buried, the earliest and greatest hero in the mythology of the central New Hebrides region. According to the oral tradition of this archipelago, the island was abandoned immediately after the chief's funeral ceremony and became taboo, a sacred location to be used exclusively as a resting place for the chief and his entourage. Legend claims that Roy Mata organized great feasts, presided over enthronement ceremonies for dignitaries, accorded power to various chiefs, all of whom viewed him as their superior, established the social structures for this part of the archipelago, and encouraged population growth in the region. Following his death, his body was displayed in the territories of the clans that came under his rule. He was then buried in Retoka, where an impressive funeral ceremony was performed in his honor; members of his entourage and representatives from each clan were either buried alive or sacrificed at their own request (so the legend goes). But is this legend correct? Seven hundred years later, Garanger was able to determine the accuracy of the legend by carrying out detailed excavations which unearthed the graves of the chief and his attendants.[23]

Roy Mata was buried with his legs apart; the skeleton of a young woman was found lying curled up between them. His remains were surrounded by the body of a man to his left, a couple to his right, and a young woman at his feet. Around this central tomb, the remains of 33 individuals (17 women and 16 men) had been placed to form an arc; some were buried alone, but most were in couples. All of these bodies were adorned with necklaces, armbands, shell belts, and wild boar teeth. The bodies of the males were laid out on their backs, as if resting, whereas the females were curled up against their companion; they held their companion around the neck, arm, or waist, as if seeking greater protection, with their feet pressed against his feet and their hands and feet clenched. It is thought that the men had swallowed a drink containing poison and were thus drugged at the time of their burial. The women, however, were not entitled to this anaesthetizing drink. It may well be that they were buried alive or, in certain cases, strangled. Other individuals were also sacrificed, undoubtedly against their will; cannibalistic practices may even have occurred, since their long bones had been gathered together in bundles. Following the funeral, access to the island was forbidden, yet this legend was passed on for 700 years. Thanks to this culture's oral tradition, archeological research into this exceptional funerary ritual could be linked directly to the mythology and its discourse. This case was, therefore, one of some individuals being sacrificed and others "sacrificing" themselves voluntarily.

Turning back now to protohistory in the ancient world, other examples of collective sacrifice can be identified, some dating from the Bronze Age, often in very different cultural contexts. One such example is the middle basin of the Yellow River in China where the Shang dynasties developed between the seventeenth and eleventh centuries BCE. One of the tombs at the Sufutun (Su-fu-t'un) burial site was placed in a vast pit with access ramps. The burial chamber was covered over by platforms with shafts carved into its base. In addition to the treasures placed in the grave (bronze axes, jade objects, stone and shell jewelry, ceramics), the remains of 48 humans and six dogs were found at various points in this underground structure – all had been sacrificed.[24]

The unification of China during the third century BCE led to a centralized empire being established. The tomb of the first emperor is indicative of a fixation with extravagance. The sovereign was buried beneath a huge pyramid 400 m across and surrounded by two walls; the outer wall surrounded an area of 2×1 km. Buried with him in the tomb were his father's concubines and all those involved in constructing the sacred tomb, to ensure that they could not divulge any of its secrets. Other tombs were discovered in the immediate surrounding areas: the tombs of princes, guarded by the bodies of executed servants, and the tombs of 70 men, all of whom had been sacrificed. It is even thought that the emperor's children were massacred at the time of his funeral. The emperor himself requested that an army of clay statues protect him after his death. The result was a spectacular troop of warriors, built to be larger than life-size. They were placed in the underground corridors, as if in sheltered barracks. There were thousands of these statues in total.[25]

Mutilated Bodies Preserved in Peat Bogs

This overview of violence during protohistoric times ends in Northern Europe. In the marshland areas of Denmark, Norway, Sweden, the Netherlands, Germany, and the UK, peat bogs have often proved an excellent means of preserving bodies deposited in water in marshy areas. In the particular physicochemical conditions specific to lakes, lagoons, swamps, and peat bogs, bodies are preserved without being significantly damaged. Excavation work carried out in these peat bogs has often unearthed spectacular discoveries since the decomposition of the bodies is greatly reduced in such environments. As a result, the skin and flesh of these mummified remains are often preserved and are of great archeological interest. This broadens the scope for investigation, unlike in most cases worldwide where the body has decomposed to a skeleton, thus restricting the range of study. In some cases, headgear, clothes, shoes, and various instruments belonging to these "bog men" were also preserved. In many cases, the protohistoric individuals found in these environments, both male and female, seem to have been thrown into water after being executed. Their bodies show signs of violent injury: slit throats, strangulation marks inflicted by laces or ropes around the neck, various wounds, and multiple fractures. Since the soft tissues have been preserved, it is easy to identify the particular act of violence that caused their death. It is, of course, possible that accidental drowning as part of a ritual sacrifice was responsible for some of the deaths. However, in the majority of cases aggression seems the most likely cause of death, especially as the "murder weapon" has often been preserved in the form of a rope used to strangle or hang the victim.

One example is the body discovered in 1984 in England during drainage work carried out in Lindow, Cheshire. The body of this "bog man" is a permanent exhibit at the British Museum. With the aid of the most sophisticated techniques available (scanners, X-ray photography, sample analysis), anthropologists called in to examine these remains were able to ascertain immediately that this individual had sustained numerous injuries as a result of violence. Ropes, which were still preserved, bound his limbs together. His throat had been slit. He had sustained numerous fractures, particularly upon his face and skull. There can be no doubt that this was a premeditated murder and that the body was subsequently thrown into the water. Archeological studies have enabled this murder to be dated to Iron Age times, in around 350 BCE.[26]

Other discoveries have indicated the existence of similar behavior. The body of a man of about 20 years old was discovered in Tollund (Denmark) in 1950, complete with a leather bonnet, belt, and rope made up of two cords twisted together with which the individual had been hanged or strangled (plate 25). It was even possible to determine what he ate for his last meal, eaten between 12 and 24 hours before his death: a mixture of mashed cereals (barley and wheat) and various types of weed that would have grown in the cultivated fields. The body dates from the Iron Age. In 1952, another discovery was made in Denmark, this time in Grauballe, roughly 20 km to the east of Tollund. These remains are slightly more recent, dating from around

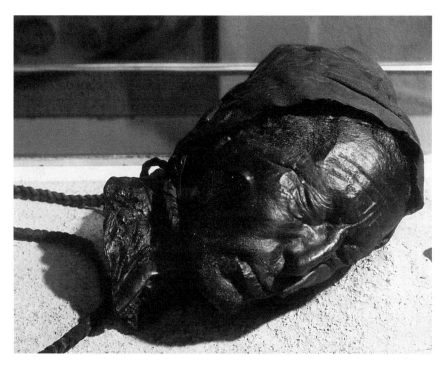

Plate 25 Tollund man, mummified human remains found in a peat bog (Denmark). Detail of the head of the tortured victim. The rope, used to strangle or hang this individual, is clearly visible. Iron Age, ca. 350 BCE. © AKG-Images.

2,000 years ago, yet are no less protohistoric in the sense that these areas were not part of the Roman empire (in this region, the period is known as the "Roman Iron Age" to indicate that it was contemporaneous with the Roman empire in those areas under Roman influence). The neck has been severed from ear to ear, cutting right through the esophagus (plate 26). It appears as though several attempts at cutting the throat were made. The body also shows signs of a fracture to the skull, level with the right temple, and an injury to the left tibia.[27] Other bodies have also been discovered in Scandinavia which show signs of having been strangled, hanged, or having had their throats cut. In a peat bog in Roum (Denmark), the decapitated body of a woman was discovered dating from the Early Iron Age.

What reasons lie behind these various executions? Sacrifice seems to be the most likely explanation. This theory was notably proposed by Professor Dieck, who in 1960 carried out the most detailed study of the day into the male and female bodies found in peat bogs.[28] The majority of these individuals were

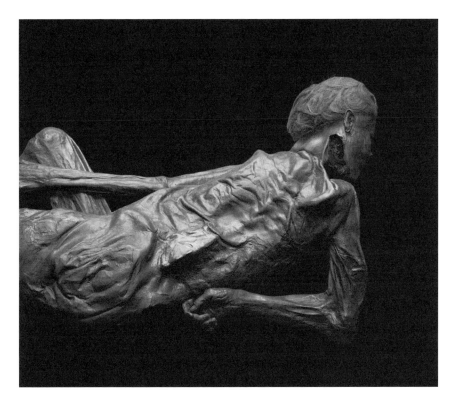

Plate 26 Grauballe man, found in a peat bog (Denmark). The throat of this individual has been slit; the deep incision across his throat is clearly visible. Roman Iron Age. Moesgard Museum, Denmark.

most likely sacrificed and then their bodies thrown into the water, perhaps to enable the community to function: the community may have required ritual violence to be carried out periodically for religious reasons. However, this theory does not rule out the hypothesis that some of these individuals were hanged, a theory that is often confirmed by the presence of ropes tied around the victims' necks. Such executions were punishments in the form of a death penalty. Acts of violence such as slitting a person's throat or smashing the skull are quick, spontaneous, and decisive acts. However, hangings and decapitations take too long to carry out to be classed as sudden acts of murder. They may have been performed as part of a punitive ritual, in the most general sense of the term. In this case, these executions may represent the beginnings of a sense of justice (be this at a religious, social, or family level) and punishment.

With the aid of such evidence, it may be possible to piece together a new and largely unexplored vision of the final stages of prehistory and protohistory involving the emergence of new social conditions and constraints which, if not adhered to, could result in death. The fact that bodies were subsequently thrown into the water could indicate that the murder, although endorsed, still had to be covered up either by disposing of or concealing the victim's body. The victim became an outcast.

Finally, all of the acts discussed – individual violence, sacrifice, punishment, concealing the body – may represent a new perception of homicide within society. Murder would have been considered a much feared and irreversible act taking the form of sacrifice or the ultimate punishment. The decision to carry out such executions would have been made within the hierarchically structured community. Yet murder would also have been considered a shameful act. As a result, vague notions of justice, social punishment, and criminal law may have begun to emerge within protohistoric societies. Thus, executions may have been ordered by repressive collective authorities, rather than being spontaneous acts of revenge on the part of an individual. The two main objectives – sacrifice and punishment – may also have combined in the one act; the victims chosen to "save" the community may already have been banished from society for various reasons: for breaking a taboo, for psychological reasons, for committing a crime for which punishment was required, or for simply being prisoners of war or individuals captured from foreign enemies.

Conclusion

What conclusions can be drawn from these various examples of violent behavior? It certainly seems that violence, according to the current definition of the term, has more or less always existed. Although proof from the early periods may be lacking, the only doubts are raised by the scarcity of available evidence or by difficulties in interpreting early evidence. From the end of the Paleolithic onwards, when evidence becomes more prolific, various types of aggression can be clearly identified.

Before progressing any further, it should be noted that the meaning of the term "violence" is relative, since each culture determines its own codes of conduct. As a result, the concept can vary according to the time and place in question. Of course, it is still possible to analyze and pinpoint this concept and archeology contributes to this exercise. However, the reality, perception, and intensity of violence can vary from culture to culture. Those involved in human sacrifice, murder, slavery, and conflict, either as officiants or as victims, may perceive these acts as the result of fate or law and may even have participated with a certain degree of pride. Indeed, for Homer's heroes and the young Sioux, there was no greater glory than that of dying in combat, no greater honor for a Hindu wife than that of throwing herself upon her husband's funeral pyre, and for the kamikaze pilot, no greater sign of grandeur than that of dying in a suicide mission by crashing his plane into an American ship in the Pacific.

Adopting a schematic approach, at least two forms of violence can be said to coexist. The first form is subtle and "internal" and is specific to a particular group during a period of peace; it is reflected in the competition that characterizes day-to-day life and the underlying tensions that exist within any given community, however calm. These tensions may end in scores being settled, revenge, and murder. Such impetuous behavior between individuals is often condemned by the group. To avoid tensions boiling over in this way and to enable society to function without confrontation occurring between its members, societies created rules and taboos that have been ingrained in religious tradition from the very outset. Groups were therefore unable to act upon any underlying tensions owing to these codes of conduct. However, the ritual act of sacrifice provided an outlet for such frictions by punishing the victim for any misdeeds and violations for which he was held responsible. This violence (for, objectively speaking, this is violent behavior) was deemed sacred and was thus justified as legitimate; it was seen to play a redemptive and salvatory role.

Violence can also be "external," expressed as a confrontation between two or more communities. Any internal conflicts within each individual community are halted or reduced on such occasions, giving way to cohesion; adopting a collective mentality is preferable to each individual following a separate approach. This type of violence may take the form of ritual warfare, duels between warriors, raids, or widespread and ruthless conflict. Not only does such activity gain the approval of all the groups and individuals involved, it is also deemed to be necessary.

One additional and essential factor must be added to this inevitably rather basic classification: the stage of social progression and thus temporal dimension under consideration. The coercion involved can be interpreted in many different ways, depending upon whether the group in question is a small and fluid band of hunter-gatherers, a small village of peasants, or a city with a population of several thousand. The way in which authority or power is exerted depends upon the hierarchy in place and thus varies greatly from group to group. Whatever the case, apart from individual aggression, the violence that takes place during sacrifice or warfare is often justified: murder is "legalized" and accepted in society.

Murder or sacrifice? As the various examples from prehistory have demonstrated, it is often difficult to separate these interpretations. Archeology is often stretched to its limit when attempting to resolve this matter with reference to preliterary times. In many cases, it is difficult to determine the cause of death: an act of revenge inflicted by one individual, a punishment inflicted upon either members of a community or outsiders, injuries sustained in battle, or sacrificial execution. It is often impossible to progress beyond the hypothetical. However, the range of weapons used in such killings can often be determined with a high degree of accuracy. Weapons have been continually improved over time. In addition to their practical role, weapons became ever more prestigious symbolically to the point where they became a symbol of masculinity and virility. Paleolithic cave paintings (Cougnac and Pech-Merle, France) as well as scenes featured upon objects (Paglicci, Italy) show figures being struck by projectiles, which appear to be javelins or assegais and which were either thrown by hand or launched with a stick-thrower. The stick-thrower was a hunting tool which could also be transformed into a formidable weapon in this way. If the "torture" featured in the Addaura rock engravings has been correctly interpreted, the level of suffering inflicted or cruelty imposed during initiation rituals (in the form of asphyxiation) some 12,000 years ago can be assessed.

The bow, invented toward the end of the Paleolithic, was the supreme weapon for firing over long distances during the Mesolithic and Neolithic, and perhaps even more recently, since it could be used to fire arrows accurately and effectively. During farming times, axes with handles and flint daggers (and later copper and then bronze daggers) were used in close combat. With the arrival of the Bronze Age new weapons of attack, most notably swords and spears, began to play a significant role, along with the bow, which was still in use. In the first cities or in "barbarian" chiefdoms, chariots and then horses began to play a part in conflict. Archeology has thus unearthed evidence relating to such techniques as well as to changes in the methods of killing. However, when it comes to the reasons behind these acts, archeology is on shakier ground.

How can we decipher the mentality of prehistoric humans? What role did violence play and how did hunter-gatherers, Neolithic peasants, and Bronze Age warriors perceive violence? At the beginning of this work, we warned readers against applying current perceptions to the study of early societies. This could easily lead us to pass judgment on customs that are unfamiliar to us, such as cannibalism. The notion of exocannibalism, i.e., cannibalism for purely nutritional reasons, may be perceived as somewhat disturbing. Yet if this prehistoric cannibalism were ritualistic, a case of "putting to death" and consuming a member of the community for a religious reason, perhaps as an offering to the ancestors, this would have been a sacred and sublime act.

Turning again to the notion of sacrifice, there is no doubt that the various examples discussed have only touched upon some of the many aspects of this issue. Sacrifice certainly involves violence, but did the "executioner" responsible for cutting the victim's throat, firing the fatal arrows, or hanging the victim consider it to be a violent act? What was the "victim's" frame of mind? Did the numerous individuals killed in Ur, Abydos, and Kerma to accompany a sovereign in death consider it to be an honor or a punishment? Did they give in to this constraint, unable to react against it in view of their inferior status? Leaders were more or less deified, yet the fact that their entourage and closest servants followed them into the afterlife in this way suggests that these leaders could not manage "elsewhere" without them.

In fact, killing close acquaintances or even separating oneself from the sovereign or leader of the community was nothing more than an imperial duty carried out to save the community. The "victim's" life was offered as a means of ensuring collective salvation and enabling life to continue. The act was an essential means of regeneration and reestablishing order. This act of "putting to death" is highly sacred and therefore, although violence is involved, the notions of murder and negative activity do not play any part. Indeed, the pharaohs celebrated their death and symbolic resurrection annually in the form of the Sed festivals. This custom may be a relic of an earlier era when communities would eliminate their "sovereigns" in impressive religious ceremonies in cases where these "sovereigns" were no longer carrying out their role as mediator with the supernatural forces satisfactorily.[1] Was the grandeur and servitude associated with such leaders vested in a fundamental post? This is a new field of research in archeology and anthropology: is it possible that some of the earliest charismatic "figures" from the Copper and Bronze Ages, when the social pyramid became more marked, were executed in grandiose ceremonies, indicated perhaps by the size of their tombs and the number of offerings buried with the bodies? This is another theory worth investigating.

However, this work has sought in particular to document the progressive increase in the role of warfare since recent prehistory. The term "warfare" has been applied in its most general sense here to mean confrontations between groups of humans, often taking the form of attacks and raids, the aim of which is to injure, kill, or pillage. Locating archeological evidence of such conflicts is far from easy. The chances of finding communal graves dating from prehistoric times, like those from Talheim, are slim. Excavations tend to focus upon settlements and cemeteries, i.e., ordinary locations. Casualties killed in confrontations taking place upon "battlefields" are generally buried far away from settlements, i.e., beyond the perimeters of most archeological excavations. It is also rare for villages coming under siege at any time to leave the remains of those killed on site; they tend to be removed very quickly.

If we were to evaluate the number of deaths attributable to warfare during historic times, based solely upon the human and material remains found to date and disregarding written sources, we would be no further advanced. Indeed, very little remains of those killed in battle over the last thousand years where bodies were abandoned where they lay or buried in makeshift graves (and the troops involved in these battles were far superior in numbers to those of recent prehistory). Any theory based purely upon the limited amount of archeological evidence available, however reasonable and rigorous, cannot claim to reflect reality. Without close study of any of the available written accounts, it would be easy to grossly underestimate the number of wars and battles, and consequently the recent past would be considered remarkably peaceful. This may well explain why the violence of prehistoric times has also been underestimated. Written accounts are evidently an invaluable source of information on such matters.

The confrontations that are known to have taken place in Djebel Sahaba seem to demonstrate the existence of conflict between communities at the end of the Paleolithic. Evidence from certain Mesolithic sites, though less conclusive, indicates that similar situations occurred here. But did confrontation between humans take place before this? Although archeological evidence is lacking, it seems reasonable to assume that it did. There is evidence of murder having occurred from the first half of the Upper Paleolithic, although the context and reasons surrounding these actions are not known. The role of warfare in hunter-gatherer society is also well documented in ethnology. A recent study of ten hunter-gatherer societies revealed that two of the societies were more or less constantly at war, five fought periodically, while the remaining three were rarely or never at war.[2]

War is often thought to be a practice associated with the development of cities, the protective role of states, and their coercive function. According to this perception of warfare, conflict in the Eastern Mediterranean first took place in 3000 BCE, at the time of the first pharaohs or Sumerian dynasties. In those areas where writing did not develop until a later date and which did not have a state system, as was the case throughout the majority of Europe, the Bronze Age confrontations of the second millennium BCE are the closest these areas came to this definition of conflict. However, it seems more relevant to view the development of such behavior over a longer time span. There was, of course, a "prehistory of warfare" in the most general sense of the term; all evidence must be meticulously recorded in order to determine the social context of this period. It goes without saying that this approach cannot be limited solely to recording isolated facts (such as deaths due to arrow wounds), since such facts do not reflect the full scale of the issue. A more extensive approach is required, encompassing evidence relating to the economy and social organization, demographic models, the hierarchical ranking of sites, defensive architectural features, types of power, and the relations between the various sources of authority. In short, a more global perspective must be adopted. Only in this way can the situations that triggered such conflicts be identified and any possible traces of evidence be found. In fact, rather than relying solely upon archeological analysis, the probability of various types and incidents of violence having occurred is best demonstrated by drawing parallels with ethnological examples; indeed, the variety of cultures documented in ethnology will serve to level out the study. The archeological record is inevitably partial and incomplete. In adopting a purely archeological approach and sticking strictly to archeological sources, researchers run the risk of overlooking relevant evidence and leaving certain lines of enquiry unexplored. This would obviously be detrimental in terms of limiting archeological theory. This is, therefore, one of the limiting factors of a purely archeological approach. Theories based too closely upon archeological evidence can only present, at best, a sketchy reconstruction of the complex reality. Those theories that do not take enough account of archeological evidence run the risk of being irrelevant and fanciful. Reconstructing the social organization and its implementation is undoubtedly the best way of detecting the potential occurrence of conflict in prehistory. This is inevitably a speculative exercise for the most part, yet it is the only way of studying behavior in preliterary societies without adopting an overly limited outlook.

As the reader will have noticed, this work has adopted a somewhat evolutionary approach. Each stage in the increasing role of conflict in society seems to be marked by changes in the economy, an exploitation of the environment, technological developments, and social hierarchy. Of course, the clashes that took place in Sudan during the Epipaleolithic and the conflicts that characterized the Copper Age in the West had little in common with the actions of the eastern sovereigns during the second millennium BCE. Warfare becomes ever more prominent as society increases in complexity. Both the troops involved and the strategies employed vary. It seems likely that those conflicts that occurred during the Epipaleolithic or at the time of the first farming communities took the form of ambush attacks, raids that may have ended in murder and confrontations between young males. By contrast, in Megiddo or Kadesh where "the first battles in history" took place, "specialized" trained troops came face to face, forming contingents and employing tried and tested techniques in battle. However, it is the mentality behind this need for confrontation which is of interest here, rather than these indisputable variations in the forms of warfare. Whatever the motives, it is evident that some areas were characterized by confrontation very early on, which even resulted in enemies being killed in some cases. This need for confrontation is one aspect of competition between humans and can be classified as one of the "activities" that form part of the masculine sphere. In this respect, there is a significant contrast between the female domain (symbolized by biological features in Neolithic and Chalcolithic art) and the male domain (represented by weapons). The ideology behind the warrior is reflected in the stone statues of the fourth millennium BCE onwards. In certain areas, warriors were widely "staged" in this way. Two thousand years later, more complex societies began to emerge with the arrival of the Bronze Age and warriors gradually became established in society. The competition, too, became more intense for those wishing to prove themselves and be worshipped as heroes, i.e., as the most determined warriors in defeating an enemy. Courage, honor, and loyalty became noble qualities through this interplay of weapons and victories. According to the idealized notions of those fighting, cruelty, barbarity, and death were no longer an issue. Warriors were motivated by the community that they were defending or representing. Yet where is Good and Evil? Can archeology incorporate aspects of Manichean theory? Tracking down the notions of violence and war in prehistory soon brings about a new level of awareness and causes us to make personal judgments.

On a final note, we shall end with some more general observations. War is merely one aspect of domination between humans, albeit a collective and cruel one. On an individual level, this begins as soon as competition enters into the equation, whether this competition is related to materials, partners, society, or religion. Freud, Marx, and Dawkins, among others, have all attempted to explain how our subconscious, our social condition, or our chromosomes can lead to confrontation with a father, mother, or brother, a boss, worker, or slave, or with those of a different color, financial status, or religion. In short, confrontation with others. Aggression and conflict from prehistory onwards could, therefore, be the result of a gradual rise in tension directed at others: rivals, family, tribes, or towns. There is a surprising paradox between the ever-increasing number of cultures and societies, which leads to exchange systems and alliances being formed, and the violence that can suddenly surface and destroy this conviviality at any moment.

However, it is important not to over-dramatize the situation. Indeed, the magnificence of the Lascaux paintings and the effort which groups must have put into building temples and megalithic tombs as well as distributing and exchanging materials and objects over long distances (which were considerable for the day) indicate not only the level of cultural sophistication attained by these societies, but also their degree of collaboration, cooperation, and desire to work together. History did not begin with the advent of writing; it is more deeply rooted in the past. Prehistoric civilizations, all based on oral tradition, were nevertheless sophisticated in some ways. Their creativity and, in particular, their economic and social systems reveal that civilizations began to develop structures similar to those of the civilizations of history very early on, in particular from the period of the first sedentary agricultural communities. It is precisely because we, the authors, are convinced that these societies were sophisticated, culturally speaking, that we have endeavored not to omit any aspect of their cultural development. Although we recognize that violence often featured in the mentality of prehistoric humans, this does not mean that this behavior should be considered "barbaric." Indeed, this shows that a degree of severity, exploitation, and occasionally cruelty has featured in the running of most human societies, both "prehistoric" and "historic" (without there being any break between the two), including those civilizations which are now considered to have been particularly noble. In view of all the dramatic events experienced throughout the twentieth century – Nazism, the Gulags, nationalism, fundamentalism – can we really say that humans have improved since prehistoric times, that humans are better? Certainly not. Yet it is unrealistic to believe that humans were peaceful and innocent in the distant past either. Keeley says that to idealize prehistoric humans is to dehumanize them. Archeological evidence and subsequent historical facts have both shown that *Homo sapiens* has continually fluctuated between better and worse states of existence throughout its already long history.

Appendix 1: Evidence of Arrow-Inflicted Injuries from the Neolithic Age in France

Maryvonne Naudet and Raymond Vidal

This information is drawn from bibliographic sources and discussions with various researchers.

1 Confirmed cases

(44 sites, 67 bones showing signs of injury, 66 individuals killed or injured)

Town (department)	Location	Type of tomb	Individuals killed or injured/total deceased	Location of the impact; possible type of arrow used	Probable date (BCE)	Period/culture; observations
1 Téviec (Morbihan)	L'îlot	Collective burial in a cemetery containing 10 tombs	1 young adult male, 20–25 years old *1 killed/6*	6th dorsal vertebra 11th dorsal vertebra	ca. 5500	Final Mesolithic
2 Quatzenheim (Bas-Rhin)	–	Individual tomb in a cemetery containing at least 13 tombs	1 young adult male less than 20 years old (tomb 10) *1 killed or injured/13*	1 right ilium	5200–4800	Neolithic Linear Band culture Arrowheads in tomb 13

Town (department)	Location	Type of tomb	Individuals killed or injured/total deceased	Location of the impact; possible type of arrow used	Probable date (BCE)	Period/culture; observations
3 Clermont-Ferrand (Puy-du-Dôme)	Pontcharraud	Pontcharraud 2: collective burial	1 adult male *1 killed or injured/7*	1 vertebra	4400–4100	Middle Neolithic (proto-Chassean?)
4 Auzay (Vendée)	Les Châtelliers-du-Vieil-Auzay	3 double burials covered with stones beneath a long earth barrow	1 adult male (tomb 3)	4th lumbar vertebra	3600–3200	Recent Neolithic – Peu-Richard culture Possibly 6 individuals executed
5 Saint-Jean-Saint-Paul (Aveyron)	Les Treilles	Ossuary – cave	1 young adult 3 individuals *2 killed and 2 injured/74*	1 left fibula 1 radius, 1 metatarsal bone 1 rib	3500–2200	Final Neolithic – Chalcolithic/Treilles culture + various other fractures and injuries
6 Guiry-en-Vexin (Val-d'Oise)	La Ferme Duport	Covered passageway	1 individual *1 killed/30*	1 cervical vertebra	3400–2900	Recent Neolithic/Seine-Oise-Marne culture
7 Presles (Val-d'Oise)	La Pierre Plate	Covered passageway	1 elderly adult *1 killed/more than 100*	1 dorsal-lumbar vertebra Other injuries to frontal and femur; skull smashed	3400–2300	Seine-Oise-Marne culture 3400–2900 or Gord culture 2900–2300
8 Coizard (Marne)	Razet	Hypogeum	1 young adult male	1 lumbar vertebra	3400–2300	Seine-Oise-Marne culture 3400–2900 or Gord culture 2900–2300
9 Villevenard (Marne)	La Pierre Michelot	Hypogeum	1 young adult male *1 killed/22*	1 vertebra	3400–2300	Seine-Oise-Marne culture 3400–2900 or Gord culture 2900–2300
10 Villevenard (Marne)	Hypogeum II	Hypogeum	1 young adult male *1 killed/?*	1 vertebra	3400–2300	Seine-Oise-Marne culture 3400–2900 or Gord culture 2900–2300

No. & Site	Name	Type	Individuals	Injured bones	Date	Culture/period
11 Oyes (Marne)	Hypogeum I	Hypogeum	1 young adult male	1 humerus	3400–2300	Seine-Oise-Marne culture 3400–2900 or Gord culture 2900–2300
12 Oyes (Marne)	Hypogeum II	Hypogeum	1 young adult male	1 skull (zygomatic arch)	3400–2300	Seine-Oise-Marne culture 3400–2900 or Gord culture 2900–2300
13 Trêves (Gard)	Le Pas-de-Joulié	Ossuary – cave	1 individual *1 killed/more than 300*	Copper blade embedded in 3rd cervical vertebra	3300–2900	Final Neolithic/early stage of the Treilles culture + 1 damaged frontal and 1 damaged parietal
14 Les Matelles (Hérault)	Suquet-Coucolières	Swallow hole cave – ossuary	4 individuals *(perhaps 6)*	1 humerus, 1 femur, 1 tibia, 1 vertebra	3300–2200	Final Neolithic – Chalcolithic
15 Marvejols (Lozère)	Le Crespin	Dolmen	1 individual *1 killed/18*	1 skull (right parietal)	3300–2200	Final Neolithic – Chalcolithic
16 Grillon (Vaucluse)	Le Capitaine	Hypogeum	2 individuals *2 killed/150*	2 dorsal vertebrae	3200–2700	Final Neolithic – Early Chalcolithic
17 Cornus (Aveyron)	Fontcagarelle	Ossuary – cave	1 individual *1 injured/30*	1 radius	3000–2200	Chalcolithic/Treilles group
18 Saint-Saturnin-d'Apt (Vaucluse)	La Lave	Cave burial site	3 individuals *3 injured/66*	1 sacrum, 1 left femur, 1 left humerus	3000–2200	Chalcolithic Other injuries upon 2 skulls, 1 humerus, 1 femur, 1 fibula, 1 ulna
19 Gémenos (Bouches-du-Rhône)	Saint-Clair	Cave burial site	1 individual *1 injured/more than 15*	1 tibia	3000–2200	Chalcolithic
20 Bertholène (Aveyron)	Maymac	Dolmen (no. 5)	1 individual *1 killed or injured/?*	1 vertebra	3000–2200	Chalcolithic/Treilles group
21 Montbrun (Lozère)	Le Sot-de-la-Lavogne	Cave burial site	1 individual *1 injured/30*	1 dorsal vertebra	3000–2200	Chalcolithic/Treilles group

243

Town (department)	Location	Type of tomb	Individuals killed or injured/total deceased	Location of the impact; possible type of arrow used	Probable date (BCE)	Period/culture; observations
22 Sainte-Énimie (Lozère)	–	Cave burial site	1 young adult male *1 killed/5*	2 dorsal vertebrae	3000–2200	Chalcolithic/Treilles group 1 fragment of a skull showing signs of trepanation
23 Fontvieille (Bouches-du-Rhône)	Le Castellet	Hypogeum	1 individual *1 killed/100*	1 lumbar vertebra	3000–2200	Chalcolithic
24 Sébazac-Concourès (Aveyron)	Puechcamp	Dolmen	1 individual *1 injured/24*	1 left metacarpal bone	3000–2200	Chalcolithic/Treilles culture
25 Cornus (Aveyron)	Prévinquières	Dolmen	1 individual	1 right femur	3000–2200	Chalcolithic/Treilles culture
26 Gijounet (Tarn)	Mauray	Swallow hole burial site	1 young adult aged 20–25 years *1 killed/7*	5th lumbar vertebra Lanceolate, large-stemmed arrow	3000–2200	Chalcolithic
27 Le Massegros (Lozère)	Aragon	Ossuary – cave	1 individual *1 killed/9*	1 lumbar vertebra	3000–2200	Chalcolithic/Treilles culture
28 Sarrians (Vaucluse)	Les Boileau	Hypogeum	1 individual *1 killed/300*	1 vertebra	2900–2500	Final Neolithic
29 Roaix (Vaucluse)	Les Crottes	Hypogeum	1 adolescent 2 individuals *2 killed/roughly 100 in the "war layer"*	1 sacrum 1 vertebra, 1 mastoid apophysis, 4 additional arrows found in thorax bones	2900–2500	Final Neolithic – Chalcolithic

30 Chanac (Lozère)	L'Aumède	Dolmen	1 young adult 1 individual *1 killed and 1 injured/40*	11th dorsal vertebra 1 tibia	2800–1800	Chalcolithic – Early Bronze Age 8 cases of trepanation and several fractures also identified
31 La Ciotat (Bouches-du-Rhône)	Terrevaine	Cave burial site (ca. 30 bodies in 5 graves)	1 individual *1 killed/7 (?)*	1 lumbar vertebra	2600–2200	Recent Chalcolithic
32 Boucoiran (Gard)	Le Chemin-de-Fer	Ossuary – cave	1 individual *1 injured/12*	1 sacrum	2600–2200	Chalcolithic/Fontbouisse culture
33 Laissac (Aveyron)	Les Caïres	Rock shelter	1 individual *1 injured/13*	1 left radius Crenulate ("pine tree") arrow	2600–2200	Chalcolithic/final phase of the Treilles culture Fractures and cases of trepanation also identified
34 Saint-Rome-de-Tarn (Aveyron)	Font-Rial	Dolmen	1 adult *1 injured/more than 5*	1 tibia Crenulate ("pine tree") arrow	2600–2200	Chalcolithic/final phase of the Treilles culture
35 Creyssels (Aveyron)	Les Cascades	Ossuary – cave (cave I)	3 young adults *2 injured and 1 killed/79*	1 tibia, 1 metatarsal bone, 1 left radius	2600–2200	Chalcolithic/final phase of the Treilles culture
36 Veyrau (Aveyron)	Les Gâches	Ossuary – cave	1 individual *1 injured/52*	1 tibia	2600–2000	Chalcolithic/final phase of the Treilles culture
37 Saint-Rome-de-Cernon (Aveyron)	Sargel	Ossuary – cave (cave V)	1 individual	1 fibula or 1 radius? Crenulate ("pine tree") arrow (made from chert)	2600–2200	Chalcolithic/final phase of the Treilles culture

Town (department)	Location	Type of tomb	Individuals killed or injured/total deceased	Location of the impact; possible type of arrow used	Probable date (BCE)	Period/culture; observations
38 Saint-Georges-de-Lévezac (Lozère)	Les Baumes-Chaudes	Swallow hole cave – ossuary	At least 10 individuals *10 injured or killed/ 300* (Prunières cites 17 cases)	Documented examples: 3 ilia, 3 lumbar vertebrae, 2 tali, 1 tibia, 1 skull Numerous undocumented examples	2600–2200	Chalcolithic/final phase of the Treilles culture; perhaps Early Bronze Age More than 60 cases of trepanation; various healed fractures; metal blade embedded in thorax
39 Saint-Rome-de-Dolan (Lozère)	Almières	Ossuary – cave	1 individual *1 injured/36*	1 talus	2600–2200	Chalcolithic/final phase of the Treilles culture + 1 pierced skull
40 Millau (Aveyron)	Le Monna	Ossuary – cave	1 individual *1 injured/ca. 30*	1 rib	2600–2200	Chalcolithic/final phase of the Treilles culture + 1 skull fragment
41 Félines-Minervois (Hérault)	Rec de los Balmos	Ossuary – cave	1 male *1 injured/3*	1 ulna Stemmed arrow with "ailerons"	2600–2200	Chalcolithic
42 Saint-Martory (Haute-Garonne)	La Tourasse	Rock shelter	1 individual *1 killed/4*	2 lumbar vertebrae	2600–2200	Chalcolithic – Beaker culture?
43 Forcalquier (Alpes-de-Haute-Provence)	La Fare	Individual burial	1 adult male aged 30–35 years *1 injured/1*	1 left ulna	ca. 2500	Beaker culture
44 Plan d'Aups (Var)	Gendarme tumulus	Individual burial	1 individual *1 killed/1*	1 femur	2500–2200	Chalcolithic – Beaker culture

2 Unconfirmed cases

(7 sites, 8 bones showing signs of injury, 8 individuals killed or injured)

45 La Malène (Lozère)	Les Monts	–	1 individual	1 bone, unspecified	–	Final Neolithic/probably Chalcolithic
46 Le Massegros (Lozère)	Les Fadarelles d'Inos	Cave	–	1 bone, unspecified	–	Final Neolithic/probably Chalcolithic
47 Saint-Georges-de-Lèvezac (Lozère)	Girons	Cave	1 individual	1 bone, unspecified	–	Final Neolithic/probably Chalcolithic
48 La Canourgue (Lozère)	–	–	1 individual	1 vertebra	–	Photo and article published 1960 by Carrière in *Lou Pais*, p. 141
49 Sigottier (Alpes-de-Haute-Provence)	–	Cave	1 individual	1 femur	3000–2200	Chalcolithic There is no evidence to confirm that the bone was discovered in the Grapelet cave, rather than in one of the other two caves at the site
50 Castelnau-le-Lez (Hérault)	–	Individual tombs	2 individuals/*80 deceased*	2 skulls	–	Unique and very early site Remains date from the Neolithic? Later?
51 Montfort-sur-Lizier (Ariège)	–	–	1 individual	1 dorsal vertebra	13,000–8000	Outside Neolithic period: Upper Paleolithic/Magdalenian or Azilian

Other evidence of violence from Neolithic burial sites

Town (department)	Location	Type of tomb	Individuals killed or injured/total deceased	Location of the impact; possible type of arrow used	Probable date (BCE)	Period/culture; observations
52 Verrières (Aveyron)	La Médicine	Ossuary – cave	2 individuals *2 injured or killed/23*	2 skulls damaged by violent blows; attempt at performing surgery upon one of the skulls	3300–2900	Final Neolithic – Chalcolithic/early phase of the Treilles culture
53 Montélimar (Drôme)	Le Gournier	–	1 child	Flint point embedded in interior of thorax, either before or after death	4500–3500	Chassean
54 (Marne)	–	Hypogea	–	Signs of injury, but no further details specified	3400–2900 or 2900–2300	Seine-Oise-Marne or Gord culture Excavations carried out by the baron of Baye
55 Salernes (Var)	Fontbregoua	Cave	At least 14 individuals	6 skulls – signs of the flesh having been stripped away; faces smashed; blows also received to other bones, notably the long bones	ca. 5000	Recent Cardial period

56 Cabasse (Var)	La Boissière	Dolmen	1 child	Arrow penetrated body	3000–2200	Chalcolithic
57 Vauréal (Val-d'Oise)	Le cimetière des Anglais	Covered passageway	2 individuals	2 damaged skulls	3400–2900 or 2900–2300	Recent Neolithic/Seine-Oise-Marne or Gord culture of the Chalcolithic
58 Saint-Hilaire (Essonne)	Les Boutards	Hypogeum	2 individuals	1 elderly individual: arrow-inflicted injury to skull; 1 child with injury to arm	3400–2900 or 2900–2300	Recent Neolithic/Seine-Oise-Marne or Gord culture of the Chalcolithic + cases of trepanation
59 Collias (Gard)	Le Terruge	Hypogeum	1 individual	1 damaged femur with evidence of arrowhead impact	3300–2200	Final Neolithic – Chalcolithic
60 Suzoy (Oise)	–	Covered passageway	ca. 10 individuals	Roughly 10 damaged skulls	3400–2900 or 2900–2300	Recent Neolithic/Seine-Oise-Marne or Gord culture of the Chalcolithic

Appendix 2: Chronological Distribution of the 44 Confirmed Sites

BCE	1	2	3	4	5	6	7	8	9	10	11	12	13	14	15	16	17	18	19	20
1700																				
1800																				
1900																				
2000																				
2100																				
2200					■									■	■		■	■	■	■
2300					■		■	■	■	■	■	■		■	■		■	■	■	■
2400					■		■	■	■	■	■	■		■	■		■	■	■	■
2500					■		■	■	■	■	■	■		■	■		■	■	■	■
2600					■		■	■	■	■	■	■		■	■	■	■	■	■	■
2700					■		■	■	■	■	■	■		■	■	■	■	■	■	■
2800					■	■	■	■	■	■	■	■		■	■	■	■	■	■	■
2900					■	■	■	■	■	■	■	■	■	■	■	■	■	■	■	■
3000					■	■	■	■	■	■	■	■	■	■	■	■	■	■	■	■
3100					■	■	■	■	■	■	■	■	■	■	■	■				
3200				■	■	■	■	■	■	■	■	■	■	■	■	■				
3300				■	■	■	■	■	■	■	■	■	■	■	■	■				
3400				■	■	■	■	■	■	■	■	■	■	■	■	■				
3500				■	■															
3600				■																
3700																				
3800																				
3900																				
4000																				
4100			■																	
4200			■																	
4300			■																	
4400			■																	
4500																				
4600																				
4700																				
4800		■																		
4900		■																		
5000		■																		
5100		■																		
5200		■																		
5300																				
5400																				
5500	■																			

SITES		
1	Téviec	
2	Quatzenheim	
3	Pontcharraud	
4	Les Châtelliers	
5	Les Treilles	
6	La Ferme Duport	
7	La Pierre Plate	
8	Razet	
9	La Pierre Michelot	
10	Villevenard II	
11	Oyes I	
12	Oyes II	
13	Le Pas-de-Joulié	
14	Les Matelles	
15	Le Crespin	
16	Grillon	
17	Fontcagarelle	
18	La Lave	
19	Gémenos	
20	Maymac	

21	22	23	24	25	26	27	28	29	30	31	32	33	34	35	36	37	38	39	40	41	42	43	44	n° site
																								1700
									■															1800
									■															1900
									■															2000
									■															2100
■	■	■	■	■		■			■														■	2200
■	■	■	■	■	■	■		■	■														■	2300
■	■	■	■	■	■	■	■	■	■	■	■	■	■							■				2400
■	■	■	■	■	■	■	■	■	■	■	■	■	■	■	■	■	■	■	■	■		■		2500
■	■	■	■	■	■	■	■	■	■	■	■	■	■	■	■	■	■	■						2600
■	■	■	■	■	■	■	■	■	■															2700
■	■	■	■	■	■	■	■	■	■															2800
■	■	■	■	■	■	■	■	■																2900
■	■	■	■	■																				3000
																								3100
																									3200
																									3300
																									3400
																									3500
																									3600
																									3700
																									3800
																									3900
																									4000
																									4100
																									4200
																									4300
																									4400
																									4500
																									4600
																									4700
																									4800
																									4900
																									5000
																									5100
																									5200
																									5300
																									5400
																									5500

Column legend (n° — site):

- 21 — Le Sot-de-la-Lavogne
- 22 — Sainte-Énimie
- 23 — Le Castellet
- 24 — Puechcamp
- 25 — Prévinquières
- 26 — Mauray
- 27 — Aragon
- 28 — Les Boileau
- 29 — Les Crottes
- 30 — L'Aumède
- 31 — Terrevaine
- 32 — Le Chemin-de-fer
- 33 — Les Caïres
- 34 — Font-Rial
- 35 — Les Cascades
- 36 — Les Gâches
- 37 — Sargel
- 38 — Les Baumes-Chaudes
- 39 — Almières
- 40 — Le Monna
- 41 — Rec de los Balmos
- 42 — La Tourasse
- 43 — La Fare
- 44 — Le Gendarme

Notes

Introduction

1   Huot, 1989, pp. 211ff.
2   Valbelle, 1998, p. 14.
3   Menu, 1996, pp. 22, 33; see also pp. 42–8 for an interpretation of the Narmer palette; Midant-Reynes, 1999, p. 24.
4   Lévêque, 1996, p. 350.
5   Arnal, 1976, pp. 92–4.
6   Colomer, Coularou, and Gutherz, 1990, pp. 135–6.
7   Evans, 1959, pp. 168ff.
8   On the theory of the Torrean-Shardana as invaders and their conflict with the Megalithic indigenous population, see Grosjean, 1966.
9   Guilaine, 1994, pp. 166–8.
10   For example, Morris, 1967, 1968; Lorenz, 1970; Van Lawick and Goodall, 1973, 1978; Ducros and Ducros, 1992.
11   Van Lawick and Goodall, in Morris, 1967.
12   Leroi-Gourhan, 1965a, p. 236–7.
13   Clastres, 1997, p. 24.
14   Ibid., p. 9.
15   Keeley, 1996, p. 90 and table 6–2.
16   Ibid., p. 30.
17   Ibid., p. 23; Clastres, 1997, p. 5.
18   Clastres, 1997, p. 11.
19   Lévi-Strauss, 1996, pp. 291–2.
20   Chavaillon, 1996, pp. 186–7.
21   Ibid., pp. 189–90.
22   Tringham, 1993, pp. 122–3.
23   Stoczkowski, 1994, pp. 13–35.
24   Laburthe-Tolra, 1984, p. 504.
25   Ibid., p. 505.
26   Godelier, 1982, pp. 169–70.
27   Morgan, 1985, pp. 29ff.
28   Keeley, 1996, pp. 25ff.
29   Ibid., p. 119.
30   Testart, 1985, p. 65.
31   Guilaine, 1959, p. 684.
32   Scubla, 1999, p. 136.
33   Girard, 1972, p. 27.
34   Ibid., p. 215.
35   Scubla, 1999, p. 137.
36   Testart, 1993, pp. 27–9.

1   Violence in Hunter-Gatherer Society

1   Hublin, 1982, p. 25.
2   Vallois, 1957, pp. 131–3.
3   McCown and Keith, 1939, pp. 74–5, figs. 37, 38, pl. XXVII.
4   Pigeaud, 2000, pp. 18–19.
5   Patou-Mathis, 1997, 1999, 2000. For further opinions on the human remains discovered in Krapina, see Trinkaus, 1985; Russell, 1987a, b; Le Mort, 1988a, b.

6   Jourdan, 1979, p. 387 details the remains discovered at the Jean-Cros rock shelter site.

7   De Lumley, 1972, pp. 615–20.

8   White, 1999, p. 128.

9   Bermudez de Castro et al., 1999, pp. 115–18; Pares and Perez, 1999, pp. 325–42; Fernandez Jalvo et al., 1999, pp. 591–622.

10 Boulestin, 1999, pp. 181ff. This work offers a well-argued evaluation of the various theories on prehistoric cannibalism.

11 Ibid., p. 248.

12 Brennan, 1991, pp. 203–6.

13 Begouen, Cugulières, and Miquel, 1922, pp. 230–2.

14 Kozlowski et al., 1993, pp. 170–1 (cf. also Kapica and Wiercinski, ibid., pp. 245–51).

15 Scubla, 1999, p. 141.

16 Leroi-Gourhan, 1992, p. 389; Cardona, 1996, p. 127.

17 Clottes and Courtin, 1994, pp. 155ff. Some experts think that the figure depicted could, in fact, be a seal: it has five fingers, also like humans; small lines around the face could represent whiskers with others forming a pointed tail. Cf. Cardona, 1996, p. 83.

18 Mezzena, 1976, pp. 66ff.

19 For further details see Blanc, 1954a, b, 1955; Chiappella, 1954; Benoit, 1955.

20 Garanger, 1992, p. 502; Muñoz Ibañez, 1999, p. 33. It is not impossible that the bow would have been used at an earlier point in time on the Iberian Peninsula where the forests are denser, thus a throwing-stick would have proved rather ineffective here (information D. Sacchi).

21 Rozoy, 1978, pp. 1012–16.

22 Bourov, 1973, p. 147; Bourov, 1981, pp. 373–88 (see figures pp. 377–84).

23 Spindler, 1997, p. 23.

24 Anderson, in Wendorf, 1968, pp. 996–1039.

25 Wendorf, 1968, pp. 992–3.

26 Balakin and Nuzhnyi, 1995, pp. 195–7. The authors refer to Morgan's observations on the rapids of America's Great Lakes, which are rich in aquatic life. These areas were an important factor in causing the Algonquin tribes to settle and group together.

27 Ibid., p. 196.

28 See Vencl, 1991, for a comprehensive summary of violence in the Neolithic.

29 See May, 1986, pp. 186–9 for further details.

30 Dastugue, in Chamla, 1970, pp. 120–6.

31 Zammit, 1991, p. 105.

32 Balakin and Nuzhnyi, 1995, pp. 196–7.

33 Brunaux, 1986, pp. 110–12.

2   Agriculture: A Calming or Aggravating Influence?

1   Keeley, 1996, pp. 137–9.

2   See Wahl and König, 1987, for further details; Alt, Vach, and Wahl, 1987.

3   Alt, Vach, and Wahl, 1997, pp. 6–7.

4   Jeunesse, 1997, pp. 50–1.

5   Lontcho, 1998, pp. 47–50. Initial investigations indicate that these excavations covered only about one-fiftieth of the area of the trenches. If the skulls are buried with the same density throughout, then there could be 1,000 to 1,500 skulls in total (cf. Lontcho, 1998, p. 48).

6   Evidence interpreted by Boulestin, 1999, p. 235.

7   Jeunesse, 1997, pp. 48–9; Boulestin, 1999, p. 236.

8   Boulestin, 1999, pp. 235–6.
9   See Villa et al., 1986, for details of the Fontbregoua human remains.
10 Ibid., pp. 159, 165.
11 Voruz, in Boulestin and Gomez de Soto, 1995a, p. 64.
12 Morgan, 1985, p. 24. In extreme situations, there have been cases of nutritional cannibalism as a means of survival: the *Méduse* raft (1816), the survivors of an Argentinean plane crash in the Andes (1972).
13 Cf. White, 1992, on the Mancos site (Colorado).
14 For example, Bouville, 1983, pp. 22–3.
15 Boulestin and Gomez de Soto, 1995a, p. 62.
16 Guilaine, 1995, pp. 35–6.
17 Ducos, 1988, pp. 95–6.
18 The bibliography on this subject is comprehensive (starting with Cabré Aguilo, Breuil, Obermaier, Colominas, Wernert, Almagro Basch, etc.). Others relevant to the present work include Hernandez Pacheco, 1918; Porcar Ripollès, 1946; Ripoll, 1963; Beltrán, 1968; Jorda Cerda, 1975; Dams, 1984; Molinos Sauras, 1986–7; Hernandez Perez, Ferrer i Marset, and Catala Ferrer, 1989, 1998.
19 Hernandez Perez, Ferrer i Marset, and Catala Ferrer, 1989, pp. 229–30; 1998, pp. 123–4.
20 Hernandez Perez, Ferrer i Marset, and Catala Ferrer, 1998, p. 162.
21 Jorda Cerda, 1975, p. 17.
22 Molinos Sauras, 1986–7, p. 295.
23 For details of the "recent" dating of the Levantine art cf. Hernandez Perez, Ferrer i Marset, and Catala Ferrer, 1989, pp. 282–4; 1998, pp. 164–6.
24 Based upon the work of Jelinek, cited in Mohen, 1995, p. 76.
25 Information provided by Rialland.

3   Humans as Targets: 4,000 to 8,000 Years Ago

1   From the extensive literature written on this topic, we will quote from Prunières, 1882; De Baye, 1872a, b, 1880; Cartailhac, 1896; Morel and Baudouin, 1928; Pales, 1930; Morel, Jr., 1957; Cordier, 1990. Cordier's article on animal injuries is worth noting; readers who are particularly interested should refer to the comprehensive bibliography contained within Cordier's work.
2   Loison, 1998, p. 194.
3   Beeching and Crubézy, 1998, pp. 150–8.
4   Birocheau et al., 1999, p. 390.
5   Information provided by Lemercier.
6   Orliac and Orliac, 1973, p. 66.
7   Gagnière and Germand, 1942.
8   Survey by Naudet and Vidal.
9   André and Boutin, 1995, propose that trepanation cases from the limestone regions of Southern France total 213; this figure has been challenged by Hibon, 1997, who claims a total of 160 cases.
10 Brenot and Riquet, 1977, p. 9.
11 André and Boutin, 1995, p. 200. Of 14 cases of trepanation in Provence, eight were male and six female (Bouville, 1991, p. 303).
12 Hibon, 1997, pp. 62–5.
13 Bouville, 1991, p. 303.
14 Hibon, 1997, p. 88.
15 See Courtin, 1974, p. 181 and Sauzade, 1983, pp. 127ff. for details of the discovery and the site itself. Different authors have different ideas about the number of individuals buried here. Bouville claims there were 58 bodies in the lower layer (layer 5) and 71 in the upper layer (layer 2), giving a total of 129. Chambon claims there were 136 in the upper layer 2 which, together

with the total cited by Bouville for the lower level, makes a total of 194 bodies (information provided by Chambon). Mahieu (1987, p. 6) proposes a total of 250 bodies. Sauzade, 1983, pp. 130–4 includes plans showing the distribution of human remains from the remaining parts of the tomb, unearthed during the 1965–6 excavations.

16 Interpreting the deposits of the upper layers remains problematic. The skeletons that were not intact when discovered may have been deposited here at a later date or may have formed part of the last layer of primary deposits which were later rearranged. It may even be the case that the first bodies to be buried in the upper layer were cleared to the sides to allow for the large number of bodies to be subsequently deposited here intact (information from Chambon).

17 Mahieu, 1987, pp. 5–7 and 1992, pp. 75–81; more recently, Chambon, 1999, pp. 61–80. The Capitaine hypogeum in Grillon is said to contain 178 bodies by Mahieu and 136 (a low minimum figure) by Chambon.

18 Chambon, 1999, p. 75.

19 The total according to Vegas, 1992, p. 15 is 336 (a minimum figure, based upon the 1991 research). Since this article was published, another count has put the minimum at 289 bodies (De La Rua et al., 1996, p. 586). Recently, a ninth body with an arrow wound has been identified (Vegas et al., 1999, p. 443) – the figure was previously thought to stand at eight.

20 It has also been noted that there was no selection process in operation: individuals of both sexes and a range of ages were buried here, not just "male" warriors.

21 Dates obtained (before the present, BP): 5070 ± 140; 5020 ± 140; 4570 ± 40;

4520 ± 50; 4520 ± 75; 4510 ± 40; 4460 ± 70; 4440 ± 40; 4325 ± 70; 4200 ± 95 (Vegas, 1991).

22 Etxeberria and Vegas, 1992, pp. 131–4.

23 Campillo, Mercadal, and Blanch, 1993, pp. 146–50 and information provided by Mercadal.

24 Campillo, in Marti, Pou, and Carlus, 1997, pp. 233–4.

4 The Warrior: An Ideological Construction

1 Spindler, 1995, pp. 110–13.

2 See the work by Casini, De Marinis, and Pedrotti, 1995, for details of the abundance of literature devoted to the menhir-statues.

3 For details of the tomb, see Peroni, 1971, p. 205; Guilaine, 1994, p. 321; Miari, 1994, pp. 351–90.

4 Ramos-Millán, 1998, p. 35 refers to a flint "policy."

5 Pètrequin and Pètrequin, 1990, pp. 487ff.

6 Heider, 1997, pp. 95–120.

7 Pètrequin and Pètrequin, 1990, pp. 506–10. See also Pètrequin et al., 1998, p. 204.

8 It is also possible that all of these groups of menhir-statues date from the same period. In this case, the French statues may reflect a certain delay in the development of metallurgy compared to the Italian statues. However, it is not known for certain whether such a "delay" did indeed occur (Guilaine, 1994, pp. 295–8).

9 A standard theory developed in various different ways – based upon either migration or invasion – by Childe, 1926; Gimbutas, 1979, taking up where several earlier works left off; Lichardus and Lichardus-Itten, 1985. More

recently, Mallory, 1997, has conducted a survey of the various different theories on the "focal point" of Indo-Europeans; whilst emphasizing the ongoing uncertainties, he claims that the Indo-Europeans of Europe and Western Anatolia are of Pontic-Caspian origin (cf. pp. 273, 298).

10 Cf. in particular Gimbutas.

11 Mallory believes the Pontic-Caspian region to have played a part in the spread of Indo-European languages (1997, pp. 295–8). At the same time, this author is more cautious about the nature of the relationship between the ornate steles from the Pontic region and the menhir-statues of the West: Mallory, 1995, pp. 70–1.

12 De Lumley, 1995, p. 366.

13 See Pedrotti, 1993, 1995 for details of the Arco steles.

14 Monks, 1999, p. 129.

15 Cf. Almagro and Arribas, 1963, pp. 203–49 for details of the main site of Los Millares.

16 Guilaine, 1994, pp. 170–80.

17 Monks, 1999, pp. 150–1.

18 Sherratt, 1997, pp. 376–402.

5   The Concept of the Hero Emerges

1 Guilaine, 1994, p. 430.

2 Audouze and Buschsenschutz, 1989, pp. 222–8 discuss several possible models of protohistoric society in Europe.

3 Brun, 1987, pp. 57–8.

4 See Gaucher and Mohen, 1972, for details of the typology of these weapons in France and the surrounding regions.

5 Brun, 1987, p. 15.

6 For further details, see Drews, 1993, pp. 174–208; Courbin, 1999, pp. 19–108. See also the exhibition catalogue "L'Europe au temps d'Ulysse," Réunion des Musées nationaux, Paris, 1999.

7 Lilliu, 1982, pp. 186ff.

8 Erman and Ranke, 1986, pp. 728–32.

9 Piggott, 1983.

10 Drews, 1993, pp. 105–6.

11 See ibid., pp. 106–9 for details of these figures.

12 Grimal, 1988, pp. 308–9.

13 Drews, 1993, p. 209.

14 Detienne, 1999, pp. 157ff.; Étienne, Muller, and Prost, 2000, pp. 82–4.

15 Telegin, 1986.

16 According to the phrase used by Albert, in Centlivres, Fabre, and Zonabend, 1998, p. 14.

17 Brun, 1987, pp. 95–115.

18 Almagro Basch, 1966; Galan Domingo, 1993.

19 Information provided by Midant-Reynes.

20 Simon, 1991, pp. 85–8.

21 Herodotus, *The Histories*, Book 4, sections 71 and 72.

22 Mohen, 1995, pp. 76–7.

23 Garanger, 1972, pp. 59–77 and 1979.

24 Chang, 1986, pp. 371–2.

25 Barnes, 1993, pp. 192–5.

26 Brothwell, 1988.

27 Glob, 1966, pp. 13–27 (Tollund) and pp. 28–46 (Grauballe).

28 Dieck, in Brothwell, 1988, p. 97.

Conclusion

1 For further details on this theory see Girard, 1972, pp. 25, 155–67.

2 Keeley, 1996, p. 186, table 2.1 (from a study by Otterbein).

Bibliography

Almagro, M. and Arribas, A. (1963). *El poblado y la necropolis megaliticos de Los Millares (Santa Fe de Mondujar, Almeria)*. Madrid: Bibliotheca Praehistorica Hispana, 3.

Almagro Basch, M. (1966). *Las estelas decoradas del Suroeste peninsular*. Madrid: Bibliotheca Praehistorica Hispana, 8.

Alonso, A. and Grimal, A. (1996). El arte rupestre preistórico de la Cuenca del Rio Taibilla (Albacete y Murcia). In *Nuevos planteamientos para el estudio del arte levantino*, vol. 2, Barcelona.

Alt, K. W., Vach, W., and Wahl, J. (1987). Verwandtschaftanalyse der Skelettreste aus dem bandkeramischen Massengrab von Talheim, Kreis Heilbronn. *Funderberichte aus Baden-Wurtemberg*, 12, pp. 195–217.

Alt, K. W., Vach, W., and Wahl, J. (1997). La reconstitution "génétique" de la population de la fosse commune rubanée de Talheim. In C. Jeunesse (ed.), *Le Néolithique danubien et ses marges, Cahiers de l'Association pour la promotion de la recherche archéologique en Alsace*, 3, pp. 1–8.

Anati, E. (1979). *La Préhistoire des Alpes*. Milan: Jaca Book.

Anatrella, T. (1998). *La Différence interdite. Sexualité, éducation, violence. Trente ans après mai 1968*. Paris: Flammarion.

Andersen, N. H. (1997). *The Sarup Enclosures*. Moesgaard: Jutland Archaeological Society Publications.

André, D. and Boutin, J.-Y. (1995). *Les Baumes-Chaudes et les trépanations anciennes dans les Grands Causses*. Association Dr Prunières.

Anon. (1999). *L'Europe au temps d'Ulysse*. Paris: Réunion des Musées nationaux.

Armendariz, J. and Irigaray, S. (1995). Violencia y muerte en la Prehistoria: el hypogeo de Longar. *Revista de Arqueologia*, 168, pp. 16–29.

Armendariz, J., Irigaray, S., and Etxeberria, E. (1994). New evidence of prehistoric arrow wounds in the Iberian Peninsula. *International Journal of Osteoarchaeology*, 4, pp. 215–22.

Arnal, J. (1976). *Les Statues-Menhirs, hommes et dieux*. Toulouse: Éditions des Hespérides.

Audouze, F. and Buschsenschutz, O. (1989). *Villes, villages et campagnes de l'Europe celtique*. Paris: Hachette.

Audouze, F. and Buschsenschutz, O. (1992). *Towns, Villages and Countryside of Celtic Europe*, trans. Henry Cleere. Bloomington: Indiana University Press.

Aufderheide, A.-C. and Rodriguez-Martin, C. (1998). *The Cambridge Encyclopaedia of Human Paleopathology*. Cambridge: Cambridge University Press.

Azémar, R. (1989). *Les mobiliers des sépultures mégalithiques du Larzac aveyronnais*. Toulouse: EHESS.

Balakin, S. and Nuzhnyi, D. (1995). The origin of graveyards: The influence of landscape elements on social and ideological changes in prehistoric communities. *Préhistoire européenne*, Liège, 7, pp. 191–202.

Barandiaran, I. and Basabe, J.-M. (1978). *El yacimiento eneolitico de la Atalayuela en Agoncillo (Logroño)*. Pamplona.

Barletta, R. (1996). *El quinto mandamiento*. Buenos Aires: Ediciones Lohlé-Lumen.

Barnes, G. (1993). *China, Korea and Japan: The Rise of Civilization in East Asia*. London: Thames and Hudson.

Baudouin, M. (1911). Classification générale des lésions osseuses humaines de l'époque néolithique. *AFAS*, 40, Dijon.

Baudouin, M. (1928). Flèche en silex incluse dans une vertèbre humaine. *La Nature*, 2785, p. 451.

Baye, J. de (1872a). Grottes artificielles sépulcrales de la Marne. *Matériaux pour l'histoire primitive et naturelle de l'homme*, vol. 3, 2nd series, pp. 494–504.

Baye, J. de (1872b). Grottes préhistoriques de la Marne. *Congrès international d'anthropologie et d'archéologie préhistorique de Bruxelles*, Paris: Claye, p. 37.

Baye, J. de (1880). *L'Archéologie préhistorique*. Paris: E. Leroux.

Baye, J. de (1888). *L'Archéologie préhistorique*. Paris: Baillère.

Bazin, J. and Terray, E. (1982). *Guerres de lignages et guerres d'États en Afrique*. Éditions des Archives contemporaines.

Beeching, A. and Crubézy, E. (1998). Les sépultures chasséennes de la vallée du Rhône. In J. Guilaine (ed.), *Sépultures d'Occident et genèses des mégalithismes*. Paris: Errance, pp. 147–64.

Begouen, H., Cugulières, and Miquel, H. (1922). Vertèbre humaine traversée par une lame en quartzite. *Revue anthropologique*, pp. 230–2.

Begouen, H. and Vallois, H. V. (1932). Un cubitus percé d'une flèche en silex. *Anthropologie*, Prague, pp. 109–12.

Beltrán, A. (1968). *Arte rupestre levantino*. University of Saragossa.

Beltrán, A. (1982). *Rock Art of the Spanish Levant*, trans. Margaret Brown. Cambridge: Cambridge University Press.

Bennike, P. (1985). *Paleopathology of the Danish Skeletons*. Copenhagen: Akademisk Forlag.

Benoit, F. (1955). À propos des "acrobates" de l'Addaura. Rite et mythe, *Quaternaria*, 2, pp. 209–11.

Bergman, C. A. (1987). Death on the Plains. *Journal of the Society of Archer-Antiquaries*, London, 30, pp. 12–14.

Bermudez de Castro, J. M. et al. (1999). *Atapuerca. Nuestros antecesores*. Junta de Castilla y León, Museo Nacional de Ciencias Naturales.

Bernard, A. (1999). *Guerre et violence dans la Grèce antique*. Paris: Hachette Littérature.

Bernheim, P.-A. and Stavridès, G. (1992). *Cannibales!* Paris: Plon.

Binant, P. (1991). *La Préhistoire de la mort*. Paris: Errance.

Birocheau, P., Convertini, F., Cros, J.-P., Duday, H., and Large, J.-M. (1999). Fossé et sépultures du Néolithique récent aux Châtelliers-du-Vieil-Auzay (Vendée): aspects structuraux et anthropologiques. *Bulletin de la Société préhistorique française*, 96, pp. 375–90.

Blanc, A.-C. (1939). L'uomo fossile del Monte Circeo. Uno cranio neandertaliano nella grotta Guattari a San Felice Circeo. *Rendiconti Accademia dei Lincei*, 29 (6), pp. 48–67.

Blanc, A.-C. (1954a). Considerazioni su due figure dell'Addaura. *Quaternaria*, 1, pp. 176–80.

Blanc, A.-C. (1954b). Il sacrificio umano dell'Addaura ed il nesso ideologico tra morte e generazione nella mantalità primitiva. *Quaternaria*, 1, pp. 184–6.

Blanc, A.-C. (1955). Il sacrificio umano dell'Addaura e la messa a morte rituale mediante strangolamento nell'etnologia e nella paletnologia. *Quaternaria*, 2, pp. 213–15.

Blumenschine, R. and Cavallo, J. (1992). Nos ancêtres, des charognards. *Pour la Science*, Paris, 182, pp. 74–81.

Bocquet, A. (1975). Les poignards néolithiques de Charavines, Isère, dans le cadre de la civilisation Saône-Rhône. *Etudes Préhistoriques*, 9, pp. 7–17.

Bonnet, C. (1990). *Kerma, royaume de Nubie. L'Antiquité africaine au temps des pharaons.* Geneva: Musée d'art et d'histoire.

Boone, E.-H. (ed.) (1984). *Ritual Human Sacrifice in Mesoamerica.* Washington, DC: Dumbarton Oaks.

Boule, M. and Vallois, H. V. (1946). *Les hommes fossiles.* Paris: Masson.

Boulestin, B. (1999). *Approche taphonomique des restes humains. Le cas des mésolithiques de la grotte des Perrats et le problème du cannibalisme en préhistoire récente européenne*, BAR, International Series, 776, Oxford.

Boulestin, B. and Gomez de Soto, J. (1995a). Le cannibalisme au Néolithique. Réalité et sens. In *La Mort: passé, présent, conditionnel.* La Roche-sur-Yon: Groupe vendéen d'études préhistoriques, pp. 59–68.

Boulestin, B. and Gomez de Soto, J. (1995b). Cannibalisme néolithique: quelques hypothèses. *Les Nouvelles de l'archéologie*, 59, pp. 35–7.

Bourov, G.-M. (1973). Die mesolitischen Kulturen in Aüsserten Europaïschen Nordosten. In S. Kozlowski, *The Mesolithic in Europe.* Warsaw, pp. 129–49.

Bourov, G.-M. (1981). Der Bogen bei den Mesolitischen Stämmen Nordosteuropas. *Mesolithikum in Europa*, Veröffentlichungen des Museums für Ur-und Frühgeschichte Potsdam, 14/15, pp. 373–88.

Bouville, C. (1980). L'hypogée chalcolithique de Roaix. Apport à l'étude de la démographie en Provence. *Bulletins et mémoires de la Société d'anthropologie de Paris*, 7, pp. 85–9.

Bouville, C. (1982). Mort violente. Les massacres. *Histoire et archéologie*, 66 (September), pp. 36–41.

Bouville, C. (1983). Types crâniens "allochtones" et "autochtones" en Provence du Mésolithique à l'Âge du bronze. *Le phénomène des grandes invasions*, Centre de recherches archéologiques, pp. 21–44.

Bouville, C. (1991). Chalcolithique de Provence et trépanations. *L'Anthropologie*, 95, pp. 293–306.

Brennan, M.-U. (1991). *Health and Disease in the Middle and Upper Paleolithic of Southwestern France: A Bioarcheological Study.* PhD, New York University.

Brenot, P. and Riquet, R. (1977). La trépanation néolithique. *Archeologia*, 104 (March), pp. 8–17.

Briard, J. (1979). *The Bronze Age in Barbarian Europe*, trans. Mary Turton. London: Routledge and Kegan Paul.

Brothwell, D. R. (1988). *The Bog Man*. London: British Museum Publications.

Brun, P. (1987). *Princes et princesses de la Celtique. Le premier Âge du fer (850–450 avant J.-C.)*. Paris: Errance.

Brunaux, J.-C. (1986). *Les Gaulois. Sanctuaires et rites*. Paris: Errance.

Brunaux, J.-C. (1988). *The Celtic Gauls: Gods, Rites and Sanctuaries*, trans. Daphne Nash. London: Seaby.

Brunaux, J.-C. and Lambot, B. (1987). *Guerre et armement chez les Gaulois*. Paris: Errance.

Bunn, H.-T. and Ellen, M.-C. (1986). Systematic butchery by Plio-pleistocene hominids at Olduvai Gorge, Tanzania. *Current Anthropology*, 27 (December), pp. 431–52.

Campillo, D. (1983). *La enfermedad en la preistoria: introducción a la paleopatologia*. Barcelona: Salvat.

Campillo, D. (1996). Paleopatologia: els primers vestigis de la malatia. *Col. Leccio Historica de Ciencies de la Salut*, Barcelona, pp. 109–122.

Campillo, D., Mercadal, O., and Blanch, R.-M. (1993). A mortal wound caused by a flint arrowhead in individual MF-18 of the Neolithic period exhumed at Sant Quirze del Vallès. *International Journal of Osteoarchaeology*, 3, pp. 145–50.

Camps, G. (1992). Guerre ou paix? Origines des conflits intraspécifiques humains. *Préhistoire, Anthropologie méditerranéennes*, 1, pp. 9–15.

Capasso, L. (1985). *L'origine delle malattie*. Chieti: Ed. Marino Solfanelli.

Cardona, L. (1996). *Art et violence au Paléolithique supérieur*. Diplôme d'Etudes Approfondies, University of Toulouse II.

Cartailhac, E. (1889). *La France préhistorique*. Paris: Alcan.

Cartailhac, E. (1896). Quelques faits nouveaux du Préhistorique ancien des Pyrénées. *L'Anthropologie*, 7, pp. 309–18.

Casini, S. (ed.) (1994). *Le pietre degli dei. Menhir e stele dell'Età del Rame in Valcamonica e Valtellina*. Bergamo.

Casini, S., Marinis, R. de, and Pedrotti, A. (eds.) (1995). *Statue-Stele e massi incisi nell'Europa dell'Età del Rame*. Notizie Archeologiche Bergomensi, 3.

Castel, C. (1991). Des premiers guerriers à l'armée de métier. *Dossiers d'Archéologie*, 160, pp. 48–53.

Cauwe, N. (1997). *Curriculum Mortis. Essai sur les origines des sépultures collectives de la Préhistoire occidentale*. Thesis, University of Liège, 4 vols.

Cazalis de Fondouce, P. (1873, 1978). *Allées couvertes de Provence*, 2 vols., Montpellier: Coulet.

Centlivres, P., Fabre, D., and Zonabend, F. (ed.) (1998). *La Fabrique des héros*. Paris: Éditions de la Maison des sciences de l'homme.

Chambon, P. (1999). *Du cadavre aux ossements. La gestion des sépultures collectives dans la France néolithique*. Thesis, University of Paris I.

Chamla, M.-C. (1968). *Les Populations anciennes du Sahara et des régions limitrophes*. Mémoires du CRAPE. Paris: Arts et métiers graphiques.

Chamla, M.-C. (1970). *Les Hommes épipaléolithiques de Columnata (Algérie occidentale)*. Mémoires du CRAPE. Paris: Arts et métiers graphiques.

Chang, K. (1986). *The Archeology of Ancient China*. New Haven, CT: Yale University Press.

Chapman, R. et al. (1981). *The Archaeology of Death*. Cambridge: Cambridge University Press.

Chavaillon, J. (1996). *L'Âge d'or de l'humanité*. Paris: Odile Jacob.

Cheney, D. R., Seyfart, R., and Smuts, B. (1986). Social relationships and social cognition in nonhuman primates. *Science*, 234, pp. 1361–6.

Chiappella, V. (1954). Altre considerazioni sugli "acrobati" dell'Addaura. *Quaternaria*, 1, pp. 181–3.

Childe, V.-G. (1925). *The Dawn of European Civilization*. London: Kegan Paul.

Childe, V.-G. (1926). *The Aryans: A Study of Indo-European Origins*. London: Kegan, Trench, and Trübner.

Clastres, P. (1994). *The Archaeology of Violence*, trans. Jeanine Herman. New York: Semiotext.

Clastres, P. (1997). *Archéologie de la violence. La guerre dans les sociétés primitives*. Marseille: Éditions de l'Aube.

Claude, C. (1997). *L'Enfance de l'humanité*. Paris: L'Harmattan.

Clausewitz, C. von (1873). *On War*, trans. J. J. Graham. London: Trübner.

Clottes, J. and Courtin, J. (1994). *La Grotte Cosquer*. Paris: Éditions du Seuil.

Clottes, J. and Courtin, J. (1996). *The Cave Beneath the Sea: Paleolithic Images at Cosquer*, trans. Marilyn Garner. New York: Abrams.

Colomer, A. (1979). *Les Grottes sépulcrales artificielles en Languedoc oriental*. Toulouse: Archives d'écologie préhistorique IV.

Colomer, A., Coularou, J., and Gutherz, X. (1990). *Boussargues (Argelliers, Hérault). Un habitat ceinturé chalcolithique: les fouilles du secteur ouest*. Paris: Documents d'archéologie française.

Cordier, G. (1990). Blessures préhistoriques animales et humaines avec armes ou projectiles conservés. *Bulletin de la Société préhistorique française*, 87 (10–12), pp. 462–81 (with comprehensive bibliography).

Courbin, P. (1999). La guerre en Grèce à haute époque d'après les documents archéologiques. In J.-P. Vernant (ed.), *Problèmes de la guerre en Grèce ancienne*. Paris: Éditions de l'EHESS, pp. 89–120.

Courtin, J. (1974). *Le Néolithique de la Provence*. Paris: Klincksieck.

Courtin, J. (1984). La guerre au Néolithique. *La Recherche*, 154, pp. 448–58.

Courvilla, C.-B. (1967). Cranial injuries in prehistoric man. In D. R. Brothwell and A. T. Sandison (eds.), *Diseases in Antiquity*. Springfield: C. C. Thomas.

Cremonesi, G. (1976). Tomba della prima età dei metalli presso Tursi (Matera). *Rivista di Scienze Preistoriche*, 31, pp. 109–33.

Crubézy, E., Bruzek, J., Guilaine, J., Cunha, E., Rougé, D., and Jelinek, J. (2001). The antiquity of cranial surgery in Europe and in the Mediterranean basin. *Comptes Rendus de l'Académie des Sciences*, 332, pp. 417–23.

Dams, L. (1984). *Les Peintures rupestres du Levant espagnol*. Paris: Picard.

D'Anna, A. (1977). *Les Statues-Menhirs et stèles anthropomorphes du Midi méditerranéen*. Paris: CNRS.

Delibes, G. (ed.) (1998). *Minerales y metales en la preistoria reciente*. University of Valladolid, pp. 13–40.

Delluc, B. and Delluc, G. (1989). Le sang, la souffrance et la mort dans l'art paléolithique. *L'Anthropologie*, 93 (2), pp. 389–406.

Detienne, M. (1999). La phalange: problèmes et controverses. In J.-P. Vernant (ed.), *Problèmes de la guerre en Grèce ancienne*. Paris: Éditions de l'EHESS, pp. 157–88.

Diamond, J. (2000). *De l'inégalité parmi les sociétés. Essai sur l'homme et l'environnement dans l'Histoire*. Paris: Gallimard.

Drews, R. (1993). *The End of the Bronze Age: Changes in Warfare and the Catastrophe ca. 1200 BC*. Princeton, NJ: Princeton University Press.

Ducos, P. (1988). *Archéozoologie quantitative. Les valeurs numériques immédiates à Çatal Hüyük*. Cahiers du Quaternaire, 12, CNRS.

Ducrey, P. (1985). *Warfare in Ancient Greece*, trans. Janet Lloyd. New York: Schocken Books.

Ducros, A. and Ducros, J. (1992). Le singe carnivore: la chasse chez les primates non humains. *Bulletins et mémoires de la Société d'anthropologie de Paris*, new series, 4 (3–4), pp. 243–64.

Dumézil, G. (1970). *The Destiny of the Warrior*, trans. Alf Hiltebeitel. Chicago: University of Chicago Press.

Eiroa, J.-J., Bachiller Gil, J.-A., Castro Perez, L., and Lomba Maurandi, J. (1999). *Nociones de tecnologia y tipologia en Prehistoria*. Barcelona: Ariel.

Erman, A. and Ranke, H. (1986). *La Civilisation égyptienne*. Paris: Payot.

Escalon de Fonton, M. (1964). Naissance de la guerre en Occident aux temps préhistoriques. *Archeologia*, 1, pp. 31–4.

Étienne, R., Muller, C., and Prost, F. (2000). *Archéologie historique de la Grèce antique*. Paris: Ellipses.

Etxeberria, F. and Vegas, S.-I. (1987). Violent injury in a Bronze Age individual in the Basque country (Spain). *Journal of Paleopathology*, 1, pp. 19–24.

Etxeberria, F. and Vegas, S.-I. (1988). Agresividad social o guerra? durante el Neo-eneolitico en la cuenca media del Ebro, a propósito de San Juan Ante Portam Latinam (Rioja alavesa). *Munibe*, suppl. 6, pp. 105–12.

Etxeberria, F. and Vegas, S.-I. (1992). Heridas por flecha durante la Prehistoria en la Peninsula Ibérica. *Munibe*, suppl. 8, pp. 129–36.

Evans, J. (1959). *Malta*. London: Thames and Hudson.

Evans, J. (1971). *The Prehistoric Antiquities of the Maltese Islands*. London: Athlone.

Fernandez Jalvo, Y. et al. (1999). Human cannibalism in the Early Pleistocene of Europe (Gran Dolina, Sierra de Atapuerca, Burgos, Spain). *Journal of Human Evolution*, 37, pp. 591–622.

Finley, M. I. (1993). *On a perdu la guerre de Troie*. Paris: Les Belles Lettres/Hachette.

Forest, J.-D. (1996). *Mésopotamie. L'apparition de l'État (7ᵉ–3ᵉ millénaire)*. Paris: Méditerranée.

Gagnière, S. and Germand, L. (1942). La grotte sépulcrale de la Lave à Saint-Saturnin-d'Apt. *Cahiers de pratique médico-chirurgicale*, pp. 1–40.

Galan Domingo, E. (1993). *Estelas, paisage y territorio en el Bronce final del Sureste de la Peninsula Iberica*. Madrid: Editorial Complutense.

Gallery Kovacs, M. (trans.) (1989). *The Epic of Gilgamesh*. Stanford, CA: Stanford University Press.

Garanger, J. (1972). *Archéologie des Nouvelles-Hébrides*. Paris: Publication de la Société des océanistes, 30.

Garanger, J. (1979). *Roy Mata*. RCP 259. Paris: CNRS.

Garanger, J. (1982). *Archaeology of the New Hebrides*, trans. Rosemary Groube. Sydney: University of Sydney.

Garanger, J. (ed.) (1992). *La Préhistoire dans le monde*. Paris: PUF.

Garcia Guinea, M.-A. (1963). Le nouveau foyer de peintures levantines à Nerpio. *Bulletin de la Société préhistorique de l'Ariège*, 18, pp. 17–35.

Garlan, Y. (1975). *War in the Ancient World: A Social History*, trans. Janet Lloyd. London: Chatto and Windus.

Garlan, Y. (1988). *Slavery in Ancient Greece*, trans. Janet Lloyd. Ithaca, NY: Cornell University Press.

Gaucher, G. and Mohen, J.-P. (1972). *Typologie des objets de l'Âge du bronze en France*, vol. 1: *Les Épées*. Paris: Société préhistorique française.

Gimbutas, M. (1979). The three waves of the Kurgan people into Old Europe, 4500–2500 BC. *Archives suisses d'anthropologie générale*, 43 (2), pp. 113–37.

Girard, R. (1972). *La Violence et le sacré*. Paris: Grasset.

Girard, R. (1977). *Violence and the Sacred*, trans. Patrick Gregory. Baltimore: Johns Hopkins University Press.

Glob, P.-V. (1966). *Les Hommes des tourbières*. Paris: Fayard.

Glob, P.-V. (1971). *The Bog People*, trans. Rupert Bruce-Mitford. London: Paladin.

Glynn, I. (1978). Le partage de la nourriture chez les hominidés. *Pour la Science*, 8 (June), pp. 87–103.

Gnoli, G. and Vernant, J.-P. (1982). *La Mort, les morts dans les sociétés anciennes*. Cambridge: Cambridge University Press/Paris: Maison des sciences de l'homme.

Godelier, M. (1982). *La Production des Grands Hommes. Pouvoir et domination masculine chez les Baruya de Nouvelle-Guinée*. Paris: Fayard.

Godelier, M. (1986). *The Making of Great Men: Male Domination and Power among the New Guinea Baruya*, trans. Rupert Swyer. Cambridge: Cambridge University Press.

Goudineau, C. (1990). *César et la Gaule*. Paris: Errance.

Goudineau, C. and Peyre, C. (1993). *Bibracte et les Éduens. À la découverte d'un peuple gaulois*. Paris: Errance.

Graziozi, P. (1973). *L'arte preistorico in Italia*. Florence: Sansoni.

Grimal, N. (1988). *Histoire de l'Égypte ancienne*. Paris: Fayard.

Grimal, N. (1992). *A History of Ancient Egypt*, trans. Ian Shaw. Oxford: Blackwell.

Grmek, M. (1989). *Diseases in the Ancient Greek World*, trans. Mireille Muellner and Leonard Muellner. Baltimore: Johns Hopkins University Press.

Grosjean, R. (1966). *La Corse avant l'Histoire*. Paris: Klincksieck.

Guilaine, J. (1959). Les sépultures en fosse de Dela Laïga. *Bulletin de la Société préhistorique française*, 6, pp. 681–4.

Guilaine, J. (1994). *La Mer partagée. La Méditerranée avant l'écriture, 7000–2000 avant J.-C.* Paris: Hachette.

Guilaine, J. (1995). Leçon inaugurale. *Collège de France*, 132.

Guilaine, J. (1998). Néolithique et société: discours anthropologiques et données archéologiques. *Annuaire du Collège de France, 1997–1998, Résumé des cours et travaux*, pp. 687–97.

Guilaine, J. and Settis, S. (eds.) (1994). *Historia d'Europa. Preistoria e Antichità*. Turin: Einaudi.

Haas, J. (ed.) (1990). *The Anthropology of War*. Cambridge: Cambridge University Press.

Harmand, J. (1973). *La Guerre antique, de Sumer à Rome*. Paris: PUF.

Harris, M. (1978). *Cannibals and Kings: The Origins of Cultures*. London: Collins.

Heider, K. (1997). *Grand Valley Dani: Peaceful Warriors*, 3rd edn. New York: Harcourt Brace College Publishers.

Hell, B. (1994). *Le Sang noir*. Paris: Flammarion.

Héritier, F. (ed.) (1999). *De la violence II*. Paris: Odile Jacob.

Hernandez Pacheco, E. (1918). Estudios de arte prehistórico. *Revista de la Real Academia de Ciencas*, 16, pp. 62–88.

Hernandez Perez, M., Ferrer i Marset, P., and Catala Ferrer, E. (1989). *Arte rupestre en Alicante*. Alicante.

Hernandez Perez, M., Ferrer i Marset, P., and Catala Ferrer, E. (1994). *L'art macro-esquematic. L'albor d'una nova cultura*. Cocentaina: Centro d'Estudis Contestans.

Hernandez Perez, M., Ferrer i Marset, P., and Catala Ferrer, E. (eds.) (1998). *L'art llevanti*. Cocentaina: Centro d'Estudis Contestans.

Herodotus (1921). *Herodotus* (with an English translation by A. D. Godley), vol. 2, books 3 and 4. London: Heinemann.

Hibon, L. (1997). *Trépanations chirurgicales et prélèvements crâniens post-mortem dans les Grands Causses préhistoriques*. Mémoire de Diplôme d'Etudes Approfondies, University of Bordeaux I.

Homer (1886). *The Iliad of Homer*, trans. J. G. Cordery. London: Kegan Paul.

Homer (1967). *The Odyssey of Homer*, trans. Richmond Lattimore. New York: Harper and Row.

Hubert, H. and Mauss, M. (1889). Essai sur la nature et la fonction du sacrifice. *L'Année sociologique*, 2, pp. 29–138.

Hublin, J.-J. (1982). Cannibalisme et archéologie, la mort dans la Préhistoire. *Histoire et archéologie*, Les Dossiers, 66, pp. 24–7.

Huot, J.-L. (1989). *Les Sumériens*. Paris: Armand Colin.

Huot, J.-L., Thalmann, J.-P., and Valbelle, D. (1990). *Naissance des cités*. Paris: Nathan.

Jeunesse, C. (1997). *Pratiques funéraires au Néolithique ancien: sépultures et nécropoles danubiennes*. Paris: Errance.

Jorda Cerda, F. (1975). La sociedad en el arte rupestre levantino. *Papeles del Laboratorio de Arqueologia de Valencia*, 11, pp. 159–87.

Jourdan, N. (1979). La fragmentation des restes osseux néolithiques de l'abri Jean-Cros. In *L'Abri Jean-Cros*. Toulouse: Centre d'anthropologie des sociétés rurales, pp. 375–87.

Keegan, J. (1993). *A History of Warfare*. New York: Alfred A. Knopf.

Keeley, L. (1996). *War Before Civilization*. New York: Oxford University Press.

Kimmig, W. (1983). Die griechische kolonisation im westlichen Mitteleuropa. *Jahrbuch des Römisch-Germanischen Zentralmuseums*, Mainz, 30, pp. 5–78.

Kirk, G. S. (1999). La guerre et le guerrier dans les poèmes homériques. In J.-P. Vernant (ed.), *Problèmes de la guerre en Grèce ancienne*. Paris: Éditions de l'EHESS.

Kozlowski, S. et al. (1993). Maszycka cave: A Magdalenian site in Southern Poland. *Jahrbuch des Romisch-Germanischen Zentralmuseums Mainz*, 40, pp. 115–252, 24 pl.

Kristiansen, K. (1998). *Europe Before History*. Cambridge: Cambridge University Press.

Laburthe-Tolra, Ph. (1984). De la guerre comme jeu. Cultures et développement. *Revue internationale des sciences du développement*, 16 (3–4), pp. 503–10.

Lafont, D. (1991). La guerre au pays de Sumer. *Les Dossiers de l'Archéologie*, 160, pp. 10–17.

Lanzinger, M., Marzatico, F., and Pedrotti, A. (2000). *Storia del Trentino*, vol. 1: *La preistoria e la protostoria*. Bologna: Società Editrice Il Mulino.

Leclerc, J. (1999). Un phénomène associé au mégalithisme: les sépultures collectives. In J. Guilaine (ed.), *Mégalithismes, de l'Atlantique à l'Éthiopie*. Paris: Errance, pp. 23–40.

Le Mort, F. (1988a). Le décharnement du cadavre chez les Néandertaliens. *L'Homme de Néandertal*, 5. Liège: ERAUL, pp. 43–55.

Le Mort, F. (1988b). Cannibalisme ou rite funéraire? *Dossiers "Histoire et archéologie,"* 124, pp. 46–9.

Leroi-Gourhan, A. (1964). *Le Geste et la parole*, vol. 1: *Technique et langage*. Paris: Albin Michel.

Leroi-Gourhan, A. (1965a). *Le Geste et la parole*, vol. 2: *La Mémoire et les rythmes*. Paris: Albin Michel.

Leroi-Gourhan, A. (1965b). *Préhistoire de l'art occidental*. Paris: Mazenod.

Leroi-Gourhan, A. (1968). *The Art of Prehistoric Man in Western Europe*, trans. Norbert Guterman, London: Thames and Hudson.

Leroi-Gourhan, A. (1992). *L'Art pariétal, langage de la Préhistoire*. Grenoble: Millon.

Leroi-Gourhan, A. (1993). *Gesture and Speech*, trans. Anna Bostock Berger. Cambridge, MA: MIT.

Lévêque, P. (1964). *L'Aventure grecque*. Paris: Armand Colin.

Lévêque, P. (1968). *The Greek Adventure*, trans. Miriam Kochan. London: Weidenfeld and Nicolson.

Lévêque, P. (1996). *Empires et barbaries*. Paris: "Livre de Poche Histoire."

Lévi-Strauss, C. (1963). *Structural Anthropology*, vol. 2, trans. Claire Jacobson and Brooke Grundfest Schoepf. New York: Basic Books.

Lévi-Strauss, C. (1996). *Anthropologie structurale deux*. Paris: Plon.

Lichardus, J. and Lichardus-Itten, M. (1985). *La Protohistoire de l'Europe*. Paris: PUF.

Lilliu, G. (1982). *La civiltà nuragica*. Sassari: Carlo Delfino.

Linden, E. (1976). *Apes, Men and Language*. New York: Penguin.

Loison, G. (1998). La nécropole de Pontcharaud en Basse-Auvergne. In J. Guilaine, *Sépultures d'Occident et genèses des mégalithismes*. Paris: Errance , pp. 189–206.

Lontcho, F. (1998). La naissance de la guerre. *L'Archéologue*, 34, pp. 47–50.

Lorenz, K. (1969). *L'Agression. Une histoire naturelle du mal*. Paris: Flammarion.

Lorenz, K. (1970). *Tous les chiens, tous les chats*. Paris: J'ai Lu.

Lumley, H. de (ed.) (1972). *La Grotte moustérienne de L'Hortus (Valflaunès, Hérault)*. Études quaternaires, 1, University of Provence.

Lumley, H. de (1995). *Le Grandiose et le sacré*. Aix-en-Provence: Edisud.

McCown, Th.-D. and Keith, A. (1939). *The Stone Age of Mount Carmel: The Fossil Human Remains from the Levalloiso-Mousterian*. Oxford.

Mahieu, E. (1987). L'hypogée des Boileau. Vers une meilleure connaissance des rites funéraires du Néolithique provençal. *Bulletin de la Société préhistorique française*, 85, pp. 5–7.

Mahieu, E. (1989). *L'Hypogée des Boileau*. Études et prospectives archéologiques.

Mahieu, E. (1992). Premiers apports de l'hypogée des Boileau à l'étude des sépultures collectives du Sud-Est de la France. *Anthropologie préhistorique: résultats et tendances.* Sarrians, EPA, pp. 75–81.

Mallory, J.-P. (1995). Statue-menhirs and the Indo-Europeans. In S. Casini, R. de Marinis, and A. Pedrotti, *Statue-stele e massi incisi nell'Europa dell'Età del Rame.* Bergamo, pp. 67–73.

Mallory, J.-P. (1997). *À la recherche des Indo-Européens.* Paris: Éditions du Seuil.

Marti, M., Pou, R., and Carlus, X. (with E. Vives, J.-F. Gibaja, J. Martinez, R. Piqué, and D. Campillo) (1997). *La necropolis del Neolithic Mitjà i les restes romanes del Camí de Can Grau (La Roca del Vallès, Vallès oriental).* Barcelona: Généralité de Catalogne.

May, F. (1986). *Les Sépultures préhistoriques.* Paris: Éditions du CNRS.

Mellaart, J. (1967). *Çatal Hüyük: A Neolithic Town in Anatolia.* London: Thames and Hudson.

Menu, B. (1996). Naissance du pouvoir pharaonique. *Méditerranées*, 6/7, pp. 17–59.

Mezzena, F. (1976). Nuova interpretazione dell incisioni parietali paleolitiche della grotta Addaura a Palermo. *Rivista di Scienze Preistoriche*, 31 (1), pp. 61–85.

Miari, M. (1994). Rituali funerario della necropoli eneolitica di Ponte San Pietro (Ischia di Castro, Viterbo). *Origini*, 18, pp. 351–90.

Midant-Reynes, B. (1992). *Préhistoire de l'Égypte. Des premiers hommes aux premiers pharaons.* Paris: Armand Colin.

Midant-Reynes, B. (1999). *La Naissance de l'État en Égypte.* Habilitation à diriger des recherches, University of Paris IV.

Midant-Reynes, B. (2000). *The Prehistory of Egypt: From the First Egyptians to the First Pharaohs*, trans. Ian Shaw. Oxford: Blackwell.

Mohen, J.-P. (1995). *Les Rites de la mort.* Paris: Odile Jacob.

Mohen, J.-P. and Éluère, C. (1999). *L'Europe à l'Âge du bronze.* Paris: Gallimard/RMN.

Mohen, J.-P. and Éluère, C. (2000). *The Bronze Age in Europe*, trans. David Baker and Dorie Baker. London: Thames and Hudson.

Molinos Sauras, M.-A. (1986–7). Representaciones de caracter belico en el arte rupestre levantino. *Bajo Aragón Prehistoria*, 7–8, pp. 295–310.

Monks, S.-J. (1997). Conflict and competition in Spanish prehistory: The role of warfare in societal development from the late fourth to third millennium B.C. *Journal of Mediterranean Archaeology*, 10 (1), pp. 3–32.

Monks, S.-J. (1999). Patterns of warfare and settlement in Southeast Spain. *Journal of Iberian Archaeology*, 1, pp. 127–71.

Morel, Ch., Jr. (1957). *La Médecine et la chirurgie osseuses aux temps préhistoriques dans la région des Grands Causses.* Paris: La Nef de Paris.

Morel, Ch., Sr. and Baudouin, M. (1928). Un cas intéressant de pathologie préhistorique. Une pointe de silex dans une vertèbre néolithique. *Le Progrès médical*, 25, pp. 1042–52.

Morgan, L. (1985). *Ancient Society.* Tucson: University of Arizona Press.

Morris, D. (1967). *Primate Ethology.* London: Weidenfeld and Nicolson.

Morris, D. (ed.) (1968). *The Naked Ape.* London: Transworld.

Muñoz Ibañez, F.-J. (1999). Algunas consideraciones sobre el inicio de la arqueria prehistórica. *Trabajos de Prehistoria*, 56 (1), pp. 27–40.

Nuzhnyi, D. (1989). L'utilisation des microlithes géométriques et non géométriques comme armatures de projectiles. *Bulletin de la Société préhistorique française*, 86, pp. 88–96.

Obermaier, H. (1937). Nouvelles études sur l'art rupestre du Levant espagnol. *L'Anthropologie*, 47, pp. 447–98.

Orliac, E. and Orliac, M. (1973). La succession des industries à la grotte de la Tourasse, Saint-Martory (Haute-Garonne). *Bulletin de la Société préhistorique française*, CRSM, March, pp. 66–8.

Ortego, T. (1948). Nuevas estaciones de arte rupestre aragones "El Mortero" y "Cerro Felio" en termino de Alacon (Terrvel). *Archivo Español de Arquedogia*, 21, pp. 3–37.

Ortner, D.-J. and Pustschar, W.-G. (1985). *Identification of Pathological Conditions in Human Skeletal Remains*. Washington, DC: Smithsonian Institution.

Pales, L. (1930). *Paléopathologie et pathologie comparative*. Paris: Masson.

Pares, J.-M. and Perez, A. (1999). Magnetochronology and estratigraphy at Gran Dolina Section, Atapuerca (Burgos, Spain). *Journal of Human Evolution*, 37, pp. 325–42.

Patou-Mathis, M. (1997). Analyses taphonomique et palethnographique du matériel osseux de Krapina (Croatie): nouvelles données sur la faune et les restes humains. *Préhistoire européenne*, Liège, 10, pp. 63–90.

Patou-Mathis, M. (1999). *Comportements de subsistance au Paléolithique moyen en Europe septentrionale, centrale et orientale*, 2 vols. Mémoire d'habilation, University of Paris I.

Patou-Mathis, M. (2000). Aux racines du cannibalisme. *La Recherche*, 327 (January), pp. 16–19.

Pedrotti, A. (1993). *Uomini di pietra. I ritrovamenti di Arco e il fenomeno delle statue stele nell'arco alpino*. Trento.

Pedrotti, A. (ed.) (1995). *Le statue stele di Arco*. Trento.

Peroni, R. (1971). *L'età del Bronzo nella Penisola italiana. L'antica età del Bronzo*. Florence: Olschki.

Pètrequin, A.-M. and Pètrequin, P. (1990). Flèches de guerre, flèches de chasse. Le cas des Danis d'Irian Jaya. *Bulletin de la Société préhistorique française*, 87 (10–12), pp. 484–511.

Pètrequin, P., Maréchal, D., Pètrequin, A.-M., Arbogast, R.-M., and Saintot, S. (1998). Parures et flèches du Néolithique final à Chalain et à Clairvaux. *Gallia-Préhistoire*, 40, pp. 133–247.

Pigeaud, R. (2000). Du rififi chez les hommes préhistoriques. *La Recherche*, 357, pp. 18–19.

Piggott, S. (1983). *The Earliest Wheeled Transport from the Atlantic Coast to the Caspian Sea*. London: Thames and Hudson.

Plutarch (1866). *Lives of Illustrious Men*, trans. John Langhorne and William Langhorne. London.

Pope, S. (1962). *Bows and Arrows*. Berkeley: University of California (reprint of 1923 edition).

Porcar Ripollès, J. (1946). Iconografia rupestre de la Gasulla y Valltorta. Escenas bélicas. *Boletín de la Sociedad Castellonense de Cultura*, 22, pp. 48–60.

Prunières, B. (1882). Blessures et fractures graves régulièrement guéries sur les os humains de l'époque préhistorique. *Association française pour l'avancement des sciences*, pp. 830–1.

Ramos-Millán, A. (1998). La mineria, la artesania y el intercambio de silex durante la Edad del cobre en el Sudeste de la Península ibérica. In G. Delibes, *Minerales y metales en la Prehistoria reciente*. University of Valladolid, pp. 13–40.

Regnault, F. (1892). L'abri de la Tourasse à Saint-Martory. *L'Anthropologie*, 3, pp. 742–3.

Ripoll, E. (1963). *Pinturas rupestres de la Gasulla*. Barcelona: Monografías de Arte Rupestre, Arte Levantino.

Riquet, R. (1970). *Anthropologie du Néolithique au Bronze ancien*. Poitiers: Tixier.

Romilly, J. de (1999). Guerre et paix entre cités. In J.-P. Vernant (ed.), *Problèmes de la guerre en Grèce ancienne*. Paris: Éditions de l'EHESS, pp. 273–301.

Rozoy, J.-G. (1978). *Les Derniers Chasseurs*, 3 vols. Bulletin de la Société d'archéologie champenoise.

Rozoy, J.-G. (1993). Les archers épipaléolithiques: un important progrès. *Paléo*, 5, pp. 263–79.

Rua, C. de la, Baraybar, J.-P., Cuende, M., and Manzano, C. (1996). La sepultura colectiva de San Juan Ante Portam Latinam (Laguardia, Alava). Contribución de la Antropologia a la interpretación del ritual funerario. *Rubricatum*, 1, pp. 585–9.

Russell, M.-D. (1987a). Bone breakage in the Krapina Hominid Collection. *American Journal of Physical Anthropology*, 72, pp. 373–9.

Russell, M.-D. (1987b). Mortuary practice at the Krapina Neandertal site. *American Journal of Physical Anthropology*, 72, pp. 381–97.

Sahlins, M. (1972). *Stone Age Economics*. Chicago: Aldine-Atherton.

Sauzade, G. (1983). *Les Sépultures du Vaucluse, du Néolithique à l'Âge du bronze*. Études quaternaires, 6.

Schiltz, V. (1991). *Histoires de Kourganes*. Paris: Gallimard.

Schulting, R. (1999). Nouvelles dates AMS à Téviec et Hoédic (Quiberon, Morbihan). *Bulletin de la Société préhistorique française*, 96, pp. 203–7.

Scubla, L. (1999). Ceci n'est pas un meurtre ou comment le sacrifice contient la violence. In F. Héritier, *De la violence II*. Paris: Odile Jacob, pp. 135–70.

Serres, J.-P. (1991). Les blessures et les accidents de la Préhistoire. *Catalogue de l'exposition au musée de Roquefort-sur-Soulzon*.

Sherratt, A. (1997). *Economy and Society in Prehistoric Europe*. Edinburgh: Edinburgh University Press.

Shipman, P. (1984). Scavenger hunt. *Natural History*, pp. 20–7.

Sicard, G. (1902). Sur quelques explorations nouvelles dans les grottes de l'Aude. *AFAS*, Montauban, 31 (2), pp. 899–903.

Simon, C. (1989). Les populations de Kerma: évolution interne et relations historiques dans le contexte égypto-nubien. *Archéologie du Nil moyen*, Lille, 3, pp. 139–47.

Simon, C. (1991). Quelques réflexions sur les sacrifices humains à Kerma (Soudan). *Méthodes d'étude des sépultures*, Saintes, pp. 85–96.

Skinner, M.-F. and Sperber, G.-H. (1982). *Atlas of Radiographs of Early Man*. New York: Alan R. Liss.

Spindler, K. (1995). L'homme du glacier. Une momie du glacier de Haulajoch vieille de 5000 ans dans les Alpes de l'Ötztal. *L'Anthropologie*, 99, pp. 104–14.

Spindler, K. (1997). L'homme gelé. Une momie de 5000 ans dans un glacier des Alpes de l'Ötztal. *Dossiers d'Archéologie*, 224, pp. 8–27.

Stoczkowski, W. (1994). *Anthropologie naïve, anthropologie savante*. Paris: Éditions du CNRS.

Stoczkowski, W. (2002). *Explaining Human Origins: Myth, Imagination and Conjecture*, trans. Mary Turton. Cambridge: Cambridge University Press.

Sun Tzu (1988). *The Art of War*, trans. Thomas Cleary. Boston: Shambhala.

Telegin, E. (1986). *Dereivka: A Settlement and Cemetery of Copper Age Horse Keepers on the Middle Dnieper*. BAR, IS, 331, Oxford.

Testart, A. (1985). *Le Communisme primitif. Économie et idéologie*. Paris: Maison des sciences de l'homme.

Testart, A. (1993). *Des dons et des dieux. Anthropologie religieuse et sociologie comparative*. Paris: Armand Colin.

Thucydides (1919–23). *History of the Peloponnesian War*, trans. C. Foster Smith. London: Heinemann.

Tringham, R. (1993). Households with faces: The challenge of gender in prehistoric architectural remains. In S. M. Gero and M. W. Conkey (eds.), *Engendering Archaeology: Women and Prehistory*. Oxford and Cambridge, MA: Blackwell, pp. 93–131.

Trinkaus, E. (1985). Cannibalism and burial at Krapina. *Journal of Human Evolution*, 14, pp. 203–16.

Trinkaus, E. (1989). *The Shanidar Neandertals*. New York: Academic Press.

Turney-High, H. (1971). *Primitive War: Its Practice and Concepts*. New York: Columbia University Press.

Valbelle, D. (1998). *Histoire de l'État pharaonique*. Paris: PUF.

Vallois, H. V. (1957). La grotte de Fontéchevade. *Archives de l'Institut de Paléontologie Humaine*, 29.

Vandermeersch, B. (1981). *Les Hommes fossiles de Qafzeh (Israël)*. Cahiers de paléontologie. Paris: CNRS.

Van Lawick, H. and Goodall, J. (1973). *In the Shadow of Man*. London: Fontana.

Van Lawick, H. and Goodall, J. (1978). *Innocent Killers*. London: Fontana.

Vegas, J.-I. (1991). El enterramiento de San Juan Ante Portam Latinam (Laguardia). *Arkeoikuska*, pp. 28–39.

Vegas, J.-I. (1992). El enterramiento de San Juan Ante Portam Latinam. Las màs numerosas señales de violencia de la Prehistoria peninsular. *Cultura. Ciencias, Historia, Pensamiento*, Diputación Foral de Alava, 5 (July), pp. 9–20.

Vegas, J.-I., Armendariz, A., Etxeberria, F., Fernandez, Ma. S., Herrasti, L., and Zumalabe, F. (1999). La sepultura colectiva de San Juan Ante Portam Latinam (Laguardia, Alava). *Saguntum extra-2*, University of Valencia, pp. 439–45.

Vencl, S. (1984). War and warfare in archaeology. *Journal of Anthropological Archaeology*, 3, pp. 116–32.

Vencl, S. (1991). Interprétation de blessures causées par les armes au Mésolithique. *L'Anthropologie*, 95, pp. 219–28.

Vercoutter, J. (1992). *L'Égypte et la vallée du Nil*, vol. 1: *Des origines à la fin de l'Ancien Empire*. Paris: PUF.

Vernant, J.-P. (ed.) (1999). *Problèmes de la guerre en Grèce ancienne*. Paris: Éditions de l'EHESS.

Vigliardi, A. (1992). L'arte paleolitica del Monte Pellegrino. Le incisioni rupestri delle grotte dell'Addaura e di grotta Niscemi. *Panormus*, 3 (2), pp. 55–93.

Villa, P., Courtin, J., Helmer, D., Schipman, P., Bouville, C., and Mahieu, E. (1986). Un cas de cannibalisme au Néolithique. Boucherie et rejet de restes humains et animaux dans la grotte de Fontbregoua (Salernes, Var). *Gallia-Préhistoire*, 29, pp. 143–71.

Vlaeminck, M. (1997). *Le Grand-Pressigny dans le Nord-Ouest de l'Europe. Le silex tertiaire, concurrent possible du Grand-Pressigny?* Thesis, EHESS.

Wahl, J. and König, H.-G. (1987). Anthropologisch traumatologisch Untersuchung der menschlichen Skelettreste aus dem bandkeramischen Massengrab bei Talheim, Kreis Heilbronn. *Funderberichte aus Baden-Wurtemberg*, 12, pp. 65–193.

Waterbolk, H. T. and Glasbergen, W. (1957). Grafheuvelopgravingen in de gemeente Anlo. Van Rendierjager tot Ontginner, *Nieuwe Drentse Volksalmanak*, 75th year, pp. 23–41.

Wendorf, F. (ed.) (1968). *The Prehistory of Nubia*. Dallas: Southern Methodist University Press.

White, T.-D. (1992). *Prehistoric Cannibalism at Mancos 5 MTUMR-2346*. Princeton, NJ: Princeton University Press.

White, T.-D. (1999). Neanderthal cannibalism at Moula-Guercy, Ardèche, France. *Science*, 286 (5437), pp. 128–31.

White, T.-D. and Toth, N. (1993). The question of ritual cannibalism at Grotta Guattari. *Current Anthropology*, 32 (2), pp. 118–24.

Xenophon (1831). *The Complete Works of Xenophon*, trans. Ashley Cooper et al. London: Jones.

Zammit, J. (1991). Lésion traumatique osseuse par pointe de flèche en silex. Étude paléopathologique et intégration. *Bulletin du Musée d'anthropologie et de préhistoire de Monaco*, pp. 97–107.

Zimmerman, M.-R. and Kelley, M.-R. (1982). *Atlas of Human Paleopathology*. New York: Praeger.

Works by Jean Guilaine

La Civilisation du vase campaniforme dans les Pyrénées françaises. Carcassonne: Gabelle, 1967.

L'Âge du bronze en Languedoc occidental, Roussillon, Ariège. Paris: Klincksieck, 1972.

Premiers bergers et paysans de l'Occident méditerranéen. Paris and The Hague: Mouton and École des hautes études en sciences sociales, 1976; 2nd edn, Paris, The Hague, and New York, 1981 (with postscript).

Récits et contes populaires du Languedoc. Paris: Gallimard, 1978.

La France d'avant la France. Paris: Hachette, 1980 (paperback edn, 1985).

La Mer partagée. La Méditerranée avant l'écriture: 7000–2000 avant J.-C. Paris: Hachette, 1994.

Au temps des dolmens. Toulouse: Privat, 1998 (paperback edn, 2000).

La Plus Belle Histoire de l'homme (with A. Langaney, J. Clottes, and D. Simonnet). Paris: Éditions du Seuil, 1998; Portuguese edn, Oporto, 1999; Catalan edn, Barcelona, 1999; South American edn, Santiago de Chili/Buenos Aires/Mexico City, 1999; Spanish edn, Barcelona, 1999; German edn, Bergisch Gladbach, 2000; Chinese edn, Taibai Art et Littérature, 2000; Arabic edn, Lebanon: Academia Publishing, 2000; Polish edn, Wydawnictwo Cyklady, Warsaw, 1999; Turkish edn, Tarih, Istanbul, 2000; German edn, Bastei Lubbe, Berlin, 2001; Brazilian edn, Difel, Rio de Janeiro, 2002; Japanese edn, Chikuma Shobo, Tokyo, 2002.

De la vague à la tombe. La conquête néolithique de la Mediterranée. Paris: Editions du Seuil, 2003.

Works edited by Jean Guilaine

Les Civilisations néolithiques du Midi de la France. Carcassonne: Gabelle, 1970.

La Préhistoire française, II: *Les Civilisations néolithiques et protohistoriques de la France*. Paris: CNRS, 1976. Preface by Valéry Giscard d'Estaing.

Le Groupe de Véraza et la fin des temps néolithiques dans le Sud de la France et la Catalogne. Paris: CNRS, 1980.

El origen de la metalurgia. Mexico City: Union internationale des sciences préhistoriques et protohistoriques, 1981.

L'Âge du cuivre européen. Civilisations à vases campaniformes. Paris: CNRS, 1984.

La Préhistoire, d'un continent à l'autre. Paris: Larousse, 1986. Reprinted in paperback, 1989. American edn, *Prehistory: The World of Early Man.* New York and Oxford: Facts on File, 1991. Italian edn, Rome: Gremese, 1995.

Le Néolithique de la France. Paris: Picard, 1986 (co-edited with J.-P. Demoule).

Premières communautés paysannes en Méditerranée occidentale. Paris: CNRS, 1987 (co-edited with J. Courtin, J.-L. Roudil, and J.-L. Vernet).

De Lascaux au Grand Louvre. Paris: Errance, 1989. Preface by François Mitterrand (co-edited with C. Goudineau).

Pays de Sault. Espaces, peuplement, populations. Paris: CNRS, 1989.

Autour de Jean Arnal. Premières communautés paysannes. Montpellier, 1990 (co-edited with X. Gutherz).

Pour une archéologie agraire. Paris: Armand Colin, 1991.

Histoire de l'Europe. Préhistoire et Antiquité, 2 vols. Turin: Einaudi, 1994 (co-edited with S. Settis).

Sépultures d'Occident et genèses des mégalithismes. Paris: Errance, 1998.

Atlas du Néolithique européen, II: *Europe occidentale.* University of Liège, ERAUL, 46, 1998.

Mégalithismes, de l'Atlantique à l'Éthiopie. Paris: Errance, 1999.

Premiers paysans du monde. Naissance des agricultures. Paris: Errance, 2000.

Communautés villageoises du 8ᵉ au 3ᵉ millénaire, du Proche-Orient à l'Atlantique. Paris: Errance, 2001.

Matériaux, productions, circulations, du Néolithique à l'Age du bronze. Paris: Errance, 2002.

Arts et symboles du Néolithique à la Protohistoire. Paris: Errance, 2003.

Le Néolithique de Chypre, Bulletin de Correspondance Hellénique, Supplement 43, Athens, 2003 (with A. Le Brun).

Monographs on archeological sites

La Balma de Montbolo et le Néolithique de l'Occident méditerranéen. Toulouse: Institut pyrénéen d'études anthropologiques, 1974.

L'Abri Jean-Cros. Essai d'approche d'un groupe humain du Néolithique ancien dans son environnement. Toulouse: Centre d'anthropologie des sociétés rurales, 1979.

Leucate-Corrège. Habitat noyé du Néolithique cardial. Toulouse and Musée Paul Valéry, Sète: Centre d'anthropologie des sociétés rurales, 1984.

Carsac. Une agglomération protohistorique en Languedoc. Toulouse: Centre d'anthropologie des sociétés rurales, 1986.

Ornaisons-Médor. Archéologie et écologie d'un site de l'Âge du cuivre, de l'Âge du bronze final et de l'Antiquité tardive. Toulouse: Centre d'anthropologie des sociétés rurales, 1989.

Dourgne. Derniers chasseurs-collecteurs et premiers éleveurs de la Haute Vallée de l'Aude. Toulouse: Centre d'anthropologie des sociétés rurales, 1993.

Les excavacions a la Balma dela Margineda, 3 vols. Edicions del Govern d'Andorra, 1995 (with M. Martzluff et al.).

La Poste-Vieille. De l'enceinte néolithique à la bastide d'Alzau. Toulouse: Centre d'anthropologie, 1997.

Torre Sabea. Un établissement du Néolithique ancien en Salento. Collection de l'Ecole Française de Rome, 2003.

Index

Page numbers in *italics* refer to illustrations.

Paglicci cave, Italy, 54, 234
Paleolithic Age
    art, 52–6, *54*, 103
    burials, 40–1
    cannibalism, 44, 99
    nature of, 30, 31, 32
    warfare, 21, 24–7
    weapons, 61–3, 235
Papua New Guinea: warfare, 20, *21*, 28
Parxubeira, Galicia: steles, 180
Pas-de-Joulié cave, Trèves: bone fragments, 136, *137*
peat bogs: bodies found in, 228–32
Pech-Merle cave, Lot, 55, *55*, 234
Perrats à Agris cave, Charente, 98
Petit-Morin valley, 145
Pètrequin, A.-M. and P., 172
phalanxes, 215
Philistines, 214
Pierre-Plate dolmen, Presles: tombs, 133
Plan d'Aups, Var: tombs, 132
Plato, 6
Polvorin rock shelter, La Cenia: battle scenes, 112
Pontcharaud, Clermont-Ferrand: tombs, 128–9
Ponte San Pietro, Viterbo: "widow's tomb," 162, *163*, 164
Popovo, 76
Porcar Ripollès, J., 109, 115–16
prehistoric man
    nature of, 29–33
    violence, 36–9
primatology, 16
Prodicus, 6
projectiles: Paleolithic Age, 61–2
Protagoras, 6
Prunières, B., 133
Puabi, Queen, 224
Pueblo culture, 99
Puechamp dolmen, Sébazac-Concourès: tombs, 137

punishment
    depiction in cave drawings, 113, *114*, *115*
    in prehistoric societies, 37
Pylos, 5
    battle frescoes, 205, 212, *213*

Qa, 225
Qadan culture, 67
Qafzeh: tombs, 33, 41
Qin, king of, 6–7
Quatzenheim, Alsace: tombs, 128
Qur'an, 6

Ramessides, 4
Ramses II, 212, *214*
Ramses III, 13, 214
Razet hypogeum, Coizard, 135
Remedello culture, 178, 184, 193
Retoka: tombs, 227
Rinaldone culture, 162, 178, 184
Riparo del Romito, tombs, 34
rites of passage, 182
rivers: battles around, 204
Rixheim-type swords, 202
Roaix hypogeum, Vaucluse: tombs, 147–9, *148*, 150, 152
Roc de Sers, Charente, 52
Rocher-du-Causse, 10
"Rodezian" culture, 130
Rosnoen-type swords, 202
Rössen culture, 94
Roum, Denmark: peat bogs, 230
Roure rock shelter, Morella la Vella: battle scenes, 110–11, *110*
"Roy Mata," 227–8
Rupestrian art, 54, *54*, 56, 61, 103, 104, 180, 184

sacrifices
    China, 228
    Egypt, 224–5
    in prehistoric societies, 33–5, 37, 234, 235–6